Dancing Into Freedom?

Heidi Giersch was born in the former German Democratic Republic – communist East Germany – where the fall of the Berlin Wall in 1989 made history. As a young child of ten, she was chosen to join the Berlin State Ballet School, an experience which resulted in her leaving her home and family to pursue her ballet career training. In 1980, at twenty-seven, she danced with the Komische Oper Berlin ballet company on their first tour to Australia. She defected after the final performance in Sydney and within days was granted political asylum enabling her to stay in Australia. She was associated with the Hofbrauhaus Melbourne for fifteen years, and performed in the floor show.

Janet Brown is an award-winning Australian writer and her work is published widely. Several of her plays have been professionally staged in Melbourne, Sydney and toured regional Victoria. *Defection*, her stage play based on Heidi's life story, was performed as part of the Making Waves touring production in 2011.

Heidi Giersch
with Janet Brown

Dancing Into Freedom?

Dedication

To the two most precious women in my life – my mother and my daughter. With my eternal love.

To you, my readers, may my journey inspire you to never ever give up and hope that dreams can come true. Mine did.

Dancing Into Freedom?
ISBN 978 1 76109 016 5
Copyright © text Heidrun Patzold 2020
Back cover photo: *Australian Womens Weekly*, courtesy photographer Kimbal Baker and Bauer Media Pty Ltd
Every effort has been made to locate copyright holders of photos. Any copyright holders who are not acknowledged are invited to contact the author through the publisher at the address below.

First published 2020 by
GINNINDERRA PRESS
PO Box 3461 Port Adelaide 5015
www.ginninderrapress.com.au

Contents

Author's Note	6
Foreword	7
Prologue	13
Act One	17
Act Two	154
Act Three	168
Finale	225
Interval	229
Acknowledgements	230

Author's Note

Some of the names in this book have been changed to ensure privacy. This story is told from my earliest memories, feelings and experiences. I have done my best to be as accurate and truthful as I can.

Heidi Giersch

Foreword

The Black Rose Restaurant was the restaurant to go to in St Kilda in 1980. It was known for its vibrant, fun atmosphere and the co-owners were my clients. On the morning of Monday 21 April, I received a phone call from one of the restaurateurs asking me if I'd seen the morning newspapers. As I didn't read newspapers, I asked him to explain.

Heidrun Giersch, an East German ballet dancer, had defected and wanted to stay in Australia. Ernst was helping her and wanted my legal advice. My law training had taught me nothing about this sort of situation, and I decided a bit of rat cunning was needed. I advised Ernst to stay with Heidi and drive around Melbourne for a few hours then to visit my office at three o'clock that afternoon. The press were already onto the story and I didn't want them or me to have to deal with the media until I'd worked out a plan. I'd been practising immigration law and had been able to get some people into Australia and granted permanent residency, but this situation was completely different and front page news. To be harassed by the press was the last thing we needed.

As there was national significance to the case, I phoned the Department of Foreign Affairs and advised the official I spoke with that I would be at their offices at twelve o'clock with my client Heidrun Giersch, although I did not intend at all for Heidi to accompany me. When I arrived at the department in Spring Street, Melbourne, the lift door opened on the floor where I'd been directed to and about twenty photographers and press were waiting for us.

The reporters rushed to me and asked, 'Are you representing the ballet dancer?'

I said, 'Why are you taking my photograph?'

'We thought you were the solicitor representing the ballet dancer,' they said.

'Do I look like I would be?' Fortunately, I was able to confuse them and they apologised and dismissed me.

I then introduced myself to the receptionist, who ushered me through to see the official. I explained to him formally that Heidi wanted to stay in Australia and offered him my reasons for not bringing her with me. He said that I'd done the right thing and that the request would be given consideration. The official left me with a strong indication that there was a high possibility that we'd be granted a visa for her to stay in Australia. I thought it was a strange case for defection at the time – spies defected to Australia, not ballet dancers.

Foreign Affairs officials decided to work back late on the case that same day. They were to interview Heidi late that night at an office in Melbourne.

When Heidi and Ernst came to meet me in my office for the first time later that day, I met a beautiful young lady, totally different from anyone else I'd ever seen. She was enthusiastic, wild, full of life – and, with no English language skills, had no idea of what we were saying.

I advised Heidi and Ernst to stay away from the Black Rose and not to go anywhere they might be found, they needed to keep away from the press or anyone else who was looking for her. She was concerned that East German officials from Canberra would be searching for her. I could not imagine the mental pressures she was experiencing, although it was obvious that she was genuinely scared and I, too, was anxious.

Several officials from the departments of Foreign Affairs and Immigration attended the late-night interview. Heidi and Ernst – as her interpreter – sat next to me on one side, and the official with whom I'd met during the afternoon sat on my other side. Heidi was the only woman in the room. Much of the meeting was taken up with Heidi being questioned about her background, her intentions, her family and then translation and interpreting of her answers.

My strategy was to co-operate with the Australian government and give them every opportunity to make their decision without wanting to embarrass the government in any way. Other solicitors, with a different philosophy, would have gone to the press, trying to make a big name for themselves. I wasn't interested in seeking publicity. I was interested in getting the best decision for my client. Foreign Affairs is a very vital department for considerations about dealings with overseas nationals and I believed that if I assisted them, then it facilitated the process. I was commended on my approach.

There were two possibilities to enable Heidi to stay in Australia: refugee status and political asylum. I thought there would be no possibility we'd get political asylum. When we hear about refugees seeking 'asylum' in Australia, it means that they will almost always, if successful in their request to stay, be granted a protection visa by the Department of Immigration.

Political asylum is a particular status that is rarely granted. It is an executive decision made at the discretion of the Minister for Foreign Affairs, and before Heidi's case it was well reported that it was granted to a Russian couple, Mr and Mrs Petrov, twenty-six years earlier in 1954. The Petrovs were KGB Russian spies. The Foreign Minister makes this decision, with the full knowledge of its importance in international relationships. Such a decision creates tension between the Australian government and the government of the home country of the asylum seeker. It is reasonable to expect political asylum to be given only if the person applying is of great value to Australia – such as spies – with knowledge and information of immense national value. It's extraordinarily rare for anyone to be granted political asylum.

So, when asked during the interview what we were applying for, I answered, 'Refugee status.'

The official sitting next to me sort of dug me in the ribs and said quietly to me, 'I would recommend you apply for political asylum.'

I said, 'Excuse me,' to the other people at the table so that I could have a chat with him. I said, 'I don't think we'd be able to get it, so I don't think there's any point asking for it. If we apply for political asylum and it's rejected, then we're in no-man's-land and we have to make further application.'

The official said firmly, 'Apply for political asylum.'

Due to his encouragement, I did so. I was then advised that the department would announce its decision promptly.

On leaving the building, the official advised he would take us outside via a back door, to avoid the press, who were staking out all the exits. We had a car waiting for us. One member of the press was at the back door of the building. I walked out first, alone.

He recognised me and said, 'Didn't I see you this afternoon at Foreign Affairs?'

I said, 'Yes, you did. And if you come over here, I've got a story for you.' I took him twenty metres down the street.

Heidi and Ernst climbed into the waiting car without the journalist realising he'd just missed her. By the time he sensed what was happening, Heidi was in the front seat of the car. Somebody managed to get a photograph, which appeared in the newspaper the next day captioned, 'Heidi Giersch with her solicitor', but it was actually Heidi with the official from Foreign Affairs.

We were delighted when advised the next day that Heidi's application had been successful and that she had been granted political asylum.

The days and weeks that followed were busy, heady times in my office – the ongoing pressure from the press grew to a crescendo requiring careful mediation, and proposals from Australian dance companies for Heidi's consideration reflected both the intense public interest and controversy that her actions created.

On reflection, why was Heidi, a ballet dancer from communist East Germany, under the control of Russia, granted political asylum by the Australian government? It is my opinion that Andrew Peacock, who was then Minister for Foreign Affairs in the Fraser government, wanted to make a political protest to the Russians of the Soviet invasion of Afghanistan. The Moscow Olympics were approaching later in the year, and the Australian government was actually considering whether or not

Australian athletes should participate or boycott the games. A full Australian boycott did not go ahead, though some sports decided not to send teams.

It is difficult to know how many other subsequent defectors have been granted political asylum. The information is extremely sensitive and such records, if made available at the National Archives, have a thirty-year embargo. It's quite possible that the National Archives may never become the keeper of these records, even after thirty years, as it is a national security consideration and, unless the media are able to reveal the information, it may not otherwise be made public.

Heidi has become a good friend to me and my wife and my children over the years, and we have enjoyed many great times in each other's company. We have always encouraged her to write the story of her unique life experiences – a childhood growing up in what was then the communist regime of East Germany, a regime which no longer exists since the fall of the Berlin Wall in 1989.

In 1980, on her defection to Australia, Heidi captivated the people of this nation. Later that year, having never been to a ballet before, my wife and I were delighted to see her perform with the Sydney Dance Company in Melbourne. She has been our dear friend ever since.

Paul Connor

Prologue

It is the evening of 19 April 1980. Tonight the curtain of the Regent Theatre in Sydney has fallen for the last time for our ballet company, the Komische Oper Berlin, after seven weeks touring in Australia. As always, I have committed to my work and my colleagues from day one when we arrived in Australia until tonight.

I am about to take a gigantic risk, the biggest ever in my life. I am very conscious of the possible fatal consequences. This is a dangerous situation. I am driven by unlimited determination, clarity and confidence that nothing and nobody in the world can stop me. I cannot go back.

It was 9.30 p.m. when I last looked at a clock. Since then, I have heard a clock ticking inside of me. I feel my heart beating incredibly fast. I tell myself calmly to keep breathing, breathe deeply. It is almost impossible. My mind must stay razor-sharp and focused, following exactly my detailed plan. There is no time to allow any negative thoughts to enter my mind. This is my biggest secret. And this is the way it has to remain perhaps for some days. I just do not know how long this process takes.

I have made my master plan of escape but pretend to the world around me that absolutely everything is okay, obediently following all duties and instructions as usual.

The atmosphere in the changing room is as always, but for me it is very different. I am so nervous just hoping that nobody will read my mind and perhaps discover what is going on in my head. Everybody around me seems rather loud, talking with each other, laughing, singing, screaming or rushing to get their stage make-up off and running to the shower. Some dancers are already packing the huge bags with our training gear and ballet shoes, which are individually named, to be collectively sent by freight back to Berlin.

I pack up too, much faster than anyone else, and am first to leave with my handbag stuffed with only a change of training gear. This little bundle of my belongings, which really should have gone into the official bag, is still in my possession today.

Everyone is happy, in a celebration mood after the final curtain and saying good bye to Australia. I feel it too, just in a different way.

I announce very loudly so all can hear, 'Bye-bye, guys. Have a great night, don't do what I wouldn't do, see you tomorrow morning.' I am a great actress.

I slam the change room door shut behind me and rush through the corridors, thinking, 'Great, well rehearsed, Heidi, an outstanding performance.' I have just told the biggest lie in my life.

I take long, fast steps towards the stage door exit. I tell myself, 'Keep on acting, Heidi. The performance is not over yet.'

So far, I have completed successfully steps one, two, three and four of my master plan. Next step, number five, is that I must be the first to leave the theatre, ahead of the other eighty-five company members, and hopefully not seeing anybody until I leave the building.

I reach the stage door, open it, and get a huge shock when I bump into five colleagues outside enjoying a smoke. I think, '*Scheisse*, that's it, they've got me.' I feel frozen, and total angst overcomes me.

But they don't seem suspicious and simply ask, 'How come you can be so fast? We only finished ten minutes ago. You're leaving already? Where are you going? What are you doing tonight?'

Completely unprepared to answer, I say, 'I'm going out all night, don't know where yet, but I will have lots of fun. See you later, and don't do what I wouldn't do.' I just keep walking away from them, hoping they won't ask anything more so I can continue to follow my master plan.

This is my most dangerous experience so far. I think I'm freaking out. The moment could turn into absolute disaster. I suspect that two of the five standing there, with sweet smiles asking harmless questions, are Stasi members. But I have no proof. I feel their eyes following me, like knives stabbing me in my back. Will they run after me, grab me, tell me that I'm trapped? Will I be delivered to Stasi officials? This could be the end of a dream and the beginning of my hell.

I am praying, for the first time in my life, asking God to please help and protect me. It must be working somehow, because I manage to keep walking. Fast, faster…now I'm nearly running. But my inner voice tells me, 'Slow down, Heidi, act confident, be patient, you've nearly made it, only a few more metres, don't look back, only forward.' I think I'm forgetting to breathe. My knees feel so weak that I don't feel the ground beneath me any more. I think I will collapse any second, that I will black out.

I am pulled by an inner force of immense power towards the lights of the main street in front of me, to the exit of the walkway of the theatre while the inner voice insists, 'You're nearly there. Please don't give up, please don't!' And I mumble, 'Okay, I won't give up, I won't!'

In this very moment of my action, I have a choice: freedom or jail. And I choose freedom.

Act One

Jugend Simfonie, Youth Symphony,
choreographed by Tom Schilling for the Komische Oper Berlin

I was born in 1953 in the former East Germany, Ostdeutschland, in the major European city of East Berlin, Ostberlin. I was born on 21 March which, in Germany, is the first day of spring. I always call myself 'the spring baby', born when life starts again, when the sun shines again and begins to melt the snow which has cuddled everything. In spring, all the detail of life is revealed and the flowers start to bloom. I lived the first twenty-seven years of my life in East Germany.

After the Second World War, England, America and France took control of West Germany and Russia ran East Germany. Although the West was twice as big as the East, Berlin, the capital city of Germany was located in the East. It was decided that Berlin be divided into East and West. In 1949, East Germany became the German Democratic Republic, a communist regime, which remained under the control of the Soviets. The ruling communist party was called the Socialist Unity Party, Sozialistische Einheitspartei Deutschlands, SED.

Between 1949 and 1961, there was a continuing exodus of East Germans to West Germany and the Berlin Wall was erected effectively overnight to prevent the migration from Berlin. The famous Checkpoint Charlie was located in Berlin Friedrichstrasse. It was one of several transit checkpoints where people who had permission could travel between the West and the East. The people of the East appeared different to the people of the West. *Die Westler* had fashionable hairstyles, make-up and glamorous colourful clothes, and were in general more confident in their behaviour.

I have lived many years in Australia. Now seems the perfect time for me to reflect on my life.

I am three years old. Mum is about to take a photo of me. I squeeze my eyes shut at the flash.

She says, 'Keep your eyes open, Heidrun.'

One of my earliest memories is being in kindergarten, where I went Monday to Friday by myself because my mum worked as a teacher. Mum left for her work as a schoolteacher early and came home late in the afternoon. She taught German and Russian to high school children. We went to school from grade one to ten, and the top twenty per cent then went on to year twelve. Most of our schools had the primary and secondary sections on the same site.

We went to kinder from aged three until we started school at six. Kindergarten was not far from where we lived in Lichtenberg and I recall playing outside at the kinder with the children and the teachers. I loved playing with the hula hoop. We had plenty of them and it was my favourite game. They were made of wood and I could do all the tricks.

One day, walking home from kinder, I stopped at the shop next door, which was like a newsagency and had two windows decorated for the Christmas season. Christmas has always been a very special time in my life. The sparkling glitter, the Advent calendars and all the beautiful Christmas tree ornaments in the window absolutely fascinated me. I stood there in a sort of dreamy state admiring the scene, surrounded by the particular street smells of Christmas. The aroma from the bakeries preparing special biscuits for Christmas filled the air, snow was falling gently, the roads a bit icy.

Suddenly I screamed, 'Yeeow!' I didn't even notice people coming in or out of the shop and my three little fingers were squashed in the heavy iron door. My dream was suddenly broken. The people in the shop kindly looked after me and then I went home, where Mum took care of me.

When I was only three years old, I often pushed the heavy chairs away from the table in the living room of our flat to make some space.

This was such an effort for me. I'd pull my socks off and get up on my tippy toes, running around the table and singing, 'La, la, la, la, la, la, la…' or I'd turn on the radio – our prize possession. I'd do this for as long as I could; I didn't want to stop. Eventually, Mum or Dad insisted that I finished, because they were concerned that I'd damage my toes. Little did I know that I was making my tootsies strong and hardening them for when I would be on *pointe* shoes one day.

One night, Dad said to Mum, 'I wouldn't be surprised if our daughter becomes a ballerina one day.'

East Berlin is a very old city, and everything was grey. When I was growing up, many buildings were about four storeys high and in the long street where we lived they all looked similar. The block of flats we lived in had been built around 1923 and surrounded by similar buildings, some which were a bit newer and more modern. To my eyes, they all looked rather ugly and some of the buildings remained damaged and still in disrepair from the Second World War. Most of Berlin was severely bombed during the war. As soon as the war was over, rebuilding began. The *Trümmerfrauen*, 'rubble-women', worked day and night seven days a week, cleaning up the rubble of the buildings that had been damaged by bombs, removing the debris in human chains from one woman to the next. As children, we sang songs celebrating and encouraging the rebuilding of Berlin.

Berlin wird wieder aufgebaut
Berlin wird wieder aufgebaut und alle sind dabei.
Ich hab den Maurern zugeschaut, ein jeder schafft für zwei.
Sie setzen hurtig Stein auf Stein es kann nicht schneller gehn.
Berlin wird wieder aufgebaut – Hallo – wie wird das schön.

Berlin Gets Rebuilt (translated by the author)
We rebuild Berlin again and everybody is part of it.
I have watched the bricklayers and everyone works for two.
The bricks are laid very fast, it can't go any faster.
Berlin gets rebuilt again – Hello – how beautiful it will be.

Our flat, *Wohnung*, was on the first floor of the building. Mum always said she felt safe living on the first floor and perhaps strangely I have always liked to live in apartments on the first floor, even in Australia. Our building had balconies, which I thought was quite posh, and Mum painted our balcony in her favourite colours. Mum loved all earthy colours like beige and brown. So everything in our flat was painted and wallpapered in Mum's colours – brown, green, beige. Mum was a very handy person: she could sew, paint, make and repair things. She was creative and artistic.

Two families lived on each level of the building. We never heard any noises from our lovely neighbours, who were much older than my mum and dad. The walls of the building were very solid. Our flat was seven by ten metres, seventy square metres. There was not much room in the flat for a family of five: my mother, *Mutter*, and father, *Vater*, who I called *Mami* and *Vati*; my older brother Kalli; me; and younger brother Wolle. Kalli is nine years older than me and Wolle is five years younger. The rent was fifty-six east marks per month. There were east marks (Ostmark) and west marks (Westmark), and a west mark was five times stronger as a currency than the East's. The east mark had no meaning in world currency at all. Our money, *Geld*, was of no value to the rest of the world. Today it costs four hundred and sixty-five euro per month to rent a similar space in East Berlin. Mum is still in shock about the change.

On entering our flat, and stepping into the hallway, a patterned curtain hand-sewn by Mum hung in front of storage space. The kitchen was to the left and beyond it the narrow bathroom, which had a toilet and a big bath. There was no shower at all. A little bathroom window was always kept open. On the right-hand wall was a square mirror and next to it a glass shelf with our brushes and combs and Mum's bottle of olive oil that she sipped from every morning. My Mum still has beautiful skin, so I'm sure the oil was very good for her. We hung our towels on our own hook on the wall. Next to the bath stood the large briquette hot water service which we had to feed briquettes and kindling hours before we wanted hot water for a bath. We seldom had a bath, and when we did, each of us would take turns sharing the same water.

We were very clean children. Our mother taught us that hygiene was very important, so to wash our faces, hands, underarms, our private parts and our feet was absolutely the norm. A wooden board fitted over the rim of the bath, and inserted in a hole in the board was a round metal bowl, *Waschüssel*, which we half-filled with cold tap water and topped up with hot water boiled on the stove in the kitchen. We always had to clean up after ourselves, so part of the process was inevitably wiping the floor after washing so that nobody would slip, leaving the area the way we found it.

The briquettes were delivered by the truckload onto the street outside the building, then we carried them in a black metal bucket, which wasn't very large, through the hallway of the building, down the stairs to the cellar, where we stacked them all. On each delivery day, we made dozens of trips of briquettes to our own particular storage space in the cellar, and the task took many hours. My older brother's pride and joy – his bike – was also kept in our cellar area, and Kalli was always in the cellar mucking around with it. I'd have to go down to the cellar when he was home to tell him to come up for meals.

Our children's bedroom was a very narrow room with two beds on one side and a big cupboard, apparently built by Kalli's father. Mum was previously married to a man who had not come back from the war and he was Kalli's father and sadly they never met. Mum was very proud of this hand-built furniture. There was a cot that Mum tells me I stood up in, holding the rails of the cot screaming and shouting at night. I know why I was screaming. Later in life in Australia, I remembered that I had childhood dreams that frightened me. I dreamed that I was surrounded by fire and flames. Years later, at the Brunswick Spiritual Lyceum, I was advised by a medium during a flower reading that my childhood dream related to a previous life when I was burnt on a bonfire in the middle of a market square because I was a white witch who had a natural skill to heal people. How awesome!

I loved to play with my two dolls – one was a baby doll and one was a black African doll. My baby doll was a Christmas gift which I wished for and cherished like a real baby. Mum knitted and crocheted different outfits for my baby doll, which was nearly the size of a newborn baby and made from hard plastic. Mum taught me how to put real nappies on my baby doll. A blue jacket Mum knitted still exists and my daughter has it today. I had a little old-fashioned wooden pusher to take my doll for walks.

I loved my black doll and a favourite dress she wore in summer was red polka-dotted with a swingy skirt and a T-shirt top. I looked after this dress so well and had to mend it carefully from time to time. Eventually, I owned a similar dress myself.

My teddy was yellow and quite big, probably about fifty centimetres high. I washed him, put baby cream on him, gave him baths. He was stuffed with straw and had a little red felt tongue. I loved him and over the years he became a very worn-out teddy bear.

I was delighted when my younger brother was born. Mum knew that I wanted to have a brother and then he arrived! I called my baby doll Wolle and told Mum that had to be the baby boy's name. My little brother was my everything. I spent virtually all my time with him and felt like I was his mum, which was just what I wanted. I put him to bed, tucked him in, changed his nappies, played with him. I remember him as always smiling with blond curly hair which eventually fell out and grew to become darker and longer straight hair. I played school with him as soon as he could sit up on Kalli's big bed. He was my 'real' student surrounded by my dolls and teddies. We loved it and he did everything I told him to do. I had an awesome time with him.

When he was a toddler, I sat up with him of a night while Mum had to make her parent visits to the families of the children she taught. We were very creative and I gave Wolle a drum to bang on while he was barely old enough to sit upright. Mum had a *Zitter* packed away, and, although I wasn't allowed to play it, when she was out of an evening, I'd get it out and Wolle and I would play it. We'd play the recorder and guitar too. Our elderly neighbours upstairs wondered why there was so much noise of a night from our flat and told Mum about our musical evenings. I was actually scared to be alone and responsible for Wolle, and making a lot of noise seemed to help. We both developed a great love of music. Eventually, our neighbours gave me a real violin to add to my musical instrument collection. What a wonderful gift! Mum then booked me in for violin lessons after school time and I was taught some lovely, simple tunes like *Alle meine Entchen schwimmen auf dem See*, 'All my little duckies swimming on the lake.'

I was creative and theatrical from a young age and enjoyed playing with my hand-made puppets. I devised puppet shows for my little brother and friends. My puppet theatre was more than one metre high, it was wooden and had two hinged flaps that opened to reveal the bright red curtain.

Sunday was the only day for visiting relatives and I remember visiting Dad's mother sometimes for afternoon tea. Whenever we visited, we followed the tradition of taking a home-made cake and a bunch of flowers. We had no garden, of course, but bought the flowers from a tiny shop around the corner from where we lived. Flowers were very cheap.

We walked for about fifteen minutes to the station of the underground train, the U-Bahn, then caught the train for six stops, then we walked for ten minutes until we reached the block of flats where Dad's relatives lived. Their block looked similar to ours – grey, plain, solid and four storeys high. I loved visiting Dad's relatives for afternoon tea because they offered us a special treat – pink and white peppermint sugar blocks. They allowed me to drink real coffee, not kinder-coffee, which was caffeine-free Karo called *Muckefuck*. Mum only ever had real coffee on very special occasions because it was expensive, and we children were only ever allowed to drink *Muckefuck*. Like grandmothers all over the world, Dad's mum spoiled me and poured me real coffee when Mum was distracted talking to the other adults.

Sometimes on Sundays we went to a huge park, Treptower Park, only a couple of stops from our home on the S-Bahn, *Schnellverkehr*, which means 'fast traffic' train. The train system in Germany was quite unique: even though the S-Bahn and the U-Bahn may be going in the same direction, they are two different forms of public transport. The U-Bahn is a huge underground system, used in the war as bunkers for safety. It is not necessarily slower than the S-Bahn and some people prefer one form of train travel over the other. In some places, the U-Bahn actually emerges from the underground for a short section and then returns underground. There's a huge network of U-Bahn lines, but a much larger S-Bahn system of lines which extends well beyond Berlin. *Zug* – trains – takes passengers to the outskirts of cities, to other cities and even to other countries. There were few cars in East Berlin, as not many people were car owners, so we all walked and I still love walking today.

There were kiosks, walking tracks and at certain times of the year fun park rides at Treptower Park, which Dad loved. We'd take a picnic, walk beside the river and enjoy the little kiddie rides and listen to live oompa-oompa bands.

Mum's family was from Pomerania, in north-east Europe. She was the oldest of thirteen children and as her mum died very early in life, she had to take on the responsibility of being a mother to the family. She had to leave her home in 1945 when she was very young to earn money to help support her family. Mum really wanted to become an actress, but because of her family circumstances she was never able to do that. She started studying medicine but was unable to pursue it. In 1949, after the war, a girlfriend in Berlin made contact with Mum through the Red Cross and encouraged her to come and stay with her as there were study opportunities available in Berlin that were not possible elsewhere. Mum studied in Berlin and became a teacher.

I never met Mum's father, who must have died when I was young. Most of her brothers and sisters lived far away and on the other side of the Berlin Wall. One sister lived in Canada. An aunt, *Tante* Tatjana, lived close to Magdeburg, three hours by train from Berlin plus a bus ride to her village called Wellen. I loved to go there, far away from the big city, the property was a small farm, a *Bauernhof*. These properties were owned by the government but in earlier times had been privately owned by families. Many families had to abandon their properties in war-time, fleeing for safety, and then after the war the government took over the property and arranged renting and distribution of the produce grown.

My aunt lived in a very old house surrounded by a lovely big garden. Apple and cherry trees lined the road leading to her house. It was a very simple place, without a proper toilet, and we had to pump water from the well. It was a treat to just pick apples and cherries straight from the trees and eat them. I loved visiting the country. It was so different from city life. It was beautiful, we stayed for a little holiday and I was thoroughly spoilt. I loved all the fresh vegetables that grew there, and, in particular, I loved cabbage soup. I love soup and I loved *Tante* Tatjana's soup. Meat was only available in country areas at certain times on certain days. So *Tante* Tatjana would not have had much access to meat, whereas in East Berlin, where we lived, the showcase for the East, much more was available.

Living in Berlin provided access to many things that other East Germans could not obtain. Berliners are very proud people, with a cheeky sense of humour. The historic city is called 'The City of Peace, the City with Heart'. We are known to be direct and have an attitude that shows in our faces, affectionately called *Berliner Schnauze*. We have two particular sayings that true Berliners grow up knowing, emphasising our difference to others. The first saying is 'Once a Berliner, always a Berliner,' *Ein Berliner bleibt immer ein Berliner*, and no matter where we meet in the world there is a camaraderie between Berliners.

The second phrase is 'I'm a Berliner, what I can do nobody else can do,' *Ik bin en Berliner, wat ike kann kann keener*! It's a cheeky saying and it just reflects our pride and humour as Berliners. Throughout history, it has been a very special city. People who grew up in East Berlin and then moved to a different city would not give up their citizenship of East Berlin because they wouldn't be able to get it back.

Berlin has its very own slang, some similarity to the slang from Cologne and it's also similar to Viennese slang. I think the people from those cities are similar to Berliners. I married a man born in Cologne and was not surprised to fall in love with Vienna when I visited there for the first time six years ago.

My father was a *Meisterkonditor*, master baker and pastry maker. He worked out the back of a shop with some friendly women who served customers in the front of the shop. He lived at home and went to work early each morning for most of the years he lived with us. I remember that later he worked as an undercover police officer. I preferred knowing Dad as a baker than as a police officer. I still have a craving for the cakes I loved so much as a child. I always loved doughnuts, which we called *Pfannkuchen*. A doughnut cost five pfennig, which was very little.

The first day of school was a big celebration in East Germany. I wore a lovely red and white dress with a collar, this was my 'good' dress, and I wanted to wear it all the time on Sundays whenever we'd go on our family outings. All parents gave their children a traditional gift called a *Schultüte* on the morning of the first day of starting grade one. The word translates to 'school bag', but it was really a container full of sweets. It is a cone made from hard cardboard, of various sizes and patterned brightly. There is a coloured tulle net cover at the top. The material is all gathered up together and tied prettily with a bow, so that the sweets don't fall out. This was one of the only times I remember that we had lots of lollies. Everyone took their *Schultüte* to school on the first day, quite heavy and clumsy for little hands, and put them on the desk ready to share with the other children. These cones were special; they were brought home and kept, and when my daughter started school in Australia, I loved being able to continue the tradition and send her off with my *Schultüte* full of lollies to share with her classmates on her first day.

From my first day at school, I made a very good friend, Helga. I came home that day and said to Mum, 'I think I have a girlfriend and a boyfriend! Helga and Peter. And, Mum, Peter will be my *Verheiratman*.'

Mum laughed. I said my 'getting married man', not 'husband'. The word *Verheiratman* doesn't exist, I made it up, but to me it meant 'the man who I would marry'.

There were thousands of children at the Lichtenberg school I attended in our area. It was a huge school. We did not wear uniforms, but I had two outfits I often wore to school. One was a grey pleated frock, which I hated the colour of, but Mum thought it was practical and every colour can be worn with grey. I love happy colours, not grey! Grey buildings, grey clothes…but I also had a lovely dark blue jumper with a V-neck and white dots on it and long sleeves to brighten up my appearance. It was not hand-knitted, although Mum was a great knitter; perhaps she had bought it from a children's department store where she shopped perhaps once a year. In winter I wore thick cotton or woollen tights and long boots, and in the summer I wore sandals. I felt always warm and cosy in the cold German winters, except my fingers were so cold that I could not move them after being outside a few minutes. My nose was always frozen and red – Mum had a special tube of cream to defrost my frozen nose!

I had very long, straight, thick, fair hair and it nearly went down to my bottom. Mum was a master of doing my hairstyles, usually plaits perhaps coiled across my head. Sometimes, Dad did my hair. They took pride in our appearance but ribbons were only for special occasions. Shoes were polished every evening in preparation for school the next day.

School was only a ten-minute walk from our flat and I loved walking to school. Mum and my older brother were often already gone by the time I left. I'd get myself up and go to the bathroom, brush my teeth and wash, then dress myself for school. There was no time for playing before school. Mum would have prepared porridge or semolina cooked in milk ready for my breakfast. Everything was cooked in milk. Nobody had a fridge in their flat. We had a very small pantry and a bread box tin for storing various kinds of bread. Mum always believed in dark bread, either dark rye or full grain, as the healthiest. We loved white rolls too and sometimes for breakfast I made myself a roll with butter and jam. I love cherry jam and strawberry jam on a fresh roll, even today. We never toasted our bread. Toast was something I experienced for the first time when I came to Australia. Mum often greeted me of a morning, standing at the stove, stirring the breakfast, dressed in her coat ready to leave to catch the bus for work. She always looked very fashionable and elegant and took great pride in her appearance.

A big three-seater brown patterned couch and two other heavy lounge chairs were arranged at either end of the huge heavy extension dining table in our living room. Two dining chairs stood in front of the table. Mum always worked at this table. Everything happened at the table – eating, working, ironing, making things, playing board games.

A large solid dark brown wooden cabinet stood against the living room wall, packed with Mum's clothes in the left and right side cupboards and her best crockery in the middle cupboard. The crockery set was very good quality Meissner porcelain that was only used on special occasions. The drawer held 'special occasion' cutlery and behind the upper glass-door cupboards, pretty glasses, ornaments and keepsakes were displayed. On top of the cabinet was a large crystal vase containing dried branches attractively arranged. A huge, heavy desk stood next to the window. Mum didn't ever work at the desk; it provided a place for ornaments, newspapers and fashion magazines to be displayed.

I always had a key for the building and the flat. Everything needed keys and had to be locked and I was trusted with keys from a very young age. Whenever we returned home, we had to take our shoes off at the door and put our-house slippers on to wear around inside the flat, put our keys on the key-board and hang our coats on a hook.

The day my parents separated, I was six years old. I came home from school and walked inside the entrance door of the building, which was wide open. That was unusual. I'd noticed a furniture removalist truck parked outside on the road and wondered who was moving. I realised it was our furniture being carried down the stairs. Suddenly, Mum was on one side of me and Dad on the other and they were both holding my hands. Somehow, I feel my father is leaving. There is a moment of silence.

Then *Vati* asks me a question. 'Heidrun, who do you want to live with?' There is no anger in *Vati*'s question, no forcefulness at all.

Responding purely on instinct, I answer, 'With Mama.'

They both let go of my hands. Mum rushed up the stairs and I followed her into the flat. It looked very empty. I found Mum sitting on the couch with tears in her eyes. I sat next to her. We didn't speak. We just were sad. I felt nervous and scared and wanted to be strong for her and I'm sure she wanted to be strong for me.

Dad left that day and I never saw him again. However, when I reflect on this now, I do so with acceptance. I know that when parents separate, it has an impact on the children, but it is up to each individual to be responsible and to live their own life. Many people grew up without a dad – dads died, dads left, dads didn't return from the war. I feel that when Dad asked me that question, he gave me the freedom of choice. It was something really important. When Dad left, I moved from the children's bedroom into Mum's room and slept on Dad's side of the bed with my mum. I somehow felt relieved.

All the furniture that was taken from the flat was gradually replaced.

The ingredients for basic home cooking such as potatoes, carrots, flour and sugar were very cheap. Mothers always baked at home on Saturday nights. Butter we couldn't get all the time. We made our own quark, a type of cottage cheese, at home from sour milk. Meat was expensive. I loved crumbed pork cutlets, and Mum was the best cook. She made tomato sauce from fresh tomatoes and macaroni. I hated fish, and the only fish I recall having at home was herrings, full of bones. Herrings were very cheap, much more economical than any other meat. I tried them once and they were smelly and the bones stuck in my throat, so never ate them again.

There were two types of meat for roasts; one was dark and one was light – beef and pork. I only liked pork, and Mum would try to trick me by placing slices of beef on my plate covered in gravy, but she never could trick me. I'd spit it out! She thought beef was more nutritious.

She was very knowledgeable about diet. Although there was not a great variety of food, there was always food on the table and Mum cooked and presented it carefully and attractively.

Restaurants were not part of our life at all, but sometimes on a Sunday afternoon we enjoyed the special treat of taking the U-Bahn and going to an ice cream parlour with Mum. Ice cream was very cheap, and that ice cream parlour was very popular. The one we used to visit still exists today. Freshly made tricoloured Neapolitan ice cream was served with plain wafers in a little aluminium bowl and we loved it.

To buy basic foods, for example butter, sugar, flour, we used vouchers, *Lebensmittelkarten*, which ensured that each person would have sufficient and nobody would go hungry. Every person was entitled to a voucher. In every home, there was a *Hausbuch* which had each person's name in it. If you had a visitor for any longer than three days, they would need to sign in so that the government knew how many people lived in the flat for how long, who was coming and going.

Sometimes we could only buy perhaps a kilo of potatoes and at other times we could buy as many as we wanted for weeks. Boiled salted potatoes and some kind of vegetables with a flavoured white sauce were the main part of our diet. We had lots of eggs, and basic milk products were available most of the time.

A favourite meal was sweet-sour eggs, *Süss-Saure Eier*. It looks like eggs in a bird's nest and I still love them today.

Sweet-sour eggs – Mum's recipe

Wash lots of potatoes three times until clean. Peel the skin with the potato peeler.
Boil the potatoes in salt water and then mash with milk.
Make a gravy by melting plenty of butter in a pan, then add plain flour and stir until smooth.
Then add cold water and stir until mixed.
Add some bay leaves, sugar and vinegar.
Boil the eggs for four minutes exactly (prick the shell at each end so they don't burst).
Peel the eggs.

Serve the mashed potato in a pile and make a dint in the middle so that it looks like a nest. Place the eggs in the hollow.
Pour plenty of gravy over the eggs.

We took our one-litre or three-litre tin containers to the little grocery shop to be refilled with milk ladled from a large container mounted under the shop counter. The grocery shop only sold dried food, milk and dairy products – no vegetables and fruit. They used a wooden box for the money, not cash registers like today.

School started around the first of September and the school year finished at the end of June, with some holidays in between. We all carried school bags that were brown leather backpacks. They were not very big as we weren't allowed to carry heavy things and didn't have to carry large textbooks to school and home. We only carried exercise books that needed to have work finished at home. Posture and health were important for all children and we were not allowed to carry our school bags in our hands or over our shoulders, only on our backs.

From our first day at school, we used fountain pens and filled them from ink bottles which rested in holders cut into the top of our wooden school desks. Two children sat at each desk. We all wrote with our right-hands; to be left-handed was not permitted. In fact, the first time I ever saw a person write left-handed was when I visited the ANZ bank on the corner of Bourke Street and Exhibition Street in Melbourne in 1981. I was amazed to see a teller writing with her left hand. I asked her, 'How do you write with your left-hand? I can't do that! That's awesome!' I thought it was very artistic.

We met our classmates along the way to school so arrived there as a little group and always felt very safe. School started at eight o'clock. The entrance was a huge archway leading into the large courtyard and we arrived before the big school bell rang to meet in our class groups and then go upstairs to the classroom. If we were late, we'd have to bring a note from a parent explaining the reason. The older children were in a separate building to the little children. Everything needed to be done in a very organised way because there were so many children at the school. Lining up in twos, holding hands with another child, was the routine. The day began with every student standing and singing a Pioneer song together to start the day. I loved singing and we could sing as loud as we wanted to.

We studied reading and writing, maths, sports, music and singing. I loved handwriting the letters of the alphabet over and over again and at home I practised writing the alphabet in my exercise book. I wanted my writing to be perfect. I enjoyed reading and writing stories mostly, and was kind of a good student, but often was told off for talking too much.

Organised exercise was a most important part of the school day. We played lots of running games and activities such as climbing poles in our huge sports hall. We competed in teams and were encouraged to scream and shout and express our excitement. I was small, fit, strong, a healthy little girl and a good gymnast. It was so much fun.

Our teacher put a little note in our diary for good behaviour – for things like keeping a tidy desk, helping somebody at recess or doing good work. Although I didn't get too many, we were all proud of every little compliment to take home and show our parents.

As Wolle is five years younger than me, when I was going to primary school I had to wheel him to crèche in the pram and pick him up after school. I was so proud to be his big sister taking him to crèche and still remember the babies all lined up in their cribs and the toddlers' rows of cots. They were well looked after. I was tiny and the pram was so big, not like the prams of today.

Helga and I were good friends until 1963, then I eventually saw her again in 1994. She was very special to me and when I was seven-years old and my mother was very sick and away from home, I lived with her family for several months as we had no family members who lived nearby and I needed to continue to go to school.

Mum was very sick. It was night-time and she was lying in her bed.

She'd had a heart attack and was nearly dead. She called me and said, 'Heidrun, I want you to really listen now. It's very important.'

I was standing at the foot end of the bed and she said, 'Touch my feet, are they cold or are they warm?'

I said, 'Why are you asking me that?' I was a bit frightened. I told her that her feet were very cold.

Mum said, 'Listen to me. I think it's something really serious with my heart. My feet are cold. Now you have to run outside and just scream, "Help, help, help, my mum is sick and needs a doctor. She's dying! *Hilfe, hilfe, hilfe meine Mama ist krank und braucht einen Arzt, sie stirbt gleich.*"'

The neighbours came and soon a doctor arrived.

I was very privileged to stay with Helga's family. Her mother was a doctor and the father was very clever too, as was Helga, who became a doctor. It seemed they had more than us, better furniture, an open balcony with a great view. I felt like I had a sister. I enjoyed the change. It was fun. I was confident that Mum would get well. She never gave me the feeling of a worry, but I was sad when I visited her at the hospital.

All our neighbours cared for each other. Everyone knew each other, some more than others, and if we heard somebody was sick we'd shop for them and take food to them to assist. We wouldn't have stayed long, just a minute, just helping, being good neighbours. I missed that in Australia, although I often created that with my Australian neighbours because I love to connect with people next to me, although it seems to happen less and less these days. It is important to be there for people both in good times and in bad times.

Generally, I loved school and I particularly liked my class teacher. In our system, the same teacher stayed with the one class all the way until the end of primary school, like Steiner schools today. She taught all the subjects of the curriculum. Frau Schmidt had a big heart.

When Mum was sick, my teacher knew what was going on. Mum had to take my little brother to a boarding house for children at this time. On Saturdays, I'd walk for about forty-five minutes to visit my little brother and pick him up with the pram and take him out walking with me for a couple of hours. I always felt safe either walking on my own or on public transport as a little girl.

It was my birthday while Mum was away recovering. Everyone was already in the classroom before me. The curtains were drawn across and the room was dark. The large teacher's table was covered with presents for me and a traditional painted candle birthday ornament with candles burning on it.

The teacher said to me, 'That's all yours!'

Flowers, home-made cakes, some clothes and lollies. This was a one-off occasion and I think my teacher was very thoughtful. It's wonderful to make somebody feel very special, to feel not alone, cared about and loved and to make them feel like they belong.

Everybody worked, fathers and mothers – only old people were at home of a day and – we were all provided with lunch at school. Lunch cost only fifty pfennig. After the junior years, our school hours were longer but they were rather varied. Some days finished early and others went on later, though I think the classes always finished by two o'clock. As there was nobody at home, I stayed after our classes with many other children for organised after-school child minding. I never felt overtired. Everything was planned, we were signed in and out of the after-school care, completed our homework first and then participated in various arranged activities.

We did not invite our school friends to visit our homes after school because living in the blocks of flats there were plenty of children to play with. After doing my home duties, such as shopping for food, picking Wolle up from crèche or kinder, bringing in the washing, preparing dinner, bringing up the briquettes and keeping the heater going, it was playtime. Other people say that I've always worked very hard, even as a child, but for me it was just my life, I didn't know any different.

My friends called out to me from the communal backyard, 'Come down, Heidi, it's time to play,' and I joined them as soon as I could.

We never played on the street, as we were fortunate to have a big grassy backyard at our flats which not everybody had. We played chasey, hide and seek amongst the bushes counting backwards from ten – *zehn, neun, acht, sieben, sechs, fünf, vier, drei, zwei, ein*s, I'm coming! – hula hoop, hopscotch scratched into the ground with a stick, catchy ball games in a circle, skipping rope – single, double, all the combinations. It was all great fun, I loved it. Most children seemed happy and friendly. Eventually, the mothers would hang out the windows, calling to us to come home for dinner time, and always before dark.

Dinner was usually only a light meal. We'd all had a hot meal in the middle of the day, so consequently there was no cooking for dinner. We usually sat at the big square kitchen table at our own set places, as Mum prepared our light snack on the wooden chopping board in front of her, such as dark rye bread, butter, tomatoes and chives. We finished our meal with a glass of milk. Pastries and cakes were only for weekends.

Two minutes each way from our flat were bakeries and the wonderful smell of the pastries and fresh bread filled the air, but Mum did not have a spare pfennig to spend on pastries. Our food was very basic, with perhaps not much variety. The communist system ensured that nobody was hungry, but we did not have much either.

There was always something cooking on Mum's large stove in the kitchen. She always prepared a big Sunday lunch, the most important meal of the week. Weekends were also washing days, which was quite a procedure. Mum rose early, long before us, and I heard her in the kitchen preparing the boiler. We boiled all our clothes, handkerchiefs, sheets and towels with washing powder for five hours in a huge boiler on the stove. Then we transferred the clothes from the boiler to the bathtub and Mum and I hand-washed every item, adding cold water to the hot water from the boiler. Two or three bathtub fulls were typical. Then it all had to be rinsed three times until the water was clear.

Sometimes, Mum left me alone to finish rinsing the clothes, and she'd say, 'Heidrun, was the water really clear?' and I'd answer, 'Yes,

Mum,' although sometimes I didn't do it as thoroughly as I know she'd have liked, but to my judgement it was close enough and I'd had enough. The skin of my fingers was rubbed raw from washing and wringing the clothes, red and painful.

We struggled with the heavy clothes basket, carrying it up several flights of stairs to the space underneath the roof of the building, and hung the washing on the rope clotheslines strung under the roof and shared by all the tenants. Each Sunday, we made four trips up and down the stairs from our flat with all the washing. My older brother came home late on Sunday evenings after weekend bike trips away cycling with his sports club. He was always so enthusiastic about how much he enjoyed himself! His cycling clothes were then washed at night-time and hung on lines on our balcony.

It was funny in the wintertime, because we'd hang the washing up on Sunday in the cold weather and then when I arrived home from school the next day I'd have a list from Mum of my duties, including bringing in the washing, and I knew I had to do it.

Mum eventually came home from work and said, 'Didn't you check your note for this afternoon? You haven't brought the washing down.'

'But Mum, it's still frozen!'

Sometimes it took more than a week for the washing to dry in the winter, and then there were times when we couldn't even hang out the washing on the shared lines because there was no space, as no washing was being brought in. But, as we didn't have very many different outfits, we'd have to bring some of the frozen clothes inside. We'd be very careful how to take them off the line, otherwise we could snap the clothes, not to mention what a freezing job it was for little cold fingers. The clothes that were required were brought in and had to be defrosted and dried overnight so that they could then be ironed in the morning. Absolutely everything was ironed, because every item was made from either cotton or wool – there were no wash-and-wear synthetics in those days.

We used rubber hot-water bottles to heat our beds, and in each bedroom and the living room we had an enclosed briquette heater called an *Ofen* to heat the room. These large, rectangular ovens made from heat-resistant tiles stood in the corner of each main room. In the living room was a brown one, in Mum's bedroom there was a dark green one and in the children's bedroom was a lighter green one. They had two doors and were about two and a half metres high. They were a feature of the rooms, and the older-style heaters were made from beautiful patterned moulded ceramic tiles. Mum taught me how to light the ovens. I'd open the little door at knee height, put in some crumpled up newspaper, then add some fine splinters of kindling. Mum always read the *Berliner Zeitung* daily newspaper and so there was always newspaper available.

Mum's instructions were, 'Light the paper at the front. When it's going, put only two briquettes on it. If you put more on you risk extinguishing the flame. Wait until it's burning brightly then add more briquettes in a criss-cross way.'

After burning for two or three hours, the surface tiles of the oven were so hot I could hardly touch them. We put things on top of the furnace to dry. We hung towels over chairs near the heater to dry. We put socks and underwear inside the top door of the heater but had to remember to take them out before they were scorched. The ashtray at the bottom of the ovens needed to be emptied every day.

These heaters were in every flat, underneath each other with a common chimney that was cleaned periodically by chimney sweepers, *Schornsteinfeger*. In every hallway of the block of flats, a noticeboard in the entry displayed information for the residents. Whenever the chimney sweeper was due to arrive, the residents were advised. Employed by the government, as were all workers, they came during the day while everyone was at work or school and the heaters were not lit, so the chimneys had cooled down. They wore black clothes and a hat, everything about them was black, and they walked from the briquette depot in each area carrying a wooden ladder on one shoulder and a huge coil of rope with a large brush on the end of it on the other shoulder. They climbed up to the roof from inside the building, onto the ladder and then lowered the brush on the rope down to the bottom of the chimney. If you happened to see the *Schornsteinfeger*, it was considered a sign of good luck. In fact, for New Year's Eve even today, you might have a special chocolate treat decorated with a *Schornsteinfeger* made from paper or clay and this is a sign wishing good luck.

Sometimes when we wanted to have fun, we walked around to the briquette depot just two minutes away from home and had a ride on the swing with a friend for twenty pfennig. It was a boat-shaped swing that two children could sit on at the same time, facing each other. Rugged up in our hats and gloves, scarves and coats, we were always dressed suitably for the cold winter weather, when temperatures dropped as low as minus twenty-four Celsius.

Mum was a great knitter, particularly leading up to Christmas time. Whenever she had some spare time on weekends or late at night, she knitted. Most of the time we received practical presents because that was what we needed and most of the time they were handmade – a jumper, a scarf. Christmas time was all about family and being together and even though I don't remember much about Kalli at home with us when I was little, he was certainly always a part of Christmas. I believed in Father Christmas, *Weihnachtsman*, for many years.

Christmas time started four Sundays before Christmas Eve, and those four weeks are called Advent. Each day for twenty-four days before Christmas Eve, children everywhere flipped open a door on their Advent calendar, a religious season in all the German-speaking lands. On 6 December, we traditionally celebrated the arrival of Nicholas, *Nikolaus*. We put a pair of winter shoes or boots, well polished, out on the windowsill and in the morning when we woke Nicholas had visited and they were filled with goodies and apples – a pre-Christmas celebration. Although Nicholas was never seen by anybody, children all knew that he wore a long, brown hooded coat that hid his face.

Christmas fairs, *Weihnachtsmärkte*, were open during the four weeks of Advent, and we loved to visit and enjoy the Christmas music, with kids singing, playground rides, market stalls piled with beautiful shiny bells and balls, angels, stars and wooden toys. Happy Christmas songs filled the air, but they were not religious Christmas songs that would be familiar to people in the West.

Oh Tannenbaum, Oh Tannenbaum…
Wie schön sind deine Blätter…

Oh Christmas tree, oh Christmas tree,
With faithful leaves unchanging…

Even the streets of Lichtenberg smelt special at Christmas – snow (or the promise of snow), Christmas biscuits baked in the shops, mothers and their children baking Christmas goodies together at home. It was the most nostalgic, magical time of year. We made little gifts and decorations with Mum at home inside the warm flat. Everyone made little gifts for their parents, sisters and brothers, aunties and uncles. Of a night, East Berlin was always a dark and dull-looking place. It was not a city that wasted electricity. But at Christmas time, it was so different. Everything was lit up with Christmas lights. It looked beautiful and I loved it. Every window in every home was decorated for Christmas. It was a very creative time in every way. We made decorations at school and at home using whatever craft materials were available for the most important event of the year – stars from paper, wood and matches. We kept our Christmas decorations year in and year out. They were special.

Each year, we bought a large pine tree, *Tanne*, from a depot that doubled as an ice cream kiosk in the summer, and struggled to carry it home. We always chose a great big tree that would reach up to the ceiling of our flat, but it stayed on the balcony until Christmas Eve.

On the last school day before Christmas, a special performance was presented at assembly time. Each class prepared for their performance and parents were invited. This began a winter holiday of two weeks.

On the day of Christmas Eve, Mum woke even earlier than usual to prepare a duck or a goose for the special evening celebration and for Christmas Day lunch. The bird was bought weeks before Christmas. As we couldn't order our poultry, we just had to line up in a queue for maybe two hours or longer, so just getting it was a big deal. The poultry was already dead, and mostly plucked, but Mum would need to tidy it up. We wrapped the poultry in newspaper and kept it outside on the balcony, the weather was always freezing at Christmas time.

Apples were a main part of Christmas cooking and sometimes when they were available we'd be able to buy two, three or four kilos at a time. Every day leading up to Christmas, we visited the fruit and vegetable shops to see what was available. It was typical to stand in a queue for two or three hours. The older I got, the more I hated queues.

The flat was cleaned in readiness for Christmas Eve. Late in the afternoon, we had the most memorable bath of the whole year, with fragrant bath salts, then we smelt lovely and Mum tucked us into bed at about five o'clock because it was going to be a late night. It was so exciting. While we were sleeping, Mum brought the tree in from the balcony and decorated it. We were supposed to be sleeping, but usually I was so excited I didn't sleep.

After a few hours, I'd call out, 'Mum, can we get up now?' and when she said, 'Yes,' we'd hurry to dress in our best clothes. I always wore something special for Christmas Eve – a pretty dress. The door to the lounge room was closed. Then we opened the door and called out to each other, '*Fröhliche Weihnachten*, Merry Christmas,' and hugged and kissed each other.

The Christmas tree was the centre of our attention and the room was filled with the sweet scent of the pine needles. It always looked beautiful, and seeing it decorated began our evening of celebration. Positioned in front of the window so it could be seen from outside, real candles alight on the branches amongst the decorations, it was a magical sight. Mum placed a little baby crib made from folded paper under the tree, but we never talked about the significance of the crib.

We couldn't wait to have the Christmas meal, which was for immediate family only. Mum makes the best red cabbage in the world, and red cabbage was part of our traditional Christmas meal, which also included potatoes. Potatoes, potatoes, potatoes…they were cooked in all different ways for most of our meals, but for Christmas it was always boiled potatoes with gravy.

Traditional Christmas Meal

1 duck
Rub the duck with plenty of salt
Stuff the duck cavity with apples and *Bohnenkraut*, a herb.
Bake the bird for at least three to four hours and enjoy the aroma of the lovely food cooking which fills the room.

Oranges were available at Christmas time because they came from Cuba, with whom East Germany traded.

Mum always served herself first, the respectful custom for the mother who prepared the meal. Kalli and I always fought over the legs of the poultry. I hated the breast but loved the tasty skin. I do not remember anybody drinking alcohol ever at Christmas in our home.

We children cleaned up the dishes as quickly as we could, Mum said that Father Christmas was on his way to visit our home. Every family found somebody to be Father Christmas to visit their children. It was only when I was older that I realised our Father Christmas was really Kalli. Mum was very creative and had made a costume of a full-length long brown heavy winter coat, a red cap like a beanie with white spots and a white fur rim, and long black boots. With a potato sack over the shoulder, filled with goodies, Father Christmas carried a bundle of twigs which was a symbol that naughty children would get a smack from him. I was so scared of him, although I was never smacked. He wore a mask over his face, which I think frightened me, although I was very excited to see him. Father Christmas spoke with a very deep voice. The first memory I have of Father Christmas was the year I was so scared that I hid under the table when he arrived at the door. Mum cajoled me to come out, so I sat very close to her as he asked me if I'd been a good girl. I shook.

We all learnt songs and poems as music and performing were a big part of home life as well as school, and for every little gift from Father Christmas's sack, each child had to do a little performance. I usually received one main gift, perhaps a doll or something for my doll house or something to wear. I enjoyed playing with a farmhouse that had been made by my older brother's father, with miniature farm animals, and at Christmas may have received a little gift of another animal to add to the collection. Father Christmas left after about half an hour and we played with our presents while Christmas songs from the radio filled the air, and it was then time for cakes. Christmas cake, *Stollen*, a German traditional fruit cake made with yeast, was served with other cakes. Without *Hausgebackenes*, home-baked food, Christmas wouldn't be Christmas – and without Christmas, Germany wouldn't be Germany.

We loved the cakes Mum made and, finally, Mum gave each of us our *Bunter Teller*, 'colourful plate', a specially designed Christmas plate from her to each of us, full of goodies, apples and nuts. She even prepared one for herself. Bought chocolates, some in silver paper and others in gold paper, chocolate ducks and Father Christmas shapes filled the plate. The *Bunter Teller* plate only came out at Christmas. Around midnight, our very special Christmas Eve celebration ended, and we went off to bed – tired, excited and happy.

We loved it if it was snowing over our winter holiday so we could go tobogganing. We visited the same area as we did in the summer, but it was covered by snow. I think I was snow-blind. I was very sensitive to light, which created a challenge for me during dance performances later on of course. I wished I had sunglasses. Every kid went tobogganing on any tiny slopes at Christmas. We all had our own wooden toboggan and it was an everyday sight to see many people heading for the slopes carrying their toboggans on their shoulders or going to the S-Bahn station.

The winter when I was eight years old, Kalli and I travelled by S-Bahn and double-decker bus to go tobogganing.

Kalli said, 'I'll lie on my tummy and you sit on my back and off we go!'

He was adventurous and so was I. He chose a long, icy, curving, challenging slope that only big kids would normally attempt. We missed the big curve, we slid, the wooden toboggan smashed into pieces. I was in shock and hurt.

He called out to me, 'Are you all right?'

I was lying somewhere screaming and crying.

He said, 'Don't be a *Memme*.' A *Memme* is a chicken, a sook.

It was such a scary experience that I never sat on his back again, but I still loved tobogganing!

A week after Christmas and we were ready for another huge traditional celebration, New Year's Eve. The day before New Year's Eve, parents or children over eighteen queued at shops for fireworks. It was huge; there were so many different types of crackers. People came home from the shops laden with big bags of various fireworks. As we did on Christmas Eve, we bathed in the late afternoon and went to bed for a few hours before enjoying the midnight celebrations. The decorated Christmas tree still stood inside the lounge room and while we were sleeping Mum was busy decorating the lounge room with coloured streamers to celebrate New Year. We listened to the radio from about three hours before midnight, waiting excitedly to the countdown to cheer in the New Year. In the meantime, we had a late dinner of Mum's traditional potato salad, with frankfurter sausages and mustard.

Zehn, neun, acht, sieben, sechs, fünf, vier, drei, zwei, eins…

The noise was incredible! From every window and balcony in every block of flats, families lit their firecrackers and threw them into the air. The air of East Berlin was alive with the colour and sounds of fireworks exploding in every direction. Littlies stood on the balconies of the flats waving pretty patterns in the night sky with their sparklers. It was the most wonderful way to start the New Year. We hugged each other and wished each other a Happy New Year, then enjoyed the special treat of *Pfannkuchens*, doughnuts filled with delicious *Pflaumenmus*, plum purée. Mum made a punch for us, *Fruchtbowle*, that contained a tiny bit of white wine, but was mostly orange juice and lemonade. We did not have juice through the year, it was too expensive, so this was special. Mum loved to celebrate with a glass of champagne and a tiny glass of advocaat. I was allowed to have a sip of the advocaat. When we were older, she gave us half a glass of champagne. One New Year's when I was still quite young, I was so tipsy, I couldn't stop laughing! Mum couldn't stop me from laughing and was worried, but Wolle thought it was hilarious. Even today, if I have one glass of wine or champagne, I'm likely to start laughing, and I don't really drink alcohol at all. Eventually, at perhaps two in the morning after all the New Year's Eve fun was over, we'd be tired and go off to bed.

New Year's Day was the only morning of the year that Mum would sleep in until seven instead of getting up at five or six. It was a family day and we always enjoyed a wonderful lunch together, then we kids went tobogganing with the other local children.

Easter, too, was a special celebration in East Germany. There was no talk of Christ dying on the cross or any other religious significance. Until I was an adult, I had no idea of the Christian tradition. Our Easter was all about eggs and chocolate and celebrated in springtime in Germany. Again, it was only celebrated with the immediate family and was a holiday from work and school. Mum was always quite serious on Good Friday, and she'd buy herrings to cook for herself, which she loved so much. My brothers and I didn't eat fish, so she'd make us sweet-sour eggs.

We all got dressed up to go out at Easter, perhaps for a stroll on the street, to Treptower Park or to the ice cream parlour. I had one dress when I was little that I loved to wear on such special occasions. Blue with tiny colourful tulips embroidered on the material, it was strapless, smocked across the bodice, and with a flowing loose skirt. Another favourite outfit I enjoyed wearing was traditional lederhosen, leather pants with braces, that never had to be washed and never wore out, they were such good quality leather. Mine had previously belonged to Kalli and I enjoyed wearing them with a plain white shirt and a little red scarf. With my hair in two plaits, it was kind of a cheeky-boyish look.

We decorated eggs for Easter. Eggs were cheap and readily available. With Mum supervising the project, the three of us worked at the kitchen table. Firstly, we pricked each end of the egg with a needle, then cupping each egg carefully in our hands, we blew the contents into a bowl. Mum used the eggs to bake her lovely cakes or for scrambled eggs.

We painted the shells using watercolours. It was entirely up to us how we decorated them. We poked a match through the centre of the shell, tied a length of cotton around it and hung the eggs on our easter branch tree, a dark brown birch branch with tiny yellow flowers supported in Mum's crystal vase. It was a lovely decoration for the flat, celebrating spring and new life. These eggs were always kept and each year they were packed away carefully for the following year. We made new decorative eggs each year and displayed them all together. On my first Easter in Australia, that is what I did too.

The three main Easter colours were yellow, brown and green. Yellow for ducks, green for grass and brown for the Easter bunny. At school, we made pretty, colourful Easter cards for our parents and friends. Fresh Easter daisies were displayed everywhere at this time. Our traditional Easter brekky was soft-boiled eggs with fresh bread and butter. I don't remember any other special tradition of Easter food.

We couldn't sleep on Easter Saturday night, so excited that Easter bunny was visiting, and when we woke on Sunday morning we all searched for our eggs. Unlike Father Christmas, the Easter bunny was never seen. Every family has a set of papier mâché eggs for each child, which, like Russian Babushka dolls, are of various sizes that fit inside each other. Each egg is made of two separate halves. Decorated with painted Easter bunnies and ducks and chooks, they look beautiful.

The rule of the Easter egg hunt was that you could only find your own eggs and if you found your brothers', you'd have to quietly put them back. Our eggs had our names on them. Sometimes it was hard to find them; they could be anywhere – on a shelf, under a chair, in a drawer, under the bed – and so it could take up to two hours to find them all. Each egg was hidden as a half, like a bird's nest, with green paper grass in the bottom and the cavity filled with various little chocolate foil-wrapped eggs. Sometimes, Mum would have to give us hints on where to find them. If we visited relatives at Easter instead of taking cake, traditionally we'd take chocolates for the hosts and a little bunch of very colourful flowers like freesias.

Mum always made my birthday a special day. I'd get up earlier than normal, I was so excited. In the lounge room on the big table there'd be a bunch of flowers for me, a home-baked cake and a present – perhaps a writing pad, a jumper, some socks – something practical. It was such a lovely way to start my special day. We'd share the cake in the afternoon after Mum came home from work. This is a tradition I have kept with my own daughter on her birthday: fresh flowers, a home-made cake and a little gift. My mother, daughter and I, we all adore flowers.

One year, my birthday was on a Saturday and I was allowed to invite Helga and Peter, my special friends from school, to join us. Mum made us treats for afternoon tea, perhaps they are best described as fried crêpes, using a flower-shaped ladle. She dipped the moulded ladle in the oil to heat up, then put it in the egg and flour and milk mixture, placed the utensil back in the oil and in a minute one flower-shaped treat was cooked. We had a huge bowl of them, sprinkled with icing sugar, thin and crispy, about the size of a doughnut. After we finished our treats, the three of us played our recorders. Everybody learned the recorder at school.

Woman's Day, *Frauentag*, a traditional special day, was celebrated on 8 March each year for all women over eighteen in East Germany. Pupils of Mum's helped her carry home all the flowers, pot plants and hand-made gifts and chocolates she was given each year on this day by her students. Our living room was an ocean of flowers; it was amazing. It looked so beautiful!

Once a year, we also celebrated Teacher's Day, *Lehrertag*, and like all students, I made a little card and took flowers or a small home-made gift to school to give to my class teacher. Again, Mum was inundated with flowers and gifts from her students. She was well respected and loved by her students.

Mum was special. She was a dedicated teacher and organised camps with her classes and sometimes I went too because they were in the school holidays. The kids slept in large cabins and the days were spent enjoying outside activities such as bushwalks, games, cooking our meals from fresh ingredients on the campfire, and picking wild fruit as we walked through the forest. Of a night we played board games called *Mensch ärgere dich nicht*, 'Hey, Don't Get Upset'. The camps almost always ended with enthusiastic singing of a night.

Once a year is carnival time, *Fasching*, and these dress-up parties were events of great fun for adults and children. In schools, they were run by the Pioneer organisations. Mothers made the hand-made costumes and it was traditional for young girls in particular to sit with their mums to help them and learn their sewing and craft skills. I don't think most women had a sewing machine, but Mum's was her pride and joy. My mother loved organising *Fasching* for her class and I'd join in on those occasions. My favourite outfit was when I was a black and white cat.

The trade unions also organised dress-up parties for workers on New Year's Eve, whether people worked in factories or shops or other workplaces, as part of the end-of-the-working-year celebration. In East Germany, our working year was from 1 January to 31 December, unlike the tax year in Australia, which is from 1 July to 30 June. Bonuses and awards were traditionally given to hard-working workers at the end of the working year and also to students at the end of the school year.

I still have certificates presented to me at school which state the bonus I received as incentives and rewards in appreciation for good work and behaviour. We loved to receive our student bonuses and one of my certificates show that I was awarded prizes of thirty marks. That was a great deal of money for a child and I remember at ballet school using my bonus to buy eggs and sugar, which I'd make a mixture of to lick from a spoon and share with my friends – it was very sweet and we loved it. I'd also buy biscuits and lollies, a whole bag of goodies to share.

Weekends were family time. Shops were closed Saturdays and Sundays. Children whose parents were in essential services and not home for weekends would go to after-school care on Saturdays. If the weather was good, this weekend care would involve excursions and outdoor activities. On Sundays, we'd often take the train and tram and walk through the forest to visit one of the many lakes, where we'd swim. There are many beautiful lakes in and on the outskirts of Berlin. People say that there are more large lakes in and around Berlin than there are months in the year. We went to Müggelsee Lake, the largest of East Berlin's thirteen big lakes. Together we prepared a picnic that always included potato salad, boiled eggs and *Bouletten*, hamburgers. There'd be thousands of people enjoying a day out. Mum always made a lot of effort spending family time with us on Sundays, especially in the summer and autumn. I loved all outdoor activities.

One night, my older brother was looking after me and Wolle, and as I was about to go to bed he asked if I'd had a wash and brushed my teeth.

I said, 'Of course I have.'

'No, you haven't, your neck is still dirty.' He took a nailbrush and tried to brush my neck clean. He realised that it was suntan. He laughed. My big brother was trying to do everything right that Mum would have expected. I have always had a very dark tan and as an adult when people sometimes ask where I'm from, for a bit of fun, I just say I'm a gypsy.

Kalli decided to teach me how to swim. We went together to an indoor swimming pool. Suddenly, I was standing on the side of the pool and he gave me a push.

'Help, help...'

'Just move your arms and legs. Swim!'

'Help...this is scary. I can't touch the bottom...' What a horrible big brother.

'Keep moving your arms and legs!'

I was really, really mad at him, but by the end of the afternoon I could swim. I learnt a great lesson that day. Sometimes you do just have to jump into life at the deep end and swim. Today I love to swim, not competitively, but just for pleasure, and particularly in the ocean. It took me years to get used to swimming in salt water.

Mum was not a happy-go-lucky person; she was serious and very thoughtful. She was not the kind of mum that would hug and cuddle us when we were kids, but I can still feel her beautiful soft and very gentle hands stroking my hair sometimes, or touching my face saying 'Goodnight' or 'Wake up' in the morning. She was very compassionate and did everything she could do for us. I've always had great respect for my mum. She has high intelligence, no doubts, lots of courage, is very organised and disciplined. Sometimes I felt overpowered by that and felt determined to do what I wanted to do and not what she said I had to do. This probably created in me the development of the kind of rebellious person I am, and was even as a child. Guidelines and boundaries were okay, I respected that, but sometimes I felt a little boxed in and the rebel in me blossomed while I was growing up. It made me feel good to recognise that I could do what I wanted to do, that I could be strong and confident enough to follow what I chose in life. Mum was a strong example to me.

Mum carried home large heavy bags of exercise books from school – how she ran for the bus carrying such a load, I do not know. Our living room always had piles of exercise books of her students and other books that she brought home to correct and to read. Often I went with Mum to the Karl Marx *Buchhandlung*, bookshop, to find books she needed as a teacher. Some nights, before she went to bed, she drank a glass of red wine with an egg yolk mixed through it. She claimed it was good for her and would keep her hair strong and healthy.

My favourite uncle worked as a truck-driver and drove a big old truck that looked rather like an army truck. He came sometimes to Berlin, and it was a real treat when he suggested to Mum to take me for a ride up front with him in his truck for a while. He always had malt beer in his truck. This is a sweet, non-alcoholic drink that kids can drink as well as adults. It is a very healthy malt drink. Truck drivers always had to be 'zero' for alcohol. I felt so big and it was an awesome experience sitting in this truck drinking malt beer beside my uncle.

At home, each night after dinner, it was one of my duties to take the rubbish tin from under the sink in the kitchen to empty into huge rubbish bins downstairs in the backyard. Paper was kept separately, stored to give to schoolkids at organised times by the schools to collect from every household and to take to small depots for recycling. The children earnt a little pocket money at the depot that they could put in their *Sparschwein*, piggy bank. Pork was the main meat available in East Germany, and the cute fat *Schweinchen* was a common symbol for money boxes. Glass bottles and jars were kept in the cellar to use for preserves. Mum never bought any tinned vegetables or fruit. She preserved peaches, apricots and cherries to have fruit to eat all year round.

Before the construction of the Berlin Wall, to go from East to West Berlin was possible, but people needed official permission and had to return on the same day. So, although the wall was not there, during the Cold War there was restricted access for many years.

I remember the day the Berlin Wall went up. On 13 August in 1961, I was eight, it was the end of summer time, and it was already dark. We'd had our dinner as usual and I had the rubbish tin in my hand, ready to take it downstairs.

Mum is washing the dishes, and says to me, 'You don't have to take it down today.'

'Why not, Mum?'

'Don't ask me why, but you don't have to do it today.'

'You mean I don't have to do my duties?' This is odd. 'But Mum, you always say I have to do my duties so why not today. Mum, what's going on?'

'It's too dangerous.'

'What do you mean, it's too dangerous? It's never been dangerous before. What's going on, Mum?'

'It's dark.'

'I know it's dark. That doesn't matter. I always bring the rubbish down when it's dark.'

Mum insists, 'You never know who's down there.' All this time she continues washing the dishes.

'What do you mean?' It is the first time I recognise that Mum feels fear. 'I don't understand, Mum. I'll take the rubbish down now.'

'No, you're not going. You don't understand. It's very dangerous, so dangerous I don't want to tell you what it is.'

I am worried. 'What are you talking about?'

'There's maybe another war coming, the Third World War. And I have experienced war and don't want to remember.'

'What's that? You mean war – bang, bang?'

'You never know. I want you to stay in here. I want us to be here, inside, tonight. Together, not going anywhere.'

I see tears in her eyes and her voice sounds croaky. Whatever is going on, it is very serious. I leave the kitchen to think about it for a few minutes, then return.

'Mum, can you please explain? I'm really scared now. I'm not taking the rubbish down ever again!'

'Heidrun, you don't understand it and I know that you can't. I've been through the war and I don't want to scare you, but it could become dangerous – I hope not – and maybe I can tell you more after I listen to the news on the radio.'

Our small dark brown radio was such an important possession in our home. Nobody had televisions. Mum had heard on the radio that citizens were forbidden to venture outside that night. When the news eventually came on, Mum sat to listen to it, the first time I remember her doing nothing but just sitting on the couch and listening intently to the radio.

I didn't understand what they were talking about, a wall, *Mauer*, what could this mean?

I tried to interrupt to ask Mum what it meant, but she said, 'Sh, sh… This is important.' She needed to listen.

After the news finished, I asked her, 'Do you understand everything now?'

She said, 'Yes.'

'Is it that dangerous'

'It could be.'

'What does it mean – *Mauer*?'

She said it was a very dangerous situation and it had something to do with politics. I had no understanding of politics at that age, but I clearly understood Mum wanted us to be together inside.

It was much later that I understood what had happened, that overnight a wall had been started to be built dividing West Berlin and East Berlin. The centre of the Berlin Wall was only about thirty minutes from our flat, by walking and on the S-Bahn, to the Brandenburg Gate in the heart of Berlin.

For so many people, the night the wall went up was a disaster. They might have been from the East, visiting the West for the day, or vice versa, and they were not able to return. Ever. Families were separated. The urgency that people felt, risking their lives climbing from windows, getting shot, is shown in documentary films of the event. I understand that the wall was built to stop the immense migration of people from East Berlin to West Berlin that had been taken place since the end of the war.

At the time, some West Berliners worked in the East and some East Berliners worked in the West. Years later, I had a close friend whose family, from West Germany, were prevented on 13 August 1961 from going back to their home. They had permission for a day out to the East. The father of the family worked in the East and simply wanted to take his wife and children for a day out to show them where he worked. They had the required travel permission. But they could not return.

Luckily, all the family was together. Had the wall gone up the day before, when the father would have gone to the East on his own as he did each day for work, while the boys and their mother went to school and work in the West, the family would have been separated. That was the fate of thousands of uncountable families.

When people heard the news, many rushed to each side of the wall, trying desperately to get from one side to the other, either to join loved ones or return home. Where the wall wasn't physically built, the army stood with arms linked creating a barrier and blocking free passage. In the absolute panic and hysteria, many people died that night, shot as they attempted to scramble through the chain of soldiers. Some slipped through, but it was complete chaos. The government order, *Befehl*, was that passage was no longer permitted.

East Germany was called a Workers' and Farmers' State, *Arbeiter-Bauern Staat*, and all citizens were considered to be of the same, equal, class. This is what the Communism ideal is all about, although different Communist states ran their societies with different structures. Although Mum was well educated, she had to be very careful how she behaved because in her position as a teacher she was expected to do her job very well, but she certainly could not be arrogant or think she was more important than others. Artists were of course much exposed to the public but had to be very cautious how we behaved and what we said when not on stage. A behaviour of 'politically clean' was the wisest.

We all had to be very careful that we didn't get prioritised by others and that we didn't prioritise ourselves. Otherwise, we'd face that kind of attention as a challenge. Nobody sought attention. I grew up being aware that it was important to fit in. Listen to the propaganda, whether you believed it or not, say nothing, keep your opinions to yourself or you'd experience consequences, *Nachteile*, and you'd never want to have consequences.

Mum's only aim was to do her work well and to always care about the kids she taught and their families. She visited many families after school at night time, to see what the home environment of the children was like and if there were any problems. She created an incredible connection to many students. Mum taught me how to do corrections of her younger students' work, so sometimes I sat beside her of a night and marked their exercise books with a red pencil as she had shown me. Mum sat working on one side of the table and I sat on the other. I loved staying up with Mum and enjoyed helping her with her work, listening to music from the radio playing in the background. Mum listened to music every night as she corrected her students' exercise books. She loved music.

All children became Young Pioneers of the East German Youth Movement, *Jungpioniere*, once we started school. This was implemented by the communist state after the Second World War as a way to indoctrinate the East German youth into socialism. We were called the Thälmann Pioneers, named after Ernst Thälmann, the leader of the Communist Party of Germany (KPD) who had died in 1944 after being shot on Adolf Hitler's orders.

Although we were required to attend government-organised political rallies and certainly there was exposure to communist propaganda at school, the Pioneer Movement provided many of our other fun activities organised within the schools. There was an expectation that we all participated and I don't remember any child who did not, although I understand it was not compulsory. I'm sure that if you didn't join, your family would have been under suspicion by the authorities. For our Pioneer activities, we were given a blue triangular scarf to wear from grades one to four, and a red scarf from grades four to eight, with a white shirt for girls and a dark blue skirt; boys wore shorts or long slacks. We sang Pioneer songs together, full of childhood enthusiasm.

> *Pioniermarsch*
> *Wir tragen die blaue Fahne, es ruft uns der Trommelklang.*
> *Stimm fröhlich ein, du Pionier, in unserem Gesang.*
> *Seid bereit, ihr Pioniere, lasst die jungen Herzen glühn.*
> *Seid bereit ihr Pioniere, wie Ernst Thälmann, treu und kühn.*

Pioneer March (translated by the author)
We carry the blue flag, the beat of the drum is calling us.

Join us happily you pioneer and sing with us the chorus.
Be ready all your pioneers, let all the young hearts pulsate.
Be ready all your pioneers, like Ernst Thälmann loyal and brave.

We all kept a diary from day one at school and our lessons and all Pioneer events were noted in the diaries. Every day, the parent had to sign it. It was a good way and ordered for parents to communicate with school. Once a week for school assembly we wore our Pioneer scarves, *Pioniertuch*. The Pioneer organisation ran many fun activities on a mass scale for the children. During school holidays, every school organised school camps because all mums and dads worked, retirement was at aged sixty-five and nobody was home to mind the children, and these were Pioneer camps. Excursions took place after school to various places with significant political or cultural history as well as to fun places like parks, forests and lakes.

Each year on 7 October, there was a celebration of the formation of the German Democratic Republic of East Germany in 1949. When I was a young child, head of state Walter Ulbricht was the East German Communist leader. He addressed thousands of Berliners in attendance at Marx-Engels Platz near the Brandenburger Tor, Brandenburg Gate. He had the appearance of a grandpa – he wore a beard and glasses, was a bit chubby and was balding; his portrait was hung everywhere – in school corridors and classrooms, public buildings and offices. He was very much for sports, inspiring children from a young age to be active in sports. The GDR always had great success in sports at the Olympic Games.

I didn't like the official marches but all the children had to attend as proud little Pioneers or FDJ with their school groups, and workers with their unions. It seemed the whole of East Berlin attended. I felt uncomfortable among the huge crowd, the noise of the repetitive cheering, the sight of the army tankers that rolled into the march with thousands of marching soldiers. Many thousands of people attended, just listening to propaganda – 'How great we in the GDR are.' I found it so boring.

Sport was my favourite subject at school and I was one of the best in my class at whatever sporting activity we did. My sports teacher entered me into inter-school competitions in gymnastics and short-distance running in older age groups because I was so good for my age. I was her girl. The year I was ten, we worked on floor gymnastics and the single horizontal bar and I was terrific at both of them. One day, my sports teacher asked me to demonstrate to my classmates a little combination on the single bar. I was confident, it was easy enough for me, and when I performed the choreography, I had some music in my head and started singing to it.

The children started giggling and asked me, 'Why do you sing while you do that?'

I didn't really know how to answer, but I said, 'Because I like it.'

Shortly after that day, our class teacher gave us a slip of paper to take home and show our parents, to bring back signed after the weekend.

She said, 'Who wants to be a ballerina?'

In our schools, when students raised their hand, it was always the right hand and we pointed our forefinger up to the sky. Not one child raised their hand.

At recess, down in the playground, my sports teacher is on yard duty. She comes up to me and says, 'Heidrun, what do you think about it? Do you want to become a ballerina?'

'What is it?'

'A dancer.'

'A dancer? Why?'

'Heidrun, you are so talented at gymnastics and so good on the bar. And when you perform on the bar, you sing, you hear music in your head. You perform to music. That's what ballet dancers do, they dance to music.'

'Really?' I am becoming more curious.

'Of all the children at this school in grade four, if there is anyone who can be a ballerina, it is you. Heidrun, tell your mum I highly recommend you. Tell her I can see you, Heidrun, being a ballerina.'

The notice explained that there would be auditions for children to join the Staatliche Ballettschule Berlin, State Ballet School of Berlin, for the first seven-year ballet course ever offered in East Germany. Before then, the courses were much shorter.

I went home and talked to Mum about it and she signed the notice, not with great enthusiasm but because I was curious about this opportunity and she was willing to see where it might lead.

The Staatliche Ballettschule Berlin was established in 1951 and, although there were two other ballet schools in East Germany, it was the largest and most prestigious. Seven hundred students attended, mostly teenagers and young adults, and the new course enrolled students to begin their ballet course younger than ever before. The audition took three days and was really heavy going. Hundreds of children arrived, full of excitement and apprehension, and we were divided into mixed groups of thirty boys and girls.

The teachers turned us inside out, physically, mentally and emotionally and at the end of the audition we were exhausted. We were tested academically in normal classrooms, then ordered to change into our sports gear, then off for lunch, then we were tested structurally for our physique. We exercised in large ballet rooms with mirrored walls. It was all completely new to me. They stretched us and pulled us and scratched us along our legs, to feel the definition of our muscles. It was such a weird experience.

We were shown a choreographed piece of music accompanied by a pianist and told to choose costumes from a big box of clothes and props. I chose to dress as a witch, wearing a black cape and pointy hat carrying a broom. I wanted to be bad! We transformed ourselves into the character we'd chosen to dress as and danced to the music in character for two or three minutes. I truly didn't know what I was doing. I was tenth in line, and just tried to copy someone whose turn it was before mine.

During the audition, the director of the school, Doctor Albin Fritsch, spoke to each group. We were in a classroom, sitting in rows. He asked if any of us had ever seen a ballet before. All children raised their fingers, but not me. I so wished to hide under the desk. He then asked each child some brief questions. 'How old are you?' 'What's your name?' 'Where do you go to school?' 'Have you seen a ballet' 'Which one?' 'Did you like it?' 'Why do you think you want to be a ballet dancer?'

I realised that there were only a couple of Berliners in the group. Most of the children had come from other cities and states. I felt so stupid and had butterflies in my tummy thinking how I'd answer the director's questions. How could I explain that I had no clue about ballet? That the only reason I was there was because my teacher had suggested it?

I want to sound interested.

'So, Heidrun, what ballets have you seen?'

'None.'

'Oh! What are you doing here?'

With a big cheeky smile, I say, 'I don't know!'

'Can you please be serious?' Dr Fritsch insists.

'I'm very serious. I don't know.'

'There must be a reason why you are sitting in this chair.'

'My sports teacher said I'm the one from the whole school who she can see as a ballerina.'

'Really? So you're good in sports?'

'Yes.'

When I went home to tell Mum all about the audition, I said to her it was *toll*, fantastic, really great. Actually, I didn't know what kind of an impression I'd made. Some things I thought I'd done well, others I was unsure about.

Later that night, Mum came to say goodnight to me in bed. This was unusual, as I mostly said goodnight to her while she was busy with school work. She tucked me in and stroked my hair and face softly and then she said, 'What do you think? How did you go?'

'I don't know, but I think not too bad.'

I was ten years old. From seven hundred children who auditioned from all over East Germany, only thirty boys and girls would be chosen. We would be advised in a few weeks whether we'd been successful or not, whether we'd be starting school in September at the Staatliche Ballettschule Berlin.

I came home from school and saw a letter addressed to Mum from the State Ballet School on the kitchen cabinet. I was so excited. We weren't allowed to open Mum's mail of course.

As soon as she came home, I said, 'Mum, open the letter, please, quickly!'

'Do you want to open it, Heidrun?'

'No! I don't want to.' I was far too excited to do such a thing.

She took her knife to neatly open the envelope, she quietly read the letter to herself and I tried to read the expression on her face. 'You made it.'

'I made it? Truly? I can't believe it. What happens now?'

'Heidrun, you are only ten years old. I don't know if it is a good idea to go. I don't want to talk about it now. We will talk about it tonight after dinner when Kalli is home.'

After dinner, we sat in the dining room. Mum in the armchair, my tall, strong handsome older brother on one side of her and myself on the other.

Mum said, 'This is very serious.'

I felt she didn't want to let me go.

'Karl-Heinz, what do you think about it?'

Kalli, aged eighteen at this stage, said, 'Why do you ask me?'

'This would have big consequences for Heidrun later in life. It's too much for a little girl. Too much training and exercising for the body is not normal. I've been thinking about this and I feel it's not right for such young children to commit for seven years to ballet. Even the medicine course at the university only takes five years! It's too much. Too demanding. Too much responsibility.'

I spoke up. 'I'm used to responsibility here. It will just be different.'

Mum continued. 'Not only will you have to do the normal schoolwork, your days will be much longer, it will be too much hard work. Heidrun, it is a boarding school. You won't live here any more. It won't be a normal life for a child. Do you understand that?'

'Is it a boarding school? That's okay.'

'You'll be scared by yourself. I think you still need me. I am your mother. You know how you always hang onto the hem of my frock… you're scared at night by yourself.'

That was true, I always clung to Mum. 'I won't be by myself there. There are lots of others.'

'So you're not scared about leaving home?'

'No. I won't be on my own, Mum.'

'Little Wolli is only four and he will miss you so much. Kalli will be studying up in the north, I'll be all by myself here. Who will look after your little brother? I need you.' Her face was sad. 'What do you think, Kalli?' She respected him, he was very intelligent, the man of our family, and she and Kalli had been through so much together.

Kalli said, 'I'm eighteen, you don't have to worry about me any more. Wolle's only little but he's going to kindergarten and while I'm home, I'll help you as much as I can. Somehow we'll find a way to look after him. What you really must think, Mum, is that when Heidrun is seventeen she will already have a diploma in her pocket. She will be made, made for life, earning money. She'll be looked after at the boarding school. You'll be all right, Mum. Let her go.'

Mum's face softened. 'Do you really think it is a good idea?'

'Yes, Mum.' He turned to me. 'Do you want to do it?'

I said, 'I can try.'

Mum said, 'No, it's not about trying, it's committing. Committing for seven years. And after that, you have to sign a contract for three more years as a professional ballet dancer. Once you start, you can't turn back, Heidrun, the government is paying about forty thousand marks for you to go to that school. That's good, it means it doesn't cost us any money, in fact it will save me money because you'll be looked after, but you can't change your mind.' She thought for a moment, paused, then added, 'Heidrun, you never wanted to be a ballerina. You always talk about being a teacher. You're so good with Wolli and you love to play school with him so much, you'd be great working with little children.'

She tried to paint a picture for me of what I could not really understand. The decision was ultimately Mum's to make. There was no crying, no shouting, but it was very intense. Mum's reservations actually made me feel more excited as I became more informed of the consequences.

'Kalli, I'll be earning money at seventeen? That's good, isn't it, Mum? I want to go.' I persuaded her. 'Come on, Mum…'

Finally Mum said, 'Heidrun, if you think it's a good idea, if you want to do this, you have my permission.'

Little did any of us know that a very short time later Kalli would be diagnosed with serious health issues. His prognosis was very grim and it was my first awareness of the importance of health, the need to look after ourselves. This perhaps was the beginning of my interest in health, of the connection between body, mind and spirit, an interest that has developed throughout my life and remained with me to this day. It was a very worrying time, and I felt extremely connected to Kalli throughout this time. We felt we all were deep in a sad, black hole.

When he recovered and then, not long after, he married, it was such a wonderful experience to see that immense sadness transform to great happiness. Mum always used to say she could not imagine any of her children leaving this planet before her. I fully understand it was a real concern for her.

After accepting the offer at the Staatliche Ballettschule, there were a couple of months until the school year finished before ballet school commenced in September. It was exciting moving into the ballet school. I never saw Mum cry, but I'm sure she did.

The ballet school was a large old building with blue cobblestoned pavements and entrances next to the massive Berlin Cathedral, which was still in disrepair from the war. It was not far from the Berlin Wall. We all knew the wall was dangerous and we couldn't and wouldn't go near there. The school was right in the centre of Berlin, near the Brandenburg Gate and Unter den Linden, a long, wide tree-lined boulevard of the most famous buildings and architecture of Berlin: the Humboldt University of Berlin, art galleries, libraries, the Academy of Arts, the Deutsche Staatsoper Berlin (German State Opera House), which was next to the Ballet School, the Komische Oper (Comic Opera House) and its world-famous museums. This is the historical cultural precinct of East Berlin. All this wonderful architecture was on the east side of the Berlin Wall.

During our first few days at ballet school, all the students were supplied with our outfits – a dark blue leotard, skin-coloured tights and beige ballet slippers. We were designated our rooms, double bunks and six to eight girls to a room. The boys occupied a separate area to the girls. Our school days were fully planned from eight o'clock in the morning, a mix of academic classes and ballet classes. We began the day with a one-and-a-half-hour ballet training session, *Klassischunterricht* before recess, where we were first taught how to stand in the five different ballet positions of the feet and then different positions of the arms. These are the fundamentals of ballet. We were taught slowly and repeated the movements over and over again. It was very difficult and hard on our muscles. We exercised to live music and always had a pianist accompanying our exercises. Those pianists were fantastically talented and skilled. They could play all kinds of music, without even a music score in front of them.

Not consciously recognising it, this exposure to music was the beginning of my love for classical music. We trained to lovely pieces and, for the young children, they were always 'feel-good' classical pieces of music. During our ballet training sessions, we were told that every single body movement had to be in flow to the rhythm of every single note which we needed to hear. At the same time, the music simply filled the background with lovely sounds, a tool to help us move our bodies. From this age, I developed the dream that one day I would love to learn to play piano. To this day, I haven't done it. Yet.

Our exercises were often accompanied by our instructors shouting, '*Und eins, und zwei, und drei, und vier… Halt.* Stop.'

After a while, the teacher stopped counting and we'd have to know what movements to perform and when to change at the correct time to the music.

'Heidrun, stretch your knee more.' 'Heidrun, extend your foot out more' 'Tuck your tummy in. Tighten your bum muscles' 'Come on, you have to work on that.'

Sometimes our teacher whispered, sometimes she shouted and when it was loud enough for others to hear, I felt embarrassed. Unlike me, many of the girls who began at the school with me had previous ballet experience and already knew the French terms for our movements. French is the world language of ballet and automatically learnt while learning the movements. I didn't feel much encouragement, just an imperative to get the movement right, my body in control, to be balanced and correct.

Our music curriculum was ballet-oriented, and we had much more music in our curriculum than in regular schools. We worked at the ballet bars mounted on the walls. At this time, Russia was the prominent country in the world for ballet and we followed the Russian history and tradition and the Staatliche Ballettschule was exemplary of it. Then, we'd have to hurry to change from our training clothes into normal clothes for our academic classes until lunchtime. It was a crowded curriculum. There was so much to learn.

We were supplied with a cooked lunch of potatoes, carrots and peas in the big canteen, served from big pots. We lined up in our class groups, all very orderly and organised. I grew up with lots of vanilla custard as part of my diet both at home and at ballet school, and plenty of milk to drink. People didn't talk about 'good nutrition' in those days but I was conscious of what Mum called 'sensible eating'. Never too much, always enough, and regular meals. I never felt hungry. I loved ice cream and chocolates and biscuits, which we never had at home or at ballet school.

After lunch, we studied again for a couple of hours in classrooms, then all went off to change for afternoon ballet or other dance training later in the day. I was never really tired – luckily, I have always had great energy and stamina. Our days were punctuated by us always running from one room on one level to a different room on another level of the building.

We didn't want to have any homework to do at the end of the day, but if our schoolwork was unfinished, we could do our homework in the multi-purpose room before or after dinner. There was no time for much else, perhaps 'girl-talk' in the bedrooms until we had to go to bed at eight o' clock. Soon after it was lights out, no talking.

The ballet school effectively had two separate sections, the boarding section, which was overseen by a principal, and the ballet school, which was run by the director. We were ordered to be very disciplined and well behaved. I was probably the only one who ever got into trouble, because I loved to talk and couldn't sleep. I've never needed much sleep. As I wasn't tired, if I had unfinished homework, I'd use a torch under my quilt so that I could complete my homework once the lights were out. I loved living with all the other students. Many nights at home I'd been alone with Wolle while Mum was visiting parents, so it had been quite lonely and I've always been a people person.

The teachers were very professional; they must have been. Only the best ballet teachers in Berlin taught there. We had our favourite staff members who'd be on duty; some we'd love and they were kind to us and others we'd not be so happy to see. I felt that most teachers had certain expectations about my behaviour but at times I was not quite that perfectly behaved child. Sometimes I had to apologise in writing, stay later at school – detention – and take a note home to Mum to sign so that she was aware I'd been naughty. At times, she needed to come into meetings because I'd been in trouble.

Four of us girls became very good friends and eventually we got to know each other's families and visited each other's homes. One day, with some friends, I decided to sneak out of the school without signing out, which was imperative. It was just after dinner, dark, and we'd planned to explore the old cathedral nearby. We weren't allowed to play in the cathedral; it was surrounded by rubble, *Trümmer*, half ruined in the war. My curiosity surfaced again. Somebody dobbed us in. Whose idea was it, we were sternly asked. I'm sure it was mine. I was lucky that the head of the boarding school liked me for some reason and she loved and respected my Mum.

I always had friends and have kept in touch with two of the girls from those days.

There were no telephones for us to use and Mum did not have a phone anyway. It was some months before we were allowed to go home to visit on weekends. Parents could visit briefly on particular days at designated times. There was no time for me to be sentimental or sad. Mum told me later that many of the children were sad and cried, they wanted to go home, but I didn't experience any of that. When Mum visited me, I loved to go with her for a walk and to show her my room.

After some months, we were allowed to go home on Saturday afternoons and return on Sunday afternoon. I walked to the U-Bahn near ballet school, changed over after a few stops to take another line, and from there walked home. I took my clothes home to be washed. I looked forward to going home on weekends but had no time for my old friends. I didn't go out to play much any more although I had one special friend at home, a boy, who was handsome and had brown eyes and dark hair and we kissed. My first kiss. I always loved boys. Home time was family time and homework time.

Many times when I arrived home, I asked Mum, 'Is there any fresh bread?'

She knew I'd love to eat perhaps a whole loaf of bread with butter and jam. Mum always had fresh bread there ready for me and one of my favourite treats – *Zuckerschnecken* and *Streuselschnecken*, sweet pastries, or doughnuts, *Pfannkuchen*. Sitting at our big dining table, listening to the radio, doing homework and enjoying bread and pastries – I loved being home. Mum couldn't believe how much I could eat. My body probably needed all the extra carbohydrate-rich food because of the amount of physical exercise that was such a major part of my life.

I'd try to show Mum what we'd learnt at ballet school but there wasn't enough space in the flat to show her any dances. At certain times, parents were invited to the school to see our little performances. Our seven-year course was new and we young ones were an experiment for the school, which kept in regular contact with our parents.

Students at ballet school, like elsewhere, were still part of the Pioneer movement. Living at ballet school in the centre of Berlin meant that we didn't have to go far to attend the political rallies and celebrations in the city.

Although I was the youngest in the class, I developed early and so looked older for my age than many of the other girls. For some reason, I actually became a motherly figure to the other girls, perhaps because of all the responsibility I'd had when I was younger. If any of the girls were sad or upset, they came to me and I comforted them. I have had this ability since I was a child of twelve and boarded with so many other children.

One day, some friends said to me, 'How come you know everything?'

I was surprised. 'What do you mean, I know everything?'

'Whenever there's a question or a problem any of us have, we always want to come and ask you, Heidi, because what you say makes us feel happy.'

I said, 'Really?'

That was the first time I had it pointed out to me that I knew something that my friends didn't know. They called me 'Little Makarenko'. Makarenko was a Russian writer, philosopher and educator who we'd learnt about at school. It made me realise that when I say what I feel, I am truthful, and that is more helpful than just saying what I think or trying to find a clever intellectual answer to anything.

I was an average student and always had respect for people who could teach me. I only had an open mind and great curiosity for things that interest me. I think the staff at ballet school knew and understood that I was a bit different to most of the other students. Growing up with a single mother, looking after my little brother, taking on so much to help Mum meant I'd come from a different environment to most of the other girls. The teachers and staff generally supported me in a way which meant that, even if I was a bit of a little rebel, most of the time I would get away with things others would not have because they knew me very well.

I wore my first tutu at twelve years old in the role of a black and yellow bird, the first time I performed on stage in a production. Actually, it was a half-tutu, giving the appearance of the little bird's tail feathers. The school ballet was called *Das Störchlein*, *The Young Stork*, and choreographed by teachers and ex-students of the school who were invited as guest choreographers. All the school was involved in some form or other. We performed at the Deutsche Staatsoper Berlin several times and all the parents were invited. We experienced how a ballet actually was produced. It was a wonderful experience.

I also danced the role of a little Babushka doll, Russian Doll. I was the second-smallest doll and the whole dance was on *pointe* shoes. The costumes were intricate and several fittings were required. I loved the fun of hair, make-up and costumes. This was also the first time I danced in *pointe* shoes on stage. We were all very proud – students, teachers and parents. It was a very high standard of classical dance for such young dancers and our classical ballet teacher, Ursula Collein, was extremely proud of us all.

After training on *pointe* shoes, all ballet dancers begin to suffer pain in their feet, as we did. Some dancers with wide toes wrapped their toes tightly in bandages to make them as narrow as possible to slip more easily into their *pointe* shoes. Toes suffered the most, cramped and blistered most of the time. Our toes commonly bled. Each injured toe was wrapped individually in bandages so that we could tolerate the pain. Feet suffer pain and we had to learn to live with it. Ultimately, dancers all end up with flat feet and walk in a particular way, with our feet facing outwards, in close to what we call 'first position', like penguins.

Our ballet shoes required special care. The training shoes were usually leather or cotton fabric, mostly pale pink or white. We had to hand-sew on every new pair the elastic strap which went across the top of our feet.

We rolled and twisted new shoes in every direction to soften them, making the sole, in particular, able to mould to fit our individual feet.

Made from cotton and satin, our pointe shoes were imported from Russia if not made in East Germany. A small block of wood had been inserted into the toe area and covered by the cotton lining of the satin shoes. I used to tear open the binding edge at the heel, to prevent blisters, and, we'd have to sew the satin ribbons securely that we laced around our feet. At the toe of the shoe, we hand-sewed a neat semi-circle of blanket stitch in thick cotton thread. This was to preserve the satin fabric as much as possible and supply more grip while we were dancing on *pointe*. When they were too worn-out to wear in performances, we used our *pointe* shoes as training shoes by removing some of the inside layers of the soles. Without the hardness of the inner soles, we can't dance on *pointe*. We scratched the soles of our ballet shoes with a fork, a knife or scissors, making criss-cross marks in the leather sole that would assist grip.

Some ballet dancers would wet their shoes with cold water, then put them on, to make the shoes a better fit and also so prevent slipping on the dance floor. With our shoes on, we'd step into powdered chalk, which helped prevent slipping on the wooden floor. Our shoes constantly needed replacing, sometimes even during a performance. All shoes, costumes and leotards were supplied and paid for by the government.

At thirteen, I developed some discomfort in my back that gradually became worse and my teachers started complaining about my restricted movement. I explained to them about the pain I was experiencing. I was told not to worry about it, that it was only the muscles which needed to get stronger in my back. When I went home one weekend, I told Mum all about it. Mum was concerned. She took me to a very good doctor who advised that I should stop ballet, otherwise there was a possibility that I might need to wear a corset later in life because my back might be damaged to an extent that I needed support if the pain continued. Mum and I talked about whether I should continue with ballet. I did not want to if it meant that I'd have to continue suffering the pain. I imagined that I'd leave the ballet school and return home to lead a 'normal' life and study at a 'normal' school. I was pretty relaxed about it. We talked about what else I might like to do as a career and I thought I'd eventually do something with languages, which I loved, and teaching. Perhaps I could travel the world knowing different languages and become a tour leader. I had no idea whether or not this was realistic. That didn't matter.

I had a recurring dream. I had never seen the ocean; my only experience of large bodies of water was the lakes we visited on weekends. But I dreamed of a huge sea, blue water, blue sky, a white passenger ship with lots of people on it, and I was on it too. I wanted to be a sailor, wearing a white uniform and a sailor's cap so that I could travel the world. I wanted to stay in my dream and experience the big, wide world. It was a lovely dream that I always enjoyed. I captured in my mind the image of this dream like a picture on a postcard. Blue big water, white waves, blue sky, lots of space, a large white ship.

One day, I asked Mum, 'How come only men can travel the world and be sailors? Why can't women be sailors?'

Mum looked at me and said, 'Why do you ask me that?'

I explained to her my dream and said, 'I have this dream so many times. I want to be a man. I want to travel the world and be a sailor. I dream this all the time, but I know in reality I can't do that, because I'm not a man. Do they ever take women in such a job? Could I do it later on when I'm grown-up?'

Mum said, 'I don't know, maybe. I haven't heard of it but, maybe, when you're grown-up.'

I said, 'That would be so cool!'

Mum made an appointment to talk to the director of the school, Dr Fitsch, about my changed plans. She came home from the meeting and said, 'Heidrun, it's not such good news. You have to finish the seven years.'

'Oh?'

'They have invested in you and they believe you have real talent.'

'Do they? Okay.' There was no choice, I had to accept it. 'But,

Mum, after that, can I go then to uni instead of doing the three-year contract?'

She explained that once I had my diploma I would be entitled at any stage to start university if I wanted to go in a different direction from dancing. So everything would be fine. I learnt to live with the pain, which came and went regularly.

I can't say that I actually loved classical ballet much in those early years, which was our main training – it was too much pain and too serious. But I clearly remember when the idea of dancing filled me with passion. In one subject, we were to learn folk dancing. I thought the teacher was not 'elegant' like our classics teacher, who was a well known ballerina from the Deutsche Staatsoper Berlin and who walked like a typical ballerina.

But my folk dance teacher, Erika Wittig, said something that was a breakthrough for me. 'From today on, for the next month, we are going to learn Hungarian folk dancing. I'll teach you about the country the dance comes from and the history of the people.' That sounded interesting; she had my attention. Then she said, 'I want to tell you something else. You need to understand, this is like a life lesson. If you want to be a successful ballerina, you need to be able to master all these different forms of dance. I want you to understand that if you do not love dancing, you will not be very successful.'

Did I love dancing at that stage? No, I enjoyed it all and was happy – the school, the children, the teachers, the curriculum. It was all good, but, quite honestly, I did not love it.

She said to us, 'I can help you. I can teach you how to express love for dancing from the inside out. Folk dancing teaches you that because if you understand the country the dance comes from, the people, the culture, the characters, the way they feel, their mentality and their emotions, then you express all these aspects in folk dancing. It is a different skill, a completely different technique, a different genre. If you understand how to express yourself from inside out, how to express the story of each dance, you can express sadness if the story is sad, express happiness if the story is happy. That's what I want to teach you, apart from the technique.'

I said to myself, 'I like the sound of that!'

Then she said, 'Come on, let's start today. I'll show you the first steps of a Hungarian folk dance and we'll all do it together. It will be wonderful and lots of fun. Dancing is supposed to be fun and I want to teach you how much fun it can be. Now, no talking while I'm explaining…' She was passionate, enthusiastic and not a bit arrogant.

I said, 'I like that!'

She heard me and I couldn't wait to get up and learn it. The pianist started and the music was fantastic; it was fiery and such a difference from what we'd learnt in all our classical ballet training. Something was changing in me. Dancing was fun. My teacher and I became great friends. I loved her to bits. We laughed, we cried, we even sang in those folk dances. She believed in me, she gave me the courage and confidence to become the best folk dancer in the class.

Even today I am still in love with the energetic *Csardas*, the Hungarian name for the national dance and its music. The *Csardas* celebrate the diversity of a rich and colourful culture. From the men's intricate boot-slapping dances to the ancient women's circle dances, with their beautifully embroidered swirling coloured costumes, the *Csardas* demonstrates the infectious exuberance of Hungarian folk dancing. The music and dancing are accompanied by women speaking, singing, shouting in high voices, expressing beautiful emotional and meaningful lyrics.

From that day on, I started to understand what being a complete ballet dancer was really all about.

We eventually learnt all different types of dance forms – folk dancing from different countries all over the world, historic dancing such as minuets. *Pas de deux* when a girl and boy danced together, jazz dance and modern dance – all these forms we eventually had to master as professional dancers.

We often had the opportunity to attend performances at the German State Opera. We had to ask for permission and sign ourselves out from school, noting the date and time. With my best two friends, I sometimes sneaked in for free. Tickets were dirt cheap, they were subsidised by the government, and many visitors from West Germany who'd come through Checkpoint Charlie filled our theatres. East German theatres always had packed audiences. We'd average seeing about ten performances every month.

Our class all went together to see a Russian ballet film, *Sleeping Beauty*, in the first big-screen cinema in East Germany. It was a beautiful movie, featuring many of the brilliant Russian dancers of the era. I appreciated and admired them all. But *Giselle* was my favourite classical ballet. It is a two-act ballet, unlike most ballets, which have three acts. I first saw it when I was twelve and loved it. It is the story of a girl who, in the first act, is living a real life with her family and friends in the country and there's a lot of folk dancing involved. It's a love story, there's kissing and giving flowers and hugs as the boy and girl get closer. Giselle goes crazy when she finds out she's been deceived and that the boy she was in love with is already engaged to another girl. She dies of a broken heart. Then the second act is classical. It's beautiful. She's been taken away from her earthly life and is a *wili*, a spirit, and her lover is searching for her. He can only find her spirit at a certain time of the night because she's in the realm of all the other *wilis*. It touched my heart.

I loved the story; that kind of innocent, loving connection between the young woman and the young man blew me away. I loved the idea of love. I adored the music. Unlike most famous ballet composers, Adolphe Adam, who composed *Giselle*, only wrote three ballets. Mostly he wrote operas. The first time I saw *Giselle*, the two principal dancers were guest artists from Budapest, Hungary – Adéle Orosz and Viktor Róna. Guest artists were not very common in East Germany. Adéle was wonderful. I wanted to be a great ballerina and famous like her one day. These two became my idols and I had pictures of them next to my bed at ballet school. It probably increased my attraction to Hungary. *Giselle* is the classic ballet I've seen most. Whenever I've had the chance to see it, I've loved to go – in Berlin, and later in Hungary when I visited there.

Most of our teachers at ballet school were East Germans. Sometimes guest teachers from Russia came to teach special classes to the older students. Maja Lepeschinskaja, a famous Russian ballerina, was a guest teacher at our school for some time. To welcome her, we had a full school assembly and all wore our Pioneer uniforms. I was chosen to present some flowers to her and give her a welcome speech in Russian. I was very proud.

My Russian language skills were excellent. I studied it at school for six years and, as Mum was a language teacher, she had high expectations that I would be exemplary with the language. We were taught in our history curriculum that Russia was our big brother: that whatever Russia says, we must do. I didn't question it.

I loved my music teacher. She was wonderful. She taught us about the composers and we read their biographies. She introduced us to their masterpieces and taught us to analyse the different parts of their music. I wanted to know more about these geniuses – Beethoven, who had such a sad life but created enormous music. I loved *Bolero* by Ravel – from nothingness building up to the full orchestra with such great energy and then falling down again delicately to nothingness. It was brilliant. It is still my classical favourite of all time.

When I was thirteen, I lived at home for a year because the boarding school did not have enough beds for all the new students. It was decided because I was a Berliner, and they thought I was mature enough and could handle it. It freed up a bed for somebody who came from outside Berlin to board. As a young child, I was very comfortable in my environment, catching trains and walking long distances. It was during the year when I came home to stay from ballet school that I became aware, like all young women I suppose, of getting attention and being noticed by men, though I didn't seek it. It made me feel rather uncomfortable.

Mum was pleased that she was able to provide me with a new pair of white pointy boots that were very fashionable, but I didn't particularly care. Following fashion was not important to me.

Our school curriculum included a subject called *Staatsbürgerkunde*, Citizenship and State Ideology, taught to us from high school age. To my understanding, it was political propaganda and I found it boring. Our teacher talked about the same thing every week, round and round in circles. I hated it and often expressed myself openly but carefully – very carefully – in these classes. The propaganda messages didn't make sense to me. I was happy as I was. I didn't care about 'baddies' and 'goodies'. We were constantly taught that communism was 'good' and capitalism was 'bad'.

Mum, as a teacher, was expected to understand politics, and approached many times to join the Communist Party, but she never wanted to become politically involved; she had so many responsibilities on her shoulders and political involvement was one she could do without. Her priority was family; she did not want to go to political meetings. I took on Mum's attitude too – I never wanted to be involved with politics. I was approached many times to be a party member, but I wasn't interested. I wanted to follow in Mum's footsteps. I have never been interested in being involved in party politics at any stage in my life.

Turning fourteen is a very special birthday in East Germany. In the German language, we use the pronoun *Du* for 'you' when talking to children, friends and family. Once a person turns fourteen, unless you know them well, the respectful way to speak to that person is to use the term *sie*. Consequently, other aspects of grammar change too. So, once the girl or boy turns fourteen, their teachers, and other adults except for family members and close friends, call them *Sie*, no longer *Du*. It is always up to an older person to offer the younger person to refer to them as *Du*. If both agree, then it is a term of affection.

In the business world, people always refer to each other as *Sie*. Students only ever refer to their teachers as *Sie*. I actually like this formality, this language distance, as it keeps business on professional terms and avoids it melting towards a personal relationship. A little bit of formality is sensible to me. We grew up calling all adults by their surname Herr or Frau or Fräulein; it would be disrespectful to use their first name.

Called *Jugendweihe*, boys and girls have a celebratory day at school during the year that they turn fourteen, to celebrate the change in status from being a child to a young adult. All the students from classes in the other year levels put on a performance in honour of this group of 'young adults'. We were presented with *Jugendweihe Urkunde* certificates stating that

> To live a happy life we must be part of creating peace and Socialism. This means we must understand the laws and orders of this society and acknowledge them, know them and live them, and understand the power of them.

The girls all received a special new dress for the occasion. Mum chose a black costume and white frilly blouse for me and new black shoes. I didn't like the outfit, as I always loved bright colours, but Mum assured me my new outfit was good quality and black and white always stayed in fashion. We wore our special clothes to school on the *Jugendweihe* day and families were invited to attend. When we came home, or on the nearest weekend, aunties and uncles were invited to afternoon tea to celebrate the day with coffee and cake.

The age of fourteen brought another change – from being members of the Young Pioneers we became members of Free German Youth, *Freie Deutsche Jugend*, FDJ. This was the official youth movement of the German Democratic Republic. We wore a dark blue shirt with a yellow emblem on the sleeve, and remained members of the FDJ at least until we began work and automatically joined the relevant trade union.

For *Jugendweihe*, Helga invited me to celebrate with her family, who'd invited lots of relatives and friends. Although their flat was no bigger than ours, it was more modern and nicer. About thirty adults squeezed into their flat for the party, mostly standing because there was not much room for so many people. Bottles of alcoholic drinks were set up on a table, which intrigued us. They were not familiar to us. Helga's dad made a speech and toasted her, *Prost*, cheers, with champagne. As the night went on, there were many tipsy people at the party, laughing and having fun, the first time I'd seen people affected by alcohol.

Eventually, Helga's dad suggested we try whatever we liked from the drinks table and he gave each of us a schnapps glass. He said, 'Try them all if you like, but don't have too much!'

Whatever he poured for us in our little glasses, I tried, just a sip, and whatever I didn't like, he finished. I tried a chocolate liqueur, which I enjoyed, and a couple of other drinks, which I didn't like at all. About ten minutes later, I felt sick in my tummy. Then I felt dizzy and tried hard to keep smiling at people. I wanted to go home, or jump off the balcony; it was awful. I didn't make it to the bathroom, unfortunately. I should already have been home; my curfew was ten o'clock for this special occasion.

Three of the men brought me home at about mid-night, after I'd woken up on Helga's bed. I felt terrible. Mum answered the door. As soon as she saw me, she was gone, out of sight, and the men left. I didn't know where she went. I figured she was in the bathroom with the door closed, and that was a no-no in our home. Usually, doors were left open. I called out to her and she didn't answer me. I'd messed up my whole new outfit.

I passed out on my bed and Mum told me later I slept for three days. She didn't talk to me for days; she was hurt and disappointed. This was the first time I was permitted to stay out until ten o'clock, and I'd let her down badly. My new *Jugendweihe* outfit needed to be dry-cleaned. Dry-cleaning cost a lot of money and was inconvenient. I was responsible for the unfortunate consequences and never forgot it.

I was popular with the ballet boys and too many of them fell in love with me. To leave the school grounds, we had to get permission to go out in our free time, but dates were not officially allowed. I planned dates and managed to make them happen. When I was fourteen, I had a secret date with a boy who was older than I. We walked around the streets for half an hour, holding hands, enjoyed a little kiss, and planned the next date – hopefully, it would be soon – then went back to school.

By the time I was fifteen, I discovered that only people from high ranks, high ranking in the arts, or politics or even the Stasi, lived in bigger, better flats than the rest of us. Perhaps they even drove cars, which was unthinkable for most families. We'd learnt at school that every country had a State Security to protect its citizens, and I knew that in East Germany it was called *Staatsicherheit*, abbreviated to *Stasi*, the East German Secret Police. I had a curious sense of *Stasi*, not a negative sense at that time. I was not anxious about it. One day, I was sure I would find out.

Eventually, one of my ballet school friends who lived near Alexander Platz invited me to her home. The buildings looked ugly to me; they were modern and large, looked like boxes and not in keeping with the surrounding architecture. When I entered the blue-tiled building, instead of stairs, I used the elevator. I thought, 'That's posh'. The flat was better fitted-out than typical homes and had central heating, although their furniture was no nicer than Mum's. Her parents were rather formal. I thought they were a bit weird. The government gave us an allowance, *Stipendium*, from age fourteen and we found out from each other that we all received different amounts to each other. This particular girl received a higher allowance than the rest of us, and we wondered why. She didn't know, but amongst us, we decided her parents might have been *Stasi* – preferred citizens with special privileges. I didn't judge her in any way – it was not her fault.

My ears and eyes were always open and I sought the opportunity to be with older people and spent more time at lunch in the canteen with the older students. I wondered where they were at about these aspects of life. I consciously made contact with older people, asking for a minute to ask questions, sit with them, and they accepted me. I kept asking questions. I knew I was growing up and I appreciated their opinions. They didn't seem to judge me. I started to get a feeling that there were secrets, that you couldn't just say anything you thought, and that in class it was better for me to not be the open book I usually was. I gradually developed borders around myself, kept my mouth shut and my honest opinions to myself.

I wondered how come certain students were teacher's pets. No longer little cute kids, we were older with greater expectations and responsibilities and I wondered about many observations I made. How come those people always sit together? How come they whisper? How come they stop talking when I come closer? How come those teachers are friends? I started to have my own opinions about the groups that were gathering together.

I became more conscious of wanting to get to know at a deeper level people who I was familiar with, either from my past or new in my life. They intrigued me. Who were they really? I wanted to look further than their façade, to find out where they fitted in. I felt there were categories of people, but I couldn't have explained it and probably didn't want to. There was an aspect of fear involved. I learnt that, depending who I was with, I'd better not say anything… If I'm not too sure, then I keep my mouth shut, before I say something wrong. I'd rather please others and go on in my life than be considered wrong and be criticised. I was criticised enough as a student ballerina, it was so challenging to achieve the perfection I understood was necessary. I didn't want to be judged for everything I did in my life. I thought, 'Okay, Heidi, maybe it's wiser to be a bit quieter and shut up.'

A new ballet school was being built at this time, and we all moved for several months up to the north, Kühlungsborn, on the coast of the Ostsee. The whole township of holiday homes was taken over by the ballet school. Our ballet rehearsal room was a large restaurant in the summer season. We trained on freestanding wobbly ballet barres and uneven flooring. This different environment was both weird as well as adventurous and fun. For the first time in my life, I saw the *See*, the Baltic Sea, and we loved our walks on the beach. I thought it was just fantastic

– enjoying all this wonderful space, wrapped up in the cold in a big, thick, tartan cape Mum had made for me. We stayed up north for several months while the new school was built, then returned to Berlin to start at the brand-new building.

By staying up north, we'd been prepared quite cleverly for the transition to the new school in the suburb of Prenzlauer Berg. We were sad not to be right in the centre of Berlin any more, where we were close to the theatres which were now about half an hour's travelling time away. The new school was in the 'old Berlin', where people lived, rather than the centre of the city, which was the cultural and government precinct. The new ballet school building became even more important as a showpiece of East German excellence in the arts. Prenzlauer Berg, though small, was an artistic suburb and is so today.

Around this time, I was chosen to dance a waltz as part of a TV show. It was a different experience, which required ballroom dancing. We were paid a little for it as it was a professional engagement. Another time, I was chosen by a photographer as the model for a poster for the Leipzig Trade Exhibition, and shortly after as a bikini model. The school became a resource for people and opportunities. I liked this kind of diversity. I loved performing, whether a small part or a major role, and although I always had butterflies in my tummy, I didn't show it. I trained myself to stay in control.

It was very easy for me to remember the lyrics of songs that I'd only heard a few times. I loved singing and organised my friends one night to have a singing competition. We all went to one room, and using a hairbrush as a microphone we sang our favourite songs.

By this time, although the academic curriculum was always adhered to and was important, ballet started to make greater sense to me. I was performing and enjoyed the opportunity of experiencing other opportunities facilitated by being a student at the ballet school. I had my eyes wide open now and understood the importance of the connections between all the other dancers, working together and what it meant to behave in a professional way. It was all great fun and I appreciated it.

We had older students coming to our school from Budapest, Hungary, and four students older than us were chosen to go to Hungary. This was a big thing. We were allowed to watch the Hungarian students training. They could show us a lot and we girls liked watching the Hungarian boys – we thought they were 'hot'. They appeared different; it was exciting. They couldn't speak German and we couldn't speak Hungarian, but we had no trouble communicating, as dancers know all about body language. We enjoyed their company and the idea of one day becoming an exchange student and travelling to a different country became my dream. I wanted to find out more about the culture. I always wanted to be around them and insisted that they took my name and address and try to find me a Hungarian pen pal my age on their return home.

Not long after they left, I received a letter, written in German, from a Hungarian ballet girl inviting me to visit her in the school summer holidays. I was beside myself with excitement. As Hungary was another eastern communist country, to travel there was possible. Not easy, but possible. I couldn't wait to tell Mum. The summer holidays were only a couple of months away, how was I going to make this trip a reality?

Somehow, I felt confident enough to ask Mum if I could go to Hungary and she said, 'But you are only fifteen!'

I said, 'That doesn't matter.'

'You don't know this family.'

'I know I'll get to know them!'

She said, 'Have you got money?'

'No. Can I go and earn some money?'

'Where?'

'I don't know.' I thought for a moment. 'I'll ask Kalli!'

Kalli organised a job for me in an electronics factory for the first three weeks of the summer holidays to earn the money I needed to go to Hungary. I put tiny little components from a box into a little electronic set, over and over again. I was paid enough for the train fare to Hungary and one hundred marks, which was the maximum amount of money we were allowed to exchange for Hungarian currency, forint. As I was not eighteen, Mum had to sign for my permission to travel and it was granted.

I stayed in Budapest for four weeks. I learnt the language – every day I worked on it, word by word, writing things down from the dictionary. The family of my pen pal were wonderful to me; they picked me up from the station and took me everywhere. I loved their family life. At night, they played cards, canasta, by candlelight, as they smoked and drank wine in their large baroque-style flat with huge rooms and high ceilings. We didn't understand each other, but it was all great fun. All theatre and culture and ballet took a holiday during summer holiday time in Hungary, so we visited the countryside, took buses, trams, saw people, events, markets, tourist attractions and partied a lot.

We visited restaurants with live *Csardas* bands. I loved the food – lots of hot paprika dishes, more flavoursome and colourful than I'd ever tasted. These were all wonderful, exciting new experiences for me. I met so many people, I felt so free, I decided that this was true life and I fell in love for the first time. I loved the sound of the language – the men's voices deep and resonant, the women's sweet and high. I wanted to stay in Hungary, I wanted to live there.

I learnt that travelling makes you open your eyes to the world. Hungary was the window of the East for the Western world, and for the communist countries, it was the 'West for the East'. Hungarians had a distinctly different mentality to East Germans; they were more open, they had more flair, were more casual and easy-going. People were happier. It was how I imagined the Western world.

This special Hungarian family invited me to return for a wedding. It was to be a three-day, typical, traditional Hungarian wedding scheduled for the weekend after school had resumed. They said to me, 'Heidiken, you have to come back!'

I planned on my fourteen-hour train ride back to Mum's in Berlin that she would help me get back to Hungary for the wedding. Nothing was impossible. But how could I make it happen? I asked Mum to write me a letter to take to school, pleading that this was an important cultural opportunity, a once-in-a-lifetime opportunity to attend a Hungarian wedding. I had to go to a meeting at school to explain. The school director allowed me to go and I was beside myself with happiness. It was the first time ever a student was granted such a request.

On returning home to pack, Mum asked me how I was planning to pay for this trip. I'd saved some money from the previous trip and my Hungarian family gave me the missing amount to ensure that I had the funds for the train trip back to Hungary.

I had five days off from school, three days for the wedding and two days for travelling to Hungary and back. My teacher insisted that I must be on time for start of training at eight a.m. on the day of my return or I'd be in big trouble. They trusted me.

A Hungarian wedding – what an experience! The wedding was held in a little village about three hours by train from Budapest and the festivities lasted for three days, a parade of celebration from village to village singing, drinking wine and cheering the wedding couple. The bride wore a traditional Hungarian costume, a colourful dress, heavily embroidered. The groom also wore a traditional Hungarian costume of embroidered knickerbockers, white knee socks and an embroidered dark blue jacket.

All together, I visited Hungary eight times. One particular family became like an aunt and uncle to me and loved me. The Hungarians, although they too were under a communist regime, could travel much more easily than East Germans and these friends joked that one day they'd put me in a suitcase, because I was so tiny, and take me with them on a ship along the Danube from Budapest to Vienna. They were convinced I would absolutely love Vienna. It was many years before I visited Vienna and they were absolutely right.

My schoolmates seemed to accept the opportunities that I was able to experience. They were excited for me about everything I did. They loved it when I shared my adventures with them and saw in me a great love for life and immense curiosity. I was courageous in creating experiences for enriching my life.

In our last school year, when I was sixteen, we prepared for the final year of our diploma. I was in full bloom physically, although some of the girls my age looked still like children, and my teachers wanted me to go on a special diet.

Mum was defiant. 'No. All this ballet school business is unnatural enough anyway. Absolutely no diet for my daughter,' she insisted.

I certainly was not fat, but boys develop later than girls and they couldn't lift me because they were not strong enough to lift a full-grown young woman. I felt a bit outcast, because during *pas de deux* lessons I was told to just sit and watch, not allowed to participate. That was so cruel, although the teachers assured me that they would find a solo for me which would be marked equally as the *pas de deux*. I wasn't too happy, but had to live with it.

I was developing as a whole person. My focus was still on finishing as best as possible the seven years, and apply in the near future for university to study languages. As time went on, my final year at ballet school was overall more enjoyable than I expected. It was full on, and I learned to live with the back pain. I was able to go to the Staatsoper near our old school for free massages, which was helpful. I grew in confidence, life was increasingly interesting, I managed academically to my satisfaction, I was happy and adventurous, curious, determined and a loved person. I was cheeky, I was rebellious, but that was part of me. I was sure life would just fall into the right place. I connected well with the older students, looked after the younger ones, and was preparing for my professional future. I started to mix more with professional dancers and kept my ears and eyes open.

East Germany was the most eminent theatre country of all the eastern communist countries at this time. There were not enough dancers for the demands of all these theatres. I understood that there were lots of opportunities. I decided that I wanted to go to Schwerin, three hours by train from Berlin, up in the north, where I'd been told the male dancers were particularly attractive and 'real men'. That appealed to me. I was doing my own research. I expected the school to tell me I would not be chosen to stay in Berlin; not every dancer could stay in Berlin of course, which meant that most of us would be contracted interstate.

The Meckelenburgische Staatstheater Schwerin had a good name in the ballet world, in musicals, in opera and operettas. It was a jumping board for performers to the next level. I knew students from ballet school who had gone there. I secretly organised to go to Schwerin one Saturday and took my training gear with me. When I arrived at the theatre, I wanted to watch the ballet company as they trained.

The director and choreographer, Teja Kremke, approached me quietly, and asked, 'Heidi, why have you come here?'

I explained that I'd heard great things about the ballet company, that I was in my final year at ballet school. I said that I knew of his wonderful reputation – he was well known, he'd studied in Leningrad – and that I wanted to meet him. 'I'm considering that I might want to come and work here when I finish at school,' I said cheekily.

Kremke answered, 'You know your school decides where you go, they delegate you.'

I said, 'I want to work here. Can't you organise it for me?'

He thought for a moment then said, 'This afternoon is another ballet training session. Have you got your training gear with you?'

'Yes, I have.'

'Okay, come and train with us.'

And so I did. I was very aware of him watching me in the training session and I started to wonder if I should have done this.

Afterwards, he said to me, 'So you want to work here?'

'Yes.'

'I'll take you.'

'Are you serious? Can we arrange that?'

'Yes. I think so.'

It was amazing. I was sixteen, I had not even finished school yet, but everything for my future was falling into place. Being cheeky, not telling anyone of my plans, I had this wonderful opportunity. I was excited and asked him, 'How do we do it?'

Kremke said, 'I don't know, Heidi. How long are you staying here?'

'I have to go back to school later today.'

He organised the contract, the theatre director signed it, Kremke and I both signed it. I was 'signed up'!

I said, 'What happens now?'

He said, 'Don't worry about it. I'll fix it. Don't talk about this at school. Good luck with your final exams and see you next year.'

Going home on the train, I sat gazing out the window and enjoying the countryside. I love travelling by train. It was a beautiful ride back to Berlin. I wondered how Kremke could make something possible that was not officially practised. I had no answer.

At this stage in my life, I had a growing awareness of the politics of my existence. I lived a full life at school with a commitment to study and to successfully complete my diploma. That was the expectation from the government, who paid fully for the course, and so I expected myself to do the best I could do and be the best I could be. In this unusual environment, having to be so responsible and committed so early in life, I developed an open mind and was equally open-hearted and curious. I wanted to know everything, I was very alert and observant, my eyes were always open to what was going on. I felt connected very quickly to people and things, I loved to listen, using all my senses. I formed opinions about where I was, why I was living that way and where it could lead me. I was determined to think positively, to be the driver of my own life. I enjoyed life and every experience, good or bad. Every night I went to bed thinking, 'That was a beautiful day,' or 'That was a very interesting day.' Reflecting on the day, I started to analyse certain things, thinking about my values, trying to find out who I was, what was my place, why was I doing this or that. Politics became a part of it in many ways. I remember someone with wisdom said this: 'It's not about what you know, it's about who you know.'

As we were high school students, the school subject called *Staatsbürgerkunde* became very predominant in our curriculum. It was all about politics – communism and capitalism – in the contemporary, 'now' world. I didn't have a feeling of 'bad' and 'good' people in general, of things being 'possible' or 'not possible'. That wasn't how Mum had raised me. I felt this subject was all about judging people and events. It made me feel uncomfortable. It was difficult to keep my opinions to myself, because normally I was very talkative in classes. I explained to Mum that I didn't like *Staatsbürgerkunde*.

She asked, 'Why not?'

'Mum, it's all about criticising people and it's about judging them and I don't like it. But I hope my attitude to it won't reflect on the way I am perceived by everyone in school.'

Mum said, 'I understand. I feel the same. I've never wanted to be involved in politics. You want people to love you and know you for who you are, not because of what somebody may consider your political opinions to be.'

I was grateful that communist East Germany, the German Democratic Republic, had given me the educational opportunity to experience ballet school, and that my teachers saw in me a great future ballerina, I appreciated it. But this whole political confusion made me ever more alert. I felt my classmates did not understand how I felt about it. I certainly did not get good marks for this subject and wondered if my classmates were pretending their enthusiasm. Was it influenced or forced by their parents, I wondered. Their attitude was very different to mine. I felt we were not just kids any more. It was interesting to observe.

I was a good organiser and from my early teenage years I realised that some people saw leadership qualities in me. I was given opportunities at school for public speaking and felt comfortable and confident in that role. For the last two years at ballet school, I was the *FDJ-Sekretär*, FDJ leader, of the school. My leadership was not something I sought, it was put upon me by my teachers, but it was good for my personal growth and gave me opportunities to attend meetings with adults. When I was sixteen, I was officially approached about the possibility of joining the Communist Party once I turned eighteen. It was explained that if my answer was 'yes', the officials would spend time with me to prepare me to become a party member at eighteen.

'Why me?'

'We think you are a good follower and a good leader. You don't have to answer now. Think about it and let us know.'

'I'll think about it.' I wasn't into politics. I found it depressing – wars, communism, capitalism. Why did I, an artist, a ballerina, need to fill my head with this bull?

I told Mum next time I went home.

Mum said, 'It's up to you. You don't have to join.'

'But Mum, if I say no, it may have negative consequences for the rest of my life.'

Mum said, 'Let me think about it.' Then she advised me to say what she'd said whenever she'd been approached to be a party member. 'Actually, I'm quite happy with my life and I'm not ready right now for party responsibilities. At this stage in my life, I don't want to be involved.'

I appreciated her advice. I was consciously pushing away anything that was involved with politics. I was an artist without politics.

Towards the end of the final year at ballet school, we'd virtually finished our academic study requirements, so it was all ballet, ballet, ballet and preparing for our very important final ballet exams. Our teacher in dance history gave us one particular lesson and announced he wanted to make a statement, his very own opinion, and we were not to take it outside the classroom. It was a piece of wisdom from him for our lives.

'You will see. Life will not remain the same. The world is changing, we are changing. My prediction is that one day it won't be Russia and America, communism and capitalism, that have world power, it will be Asia. The Asians will take over the power in the world.'

I did not know what he meant but understood not to say anything. I thought about what he claimed…China, Asia… isn't that interesting. However, I was pleased to hear that this teacher had a worldly opinion. He explained also that art and politics are interconnected. This was interesting and something I'd not previously been aware of.

We never had the types of free political discussions in East Germany that take place amongst friends and colleagues in Australia over meals or having a drink in a pub. We knew not to criticise our leaders or the state, always aware that somebody amongst us could well be a Stasi member or informer, ready to report any negative opinions to the authorities. It was believed that about one in six adults were Stasi informers or members.

I needed to keep my pre-organised contract at Schwerin a secret. At the end of school after exams were over, choreographers and ballet directors from theatres all over the country came to see the graduation performance, as did all the parents and relatives. Our class was special, the first group of students who'd completed the inaugural seven-year course. It was a huge thing. When I got up on the morning of the graduation performance, I was sick, I had diarrhoea. Of course it was nerves. But the show must go on. And it did. I danced a classical solo variation which I'd been rehearsing all the year, and wore a light blue tutu, the first time I wore a real tutu. I felt so grown-up, like a truly professional ballerina.

A few days later, each of us attended the panel interview, face-to-face with all our teachers and the director of the ballet school. Each interviewer scored us individually. Depending on the score of the judges and the notes made by the directors and choreographers on graduation day, every student was delegated to the appropriate theatre and contracted for the following three years. We were called in one at a time. What did they think about me, I wondered. I had no clue how my interview would go. I had told nobody about my agreement with Kremke. I hadn't even told Mum. There were about twenty people, including the principal, in the interview room. I was about the fifth one to be interviewed, and had watched my fellow students come back into the waiting room announcing to us with great excitement where they would be going.

'We have decided that with your results, Heidrun, after seven years at the Staatliche Ballettschule Berlin, you will be contracted with the Komische Oper Berlin. Congratulations!'

'Really?' I was shocked that I was appointed to that prominent ballet company in Berlin. What an unexpected surprise and compliment! Good for me! I thought I had to appear happy and surprised.

'Congratulations, Heidi, we are really happy for you.'

'Thank you, I'm happy too. But I can't go there.'

'Oh, why not?'

'Well, I'm sorry, I know I shouldn't have done this, but I have actually organised and already signed my own contract somewhere else.'

The panel members had stern, stony faces.

Eventually, the director spoke, 'What do you mean?'

'I have signed a contract with the Schwerin State Theatre.'

'How did you do that?'

'I just did it. I went for an audition there. I felt over the last few years here that I was not perhaps the quality of dancer you expected me to be. I wasn't expecting you to ask me to stay in Berlin. I had heard a lot about the Schweriner State Theatre and many students I know from this school have gone there. I thought I'd go and have a look one day, and I did. I was asked to do training with them. Kremke arranged a contract. We signed. It's done.'

'This is impossible! We will investigate this. Leave the room now.'

I wait outside for about five minutes and feel like I am a very bad girl. Whatever happens, happens. If they say 'no' and I go to the Komische Oper, that's fine too. They can sort it all out.

I was called back in.

'We've decided we are not very impressed with your actions, but we wish you good luck.'

'So that means, it's all okay? It's all right I start at Schwerin?'

'Heidi, you do whatever you want to do and good luck. Now your place at the Komische Oper will be freed up for somebody else.'

'That's fine by me!' I ran out the door, full of excitement, and only then told all my friends about what I had organised.

Mum hoped of course that I would stay in Berlin but I explained to her that I would be much happier in Schwerin, where everyone knew each other. I thought it would be a great environment to work in, where all the different genres of the art in theatre were brought together.

'Mum, it will only be for three years.'

The three-year contract was a protection for both sides. As our first professional contract, it offered us security, knowing that the company couldn't get rid of us if they didn't like us. It gave us a chance to have the time and space to develop further. The company was obligated to support and encourage us. I thought this was a good idea. I would be at least twenty before I would have to make another decision about my professional life.

To celebrate the year happily, I'd planned one more holiday to Hungary. I was used to organising my visa now and as I wasn't on the blacklist, I had no problems about getting it. I had a fantastic time with my Hungarian friends.

On my return, I was excited leaving Berlin, although very aware that 'once a Berliner, always a Berliner'.

I packed my suitcase and other bags, and kissed Mum goodbye as she said, 'Take care of yourself.' Her voice was shaky and sad. She knew her girl was definitely going now. She said to me, 'I wish you would have stayed in Berlin.'

I assured her that I would come back regularly. She was sad to see me leave. I was seventeen and felt twenty-five.

I arrived at Schwerin, after taking the train from Berlin. Schwerin is a beautiful place, very historical with beautiful architecture, a much smaller city than Berlin, with very old narrow streets, the most fascinating castle and market square with many lakes, parks and forests surrounding the city.

The theatre had organised my accommodation, quite some distance away. It was typical to be accommodated in a spare room of a person's flat and I shared a room with another girl from school. We walked together to the theatre of a morning.

It was time to focus on my career now, all the new people I met, attending evening performances at the theatre where we worked, as I had no rehearsals at night yet. I watched operas, operettas and plays, enjoying a rich cultural life. The canteen was the central meeting place to catch up with colleagues and friends. The theatre had about four hundred and fifty members – including all the orchestra musicians. It was awesome.

The first time I officially entered the theatre via the stage door, I went straight into rehearsals. The company was preparing for its production of *Swan Lake*. The dancers were aged twenty-two to about thirty and I joined as the youngest chick in the history of the company.

I had a sense that thirty-five was an 'old' dancer. I was aware that a dancer's career didn't last very long. I had often talked with Mum about it, and she encouraged me to focus on what would I do later when the time was right.

I always said, 'Don't worry about me, Mum. I'll do languages.' Languages and travel, that was my long-term vision. I never wanted to finish my career as an old wreck – some were still on stage when they were long past their prime. I realised this when I saw ballets as a student in ballet school. I wanted to finish in my prime, not past it. Asbach Uralt is a brand of German cognac; uralt means very old. We had a saying that if a person was Asbach Uralt, they were too old and shouldn't have been doing what they were doing. I never wanted to be described as an Asbach Uralt ballerina.

Rehearsing *Swan Lake* was a very busy time, and I also had a little part in a ballet scene in an operetta: it was great fun to get to know everybody and to try different genres. I was truly enjoying my fresh start and embraced the whole theatre environment and I absolutely adored it all. During *Swan Lake* rehearsals, I was approached by Kremke to take on a little solo – it confirmed how highly he regarded me when he'd made the decision to hire me over a year before. This gave me a wonderful push of self-confidence. I did very well. Most colleagues were very supportive and friendly, even though they must have been surprised that this young newcomer was offered the solo. Others were very jealous; they'd been there for years and hadn't been chosen to dance solo.

I think Kremke took a particular interest in me because, at seventeen, I had come from the first seven-year course of the State Ballet School and previously East German dancers would only have had three years or five years of training. Kremke himself was a Berliner and had studied in Russia, where the tradition was to study ballet for nine years. It was said that he had been a wonderful dancer and he progressed to become a highly regarded director and choreographer. It was not in my nature to compare myself with other dancers at that stage. I was a newcomer and appreciated everyone around me. As the youngest there, I would learn from the others. But he saw more in me, and when I eventually danced my solo in the opening night premiere of *Swan Lake*, wearing a snow-white tutu and pink *pointe* shoes, I felt beautiful. Some of my colleagues probably wished I would muck it up, which I did in a sense, because I lost one of my *pointe* shoes in the middle of the pirouettes. I didn't stop and just wiggled it off and flicked it to the side of the stage, finishing my solo with one shoe on and one shoe off.

Kremke was so proud of me. I heard some of the others sniggering and giggling about me, but he said, 'Don't worry about it. That could have happened to anyone. You handled it very well.'

I could feel the atmosphere of competition, but I was not going to buy into it. I am so grateful to have had a director like Kremke. All of my other ballet school friends who went on to different theatres did not experience the inspiration and encouragement that I did with him. It created such a smooth transition for me after seven years of schooling. Kremke was a great mentor for me, which helped me to stand up for myself out there in the big new world.

I couldn't wait when I had no rehearsals at night time so I could go and watch other performances. Unlike in Australia where you have a season, or gaps between productions, in East Germany performances were organised for the whole year other than over the summer holidays, about six weeks. Otherwise, there were performances every night that I was either dancing in or able to go and watch. I so loved sitting at the side of the stage, enjoying it all.

At the beginning of my time at Schwerin, I did not keep in touch with my old ballet school friends. There was no time, and no private phones. For most people in East Germany, this was still a time of no phones, no TV, no cars, no fridge, no washing machines. Certainly only privileged people had televisions. They were uncommon and I expect only to be found in the homes of high-ranked people or Stasi people – wherever they got their money from – and even if I had a TV, I wouldn't have had time to watch it. I was working very long hours, trying to be someone, striving to develop my career. I made new friends wherever I went. I was fully involved and as a professional dancer earnt a monthly salary, *Gage*, with a possibility to be increased over the years, so I heard. I was happy to earn my own money.

Within the first few months at Schwerin, I was sitting in the audience watching an opera and during interval, a man tapped on my shoulder. I had never seen him before.

He said, 'Heidrun Giersch?'

I said 'Yes?'

'When you have some time, I want to talk with you for a few minutes. I am an opera producer.'

'But I'm a dancer.'

'I know,' he said.

Intrigued, I said, 'Okay, let's do it now.'

So we went outside.

He said, 'I want to introduce myself to you. I'm new here at this theatre.'

I said, 'I've only been here a few months myself.'

He said, 'Yes, I know. I'm watching you whenever I can and I want to ask you if you'd be interested in taking one of the main parts in the children's opera I'm producing right now. It will be the world premiere. It's a stage play, adapted from the novel by Benno Plundra, called *Tambari*.' He explained that it was the first time ever in East Germany that a children's novel had been adapted into an opera, and that its world premiere would be here.

'But I'm a dancer.'

'I know, but I'm looking for somebody like you, small with a tiny build and with a very young appearance like a twelve-year-old girl.'

'I'm seventeen!'

'Are you? You look as though you're twelve...'

'No!'

He explained it would be happening later in the year.

'Okay. You have to speak to my ballet director.'

I got the part and so became involved in that production – such a different experience to ballet – very early in my career. I still undertook all the ballet requirements expected of me, which meant I had to find spare time, extra time, in the afternoon or evening for singing lessons and to rehearse with all the other cast, and I loved it. I have always found it hard to say no to opportunities and challenges, and that is the same for me even today.

I finally learnt how to ride a bike for this stage role, playing a cheeky twelve-year-old, and had to ride from one side of the stage to the other. It was a big, old, heavy iron bike with huge wheels and it was far too big for me. I could hardly get on it. The stage manager helped me climb on, and after counting *eins, zwei, drei*, she pushed me from one side of the stage to the other, where others had to catch me. That was a challenge and we all laughed our heads off in rehearsals, it was so funny. At the final dress rehearsal, which included the orchestra, I actually couldn't guide the bike straight and fell in the orchestra pit, smashed onto one of the drums, with the bike, and I broke my little toe. How crazy! The noise was incredible, the fuss was amazing – everyone thought I killed myself.

The show must go on... Every performance after that night became a nightmare, but I had to go through with it. Of course, my toe ached. The doctor said I must take time off but I was irreplaceable in the role. We won awards and prizes for the production and people came from all over East Germany to see *Tambari*. It was fantastic. This was the first time my mother and little brother came to see me in a show. They were so proud of me and I was delighted to have them in the audience.

I moved from my original accommodation to live alone within walking distance to the theatre. That improved life greatly, although my new accommodation was terrible, a rented room in a woman's flat. It was dark, under the roof, small, narrow and cramped. Not long after I moved in, I was very tired and about to go to bed when I pulled the quilt back and screamed. Ahhhhh! Hundreds of tiny little things wriggled in the middle of the white sheet. I had no clue what they were. It freaked me out. I learned that my bed was alive with fleas! The woman sprayed them, wiped them off, and then they were gone. But I was too scared to ever go back into the bed, so I slept at my friends' places after that night.

In 1971, I was one of five ballet delegates chosen from all the theatres throughout East Germany to visit Moscow to attend a major international ballet competition at the Bolshoi Theatre. It was to be the first time I'd travelled in an aeroplane. Arriving at the airport with another delegate, we were so excited and talking so much we missed the flight and had to wait for another plane.

The Russian people who I met I liked. They had such a strong sense of their artistic culture. People came to the theatre carrying shopping bags; the arts were part of their everyday life. I experienced Moscow as much poorer than East Germany. There was hardly any food in the shops – only cheese and bread. East Germany was known as having the highest living standard in Eastern Europe under communism.

At this time, Erich Honecker replaced Walter Ulbricht as the communist leader of East Germany.

I applied to the Schwerin Theatre for different accommodation and then moved into rooms on the first floor of a very old building within spitting distance of the theatre. It had two tiny empty rooms with two crooked windows that didn't close properly and the glass rattled loosely in the rotten frames. The building had squeaky wooden floors and stairs. I had nothing, no furniture at all. I painted the rooms and wallpapered them because they looked so awful and dull and I built my own kitchen furniture. Workers, carpenters from the theatre, gave me a hammer and-nails and some timber offcuts which I used to make a kitchen unit of three shelves which I hammered together. I painted the shelves red and hung a blue and white check curtain in front. Red, white and blue are my favourite happy colours. I also made a little bench for my two-ring electric cooker, which altogether cost me the princely sum of five marks.

I went by train to various villages in the countryside and knocked on doors to ask people if they had any furniture they didn't need. This is what cheeky, courageous Berliners did, and if people had anything to spare, they'd be happy to sell it or give it away. I bought a huge old, ugly brown wardrobe and arranged for a farmer to bring it to me on his old hand-made trailer when he next came to Schwerin. I stripped the wardrobe and painted it blue with white daisies. I returned to that village, knocked on doors again, and this time bought some lounge room chairs too and a writing desk. I slept in the lounge room on a mattress which I creatively transformed to look like a couch in the day time. I simply rolled up the quilt and placed it lengthways against the wall as the back of the couch, covering it all with a blanket. Now I was able to buy myself a black and white television and started to get more of my own stuff. I don't think I ever watched the television – I really had no time.

There was only one cold water outlet for all the tenants in the building and it was on my floor level and wall-mounted to a small, rusty iron sink. In winter, the water pipes froze and the tap did not work. The toilet over the staircase leaked most of the time and so I had to take an umbrella up the stairs to get into my room. It was close to the theatre but I'd been a bit scared walking home by myself late at night, although it was only a two-minute walk.

I was becoming more fashion conscious at Schwerin, taking more notice of such things and learning from my colleagues. They taught me to knit, and it was how we spent time waiting in rehearsals. We knitted leg warmers, frocks, jumpers and scarves. I became a good and fast knitter. It was practical, it was fashionable and we were a bit competitive with each other – wanting to make the coolest items. Wool was cheaper to buy than manufactured knitted clothes. I'd enjoyed craft lessons in the early years of ballet school, where we learnt all forms of embroidery and tapestry, and I was very good with my hands. I had to be! Clothes needed mending of course, even socks. Knitted hot pants were fashionable and sexy at the time. One particular outfit I knitted that I was very proud of was a beautiful dark blue one-piece short hot pants suit with a full-length zip and a white flared miniskirt which I wore sometimes on top of it. It looked so hot on me! I was getting too much uninvited attention from men in the street, and so never wore it again. I knew I was attractive, but too much attention scared me.

Growing up in a communist country, I had no sense of religion.

When I was eighteen, a man knocked on my door and introduced himself as a church official. He said to me, 'You owe us some money.'

I said, 'What do you mean? I have nothing to do with a church, I've never had anything to do with a church. How did you even get my name?'

He looked at me and said, 'Your mother always paid membership for you.'

Until that day, I never knew that my mother had any religious involvement. Mum was actually religious, as was my older brother. They were members of the Evangelical Church. But during the Cold War time it was not really acceptable to practise religion. Mum decided it was better to stay away from religion and not be connected with it, rather then be noticed and questioned about it. Nobody wanted to be noticed and questioned in East Germany. You just wanted to live your life and do the best you could as Mum did, and any other possible difficulties were best to stay away from. Apparently, Mum had paid the church membership for herself, my brother and for me, although I did not know about it.

I made new friends easily in Schwerin. Some of my friends were married, some were single and I enjoyed socialising with them all. Often, couples were theatre couples. One colleague who drove a car took me out with her family on Sundays. This gave me beautiful opportunities to get to know further areas away from the city centre of Schwerin, especially our trips to the Ostsee. I still thought that only privileged people or Stasi had cars. My friends drove a Trabbi. There were only two different models of cars, Trabant, nicknamed Trabbi, which had the reputation of being the only car that started in wintertime in East Germany. Today they are collectors' items. The other model was Skoda, made in Czechoslovakia, another communist country at the time. Some people were driving Volvos, but they were definitely high-profile citizens.

In wintertime, up at the Ostsee, rumours abounded that when the sea was really frozen and it was dark and foggy, when you couldn't see one metre ahead, people escaped by walking over the frozen sea. Whole families and many other people, all at once, walked across the border to Denmark. Over time, thousands had escaped. To stop that, the water police guards were positioned so that it was no longer possible. Any subsequent attempt most probably would have been deadly. These are the sorts of stories I grew up with an awareness of. Up in the forest near the East and West German border in Schwerin, I saw signs that read 'Stay back. Stop. Border, Halt. *Stehenbleiben. Nicht Weitergehen-Grenze*', and soldiers patrolled the area.

In summertime, my friends planned for us to go to the beach.

'Oh, cool,' I said, 'but I haven't got bathers.'

'Don't worry about it,' my friend said. 'You don't need bathers.'

'What do you mean, we don't need bathers?'

'We go naked.'

I said, 'Are you sure?' This was something new to me.

My friend explained. 'It's called FKK.'

'What does that mean?'

'*Frei Körper Kultur* – free body culture. The places where we go, there are not many people and everybody who goes swimming is naked. It's good for your body and good to feel the sun all over. Haven't you heard about it in Berlin?'

'No. If we ever went swimming in the lakes near Berlin, we'd wear bathers. It would never have occurred to us not to.'

'Didn't your mum ever tell you that when you go swimming, wearing wet bathers is no good for your kidneys?'

'Yes, that's why she made us change into dry bathers after swimming.'

'FKK is very popular. You don't have to wear bathers, you don't have to dry them, you don't have to change, you only need your towel and you'll have a good time.'

I thought, they are a nice family, they are trustworthy, why not? 'Okay.'

There were not many people at the beach, just a few, and they were naked. My friends explained to me that there were several places around the Ostsee that were FKK beaches. In fact, Westler, people from the West, visited the East Sea in the holiday time, as the FKK beaches were especially popular with tourists. We East Germans didn't really have the money to holiday at those expensive places.

I wonder if FKK started in East Germany as our way of feeling free. In experiencing nude bathing, I felt very free, I felt awesome. I really think it's very good for the body. Sun is necessary to activate vitamin D, it is healthy and feels lovely. It is an experience to this day that I practise where I can. If I know the people I'm with well, I feel very free and I don't mind. I am not a sexist, I am not an exhibitionist, I do it when I feel like it and when I feel safe, with friends who I choose to go with to a place I want to be. I'm happy to have been introduced to FKK in a moral and friendly environment. However, here in Australia, nudist clubs are a completely different thing to what I'm talking about. I'm not for them. I do respect my body and every one else's the way that God made us – we were all born naked and pure.

At home, Mum was pretty open and relaxed about behaving naturally. At ballet school, it was normal to see each other naked. In Schwerin, there were about thirty dancers in the company and the men and women had separate changing rooms but not separate showers. There was only one largeish shower cubicle that had two outlets. Rather than waiting, some people didn't mind showering with another person

– male or female – but others were more private. After a few months, I didn't care at all about showering with any colleague.

On Sundays, I took all my laundry to the theatre and washed all of it under the shower. I was not the only one without facilities at my accommodation, so others did this too, and we hung it up to dry in our changing rooms. The theatre was very much our home, the centre of our lives.

Mum and my brothers visited me more often in Schwerin. They called me 'our ballet star'. It all happened so quickly. People from the ballet school came too, as they were wondering, 'What's happening to the Gierschen? What is she about?' Everyone was interested in what was happening in Schwerin. Under Kremke, the ballet company developed a rising reputation. News travels fast in the arts world.

My life was full on. Kremke and I developed a good relationship. I became more and more involved with all the different genres and had many different opportunities. Theatre people appreciated my talents and skills and thought well of me and my career path developed further, unusually quickly. Although it was completely unexpected, Kremke gave me the confidence to feel I was beautiful and I was special, something that ballet school didn't really give me.

I went once to Kremke's apartment for an opening night after-party. He intrigued me; he was a very quiet, reserved person and I thought it was amazing he created such wonderful choreographies and it surprised me that he had such a position. Most theatre folk are loud, but he was different, he was a training master and I appreciated his presence and admired him and felt very privileged to be invited to their home, even if it was only once. I have recently read that Kremke and Rudolph Nureyev were lovers and that a BBC documentary and book have been published about them.

Working in the theatre involved many union activities, socially integrating our artistic and domestic lives. Elections for union leaders were held each year. Union officials and colleagues thought I'd be a good union leader. Obviously, they believed I had leadership skills. I'd always been encouraged and praised for public speaking and was a good organiser at school, so I suppose this was a natural progression. If they wanted me to take it on, and would support me, why not? In general, I'm a very social person and love people so, when asked, I said 'Yes.' If I was to be partly responsible and involved with meeting the goals of our ballet ensemble and the artistic development of our members, and increasing the status of the whole Schwerin Theatre within East Germany, yes, I was for that. I was curious and I like new challenges. I felt good about it – people trusted me in this adult world.

The union leader role involved my attendance at certain meetings of the *Künstlergewerkschaft*, the Artists Union, and I had to arrange meetings where we talked about our artistic development within the ballet ensemble, within the Schwerin Theatre as a whole, and even interconnecting with other ensembles within East Germany, particularly East Berlin, the centre of culture. My role was as a mediator, or communicator, between the ensemble members and the director or choreographer. I felt trusted, and trusting others was my way of operating. I took it seriously and was re-elected each year. I wasn't into politics as such, but always wanted to know more.

My days were extremely long, there was limited spare time for myself, I was passionate about what I was doing and I had great responsibility. I felt I was not a natural follower and grew to realise I was different from others and wondered why this was so.

'Why am I different?'

'Why am I taking on even more responsibility than I need to?'

I couldn't necessarily answer these questions, but I felt good. My ballet directors appreciated my cooperation and assistance and the fact that I naturally took on board issues that I could see needed to be addressed. While being a dancer is very much about working on yourself, I found my union work in particular to be a good balance – communicating with and working for others. I liked assisting others to create a happier, more fulfilled life, simply to have an inspirational impact on others. My motto was fairness, *Gerechtigkeit*. That was how I wanted to be treated and how I wanted to treat others.

Of course by this time I learned that many of my colleagues, acquaintances and friends were party members; there was no secret about their involvement. I knew that my friendships with these people could only go to a certain level. I would never talk with them about politics at all. I had only three friends ever who I'd confide in to the extent of saying to each other, 'Be careful what you say to that one, he might be a Stasi.' We did not know if we could trust the person next to us – our best friend, our mother, our sister or our lover. So we kept our thoughts to ourselves. In my opinion, life in such a society was not fair. I think people lived with a sense of fear, although everybody had their place. There was also an intense desire and passion of competition. Competition to be more, have more, be better is probably human nature. I prefer a life rather of comradeship and not encouraging competition.

The Schwerin Theatre was in the top three of the two hundred theatres in East Germany. Our ensemble wanted to be an example of great comradeship. We were all proud and motivated to follow and live our goal to be the best we could be. It was important to me that our ensemble was given recognition for our work, and I aimed to organise a trip to Hungary as a reward. We didn't have the opportunity to travel to other communist countries as an ensemble to perform, but somehow I thought it could be inspiring for all of us to get connected to ballet companies in other countries. I thought we should be supported for our efforts.

Let's go to Budapest! I thought it would enrich our lives to share a new cultural experience. If we could do it around some time when we were to have a few days off anyway, why shouldn't we pursue it? I put the idea to a few close friends and they thought it was exciting. I proposed it to our directors and they said, 'Why not?' So, with their approval, we applied to the union for support for the trip. Everyone saved sufficient money, we gained financial support and spending money and I applied for all the visas – thirty - and had to go to Berlin to collect them all. Only one person wasn't granted a visa, our dramaturge, and although I asked the authorities, they would not tell me why. I asked him why he thought he was rejected and he had a look of fear in his eyes, and just said he had no idea. I knew it must have had something to do with politics. Perhaps he had too many contacts in the West; he mustn't have been 'clean'.

At this stage – I was about twenty – I met Gerhard. He had an audition at Schwerin Theatre and I was invited to the audition to be part of the selection panel. I didn't think he had quite the quality we wanted. Although he was engaged by the company, understandably he felt that I was against him. He had respect for me, but was a bit distant from me and I felt some tension between us.

I thought he was a funny, rather strange guy until one day when he approached me in the canteen most respectfully and formally, and said, 'Excuse me, Heidi, if you need any help organising the trip, I can assist you if you like.'

I felt he was trying to make a connection with me. I said, 'Okay, I'll let you know if I do.'

A few days later, he came to me and said, 'Do you have anything for me to help you with? I really would love to help. You have so much to do.'

We eventually became lifelong friends.

When we arrived in Budapest after our fourteen-hour train trip, everyone wanted to know where we'd sleep.

I said not to worry about it. 'I know two families here. They will look after us.' I knew anything was possible!

Some stayed with my dear friends, an elderly couple, and five of us slept in a double bed, ten of us in one room together. The others I organised to stay with other friends. No problems – Hungarians are spontaneous like I am sometimes.

One night we went for dinner at a restaurant on the Gellertberg, in Budapest. We drank sweet Palinka, schnapps, made from apple or peach or pear, in a shot glass.

My colleagues cheered me, *Prost* to Heidi for organising the trip!

They planned to get me drunk, wanting to see me out of control for once, but I only got a little bit merry and giggly. It was such a happy night and I danced on the tables. They tried many times over the years to get me drunk, but it never happened.

The trip was absolutely successful. The Schwerin Theatre thanked our ensemble for doing such great work and acknowledged our efforts. What a success! I had to report back to the union about our incredible experience.

Eventually, we had the opportunity to travel to Poland, which I organised and, privately, I visited Czechoslovakia with my brother on a ski holiday. I had some terrific travel experiences and remain very grateful for that today, it fed my desire to experience more travel to other countries and learn more languages.

I lost contact with Kremke when he left and I still wondered, having been too shy to ask and not wanting to rock the boat, how he was able to give me my contract. He didn't want anything from me. I was already familiar with the idea of people's careers progressing because they 'slept their way up'. Colleagues of mine may have thought I was sleeping my way up. That was just not my style. I had my moral standards. I was grateful that I had never experienced that pressure. I expected people to take me as I am and I'd show them what I could do.

I became a soloist, rising quite quickly through the ranks, and with that was earning more money. I danced the *Legend of Love, Die Legende der Liebe*, with a very experienced well-known male dance partner, Zwetan, from whom I learnt so much. He was tall and strong and loved to dance with me because I was so light and tiny and easy to swirl and move with. I had developed a good technique and loved expressing every emotional detail of the particular part I danced.

New directors arrived at Schwerin – Lothar Hanff as ballet director and choreographer, and Eva Reinthaller as assistant director and choreographer. Eva and Lothar had the knack of combining classical and contemporary dance movements. They both had been dancers themselves and finished dancing early because they recognised they worked together as a great team choreographing for years many new ballets and we were very privileged to have them at Schwerin.

People of the ballet world from all over the country attended our opening nights, as we'd developed a great reputation. A breakthrough production called *Freedom*, choreographed by Lothar and Eva, a short contemporary ballet which included music by Mahalia Jackson, told a political story about blacks and whites getting together and fighting for freedom. We had no black dancers, so to put black foundation on some dancers, all over their bodies, was great fun. The theme was unity, a ballet of heart and soul. The success of the production made news throughout East Germany.

Lothar and Eva had a huge impact on extending my career. In fact, Eva likes to say that she 'discovered' me. Certainly they gave me wonderful opportunities. I was privileged to be chosen to dance a new contemporary version of the role of Carmen. Eva expected Carmen to be petite and, most importantly, strongly animated, like a gypsy who found it difficult to be accepted by conventional society. Carmen's characteristics are love, pride, pain, passion and humour. She is intelligent, sensible, innocent and fun-loving and they are the qualities Eva discovered in me. Eve in *La Creation du Monde, The Creation of the Earth*, was another character I loved to dance, in bare feet, no *pointe* shoes for a change.

Another favourite role was as Anna Two in Bertolt Brecht and Kurt Weil's *Die Sieben Todsünden, The Seven Deadly Sins*. It combined dancing, acting and singing together which was not often done in ballet. Anna One was an actor, Anna Two was a dancer. We shared the stage with opera singers during this production, a contemporary ballet – a deeply philosophical and political story about the guts of the diversity of society. It was a fantastic experience.

The State Theatre Scherwin was known for its musical productions from the west. Shows such as *Sweet Charity* and *Cabaret* were popular musicals and dancers always had a big part in the success of these shows. Luckily I had in each a small part to perform, where I could prove my versatile talents and skills – singing, dancing and acting. I loved every second of it.

At twenty, I completed my three-year contract and remained at Schwerin, renewing the contract yearly, while progressing well in my career. I'd grown to realise that economically Schwerin did not have the possibilities and opportunities of everyday life that were available in Berlin. Sometimes I had to go home to Mum's over the weekend so that I could go shopping for toilet paper and toothpaste in Berlin. We couldn't get these things all the time in Schwerin. Often the shops were just empty of basic goods. Shops were often empty in Berlin too, but there was more chance of being able to buy basic items.

At times, we could buy things in Schwerin in a shop that was run by Russian soldiers stationed there and only open on certain irregular days. For instance, one day all you could see in the shop were bananas on every trestle table. They didn't look like they were great quality, but there were plenty of them. I have no idea where they got them from, but they were cheap and we could buy as many as we wanted.

Another nearby shop one New Year's Eve stocked only one particular type of white wine from Hungary. It was fruity and sweet and I loved it. I observed that many of my colleagues loved to drink alcohol, but I wasn't really interested in it. Besides, I worked so hard and had so many responsibilities, it was not in my nature to be out of control. I could laugh and have fun without other substances, but I want to confess that I smoked cigarettes. The only brand I smoked was Duett, because they were long and shiny and looked elegant between my fingers. I have been a non-smoker for many years now and can't imagine how I smoked for years while I was dancing. I think my physical overactivity helped me to not experience major side-effects.

My daily routine involved a quick meditation nap in the afternoon because after performing it was always late at night before I got to bed. I shared my life most of the time with someone close and we lived together for some time. I experienced different romantic relationships and loved all of it at that time and don't regret anything. I loved harmony in my life, but my job was my priority.

I was introduced to an East German champion boxer who asked

me to teach him some classical ballet exercises to improve his performance. He believed he wasn't using his legs properly and that training with me would help, which it did. For six months, we met regularly to train at the sports centre and I taught him how to find the music in his legs. He appreciated the help and invited me to his house in Schwerin and gave me a thank you gift of a dark blue leather jacket. I was so thrilled; such a beautiful piece of clothing wasn't something that could be bought in East Germany. So many different sports today incorporate classical ballet into the training because it enhances such an understanding of body control and movement.

At Christmas, I arranged to go and spend a few days with Mum in Berlin. It was the first time for several years that I'd been able to share this special time of the year with her. It was an unusually severe, icy cold winter. It snowed and snowed and snowed. On leaving, Mum was worried about how I'd make it back in the train from Lichtenberg Station, which was the main station in East Berlin. The tracks were all blocked, transport was at a standstill. We waited for hours, some people for days, to catch trains. The Red Cross provided cups of tea on the platform for the cold commuters. It took me nearly twenty-four hours to get back to Schwerin, a trip that usually took three hours. It made me think about the conditions of wartime and what people went through then. It was horrifying to be part of thousands of people who couldn't move, didn't know where to go; kids were crying – perhaps because it was so cold at minus twenty-five degrees Celsius. We were just waiting, not knowing when we would get to where we needed to be. It was chaotic and getting colder by the hour. The kiosks sold out and eventually the Red Cross only had water to offer the stranded commuters.

Kalli arranged to visit Schwerin to see me perform. As he was nine years older than me, and we'd lived so much of the time apart, we were not really close, but I have had some profound experiences with Kalli. I wondered how to entertain my big brother after the show. I decided we should go to a restaurant, which we seldom did because my ballet friends and I loved to cook at home, and it was cheaper of course. I had a favourite restaurant – Uhle – in a little tiny lane in old Schwerin. It was a very special place with private niches, it was romantic, nostalgic, expensive, with first-class food. I asked my dear girl friend Ulla to join us. I was so proud of my handsome, gorgeous hot-looking brother – tall, dark-haired and strong, a bit wild-looking, Kalli had the good looks of a film star. He'd married very young, at nineteen, and his former wife is a talented fashion designer with whom I am still in contact. He was single again when he came up to visit me to see his little sister on stage. In his eyes, I was a star, and he suggested I change my name to Minola Minoletti, which he thought sounded more famous.

I said to Ulla, 'Come out to Uhle with me and meet my brother, but don't fall in love with him, even though he is the best-looking man on this earth.'

They fell in love almost instantly and married soon after. He wanted to move up to Schwerin to live and found a farm advertised in the newspaper. That was something different! He'd had no farming background. Kalli moved to an old northern-style farmhouse in a tiny little village near Schwerin and he and Ulla still live there today. They love it. I thought he was crazy, a boy from the vibrant city of Berlin.

Kalli's farm had sheep and horses and cats and dogs, a straw roof that needed repairing, stables for horses, farm machinery and an old horse carriage. One day we went by horse carriage from his place to the next township, about seven kilometres away, and it was hilarious, like something out of the olden times. The farm included an apple orchard and when they harvested the apples they were required to give so many kilos to the farmers union to make juice – so living there was under government control. My brother loved the lifestyle from the first day on the farm, but I found the farm life too old-fashioned, a bit too primitive for me. Kalli was educated as a French teacher, who were very rare in East Germany and in demand.

Mum came to see me perform at Schwerin whenever she could and she understood that it had been a good decision for me to go there. My younger brother expressed his intention to be a ballet dancer too, but I did not approve of it for him. At the time I said, 'It's just for girls, not for boys', and advised against it. Of course my explanation was a bit weird, but I truly didn't think it was for this special boy. He was so much more talented with his hands. Wolle studied and became a *Stukateur*, in the building industry, restoring ceilings in old buildings and churches.

On leaving ballet school to work at the Schweriner Theatre, I understood that there were 'personal files' on people that held information collected and reported to 'authorities'. My file was added to with notes of my union involvement. My union involvement informed me much more of what was going on in the society than what others would have been aware of. Some people may not have known that they would have had a personal file, added to at every change of employment and perhaps with any information of their personal life that some informer had been asked to reveal.

I was again approached if I wanted to join the party. I maintained my decision not to be pushed into anything that I didn't want to. I said no as diplomatically as possible. 'No, I have enough on my plate.'

That was my excuse, but, inside of me, I definitely did not want to join the party – ever. I felt that those people I knew who did join were goody-goodies and I certainly did not see myself as being like them. I'm too creative to be a goody-goody; too much of a Berliner, too open-minded…too much 'me' to be like 'them'. Party members were too fake, stagnated and 'correct' and I had no desire to become like that. I did not want to go to more meetings. I hoped they would not ask me again. I'd been clear and direct twice now with my answer. The older I got, the more I liked my mum's attitude.

How could I know what negative consequences might eventuate by resisting attempts to be involved in the Communist Party? After all, our newspapers were only full of 'good news' stories about the political regime of the German Democratic Republic, how great it was. Everything was fine on the surface of our lives, but in the undercurrent of conversations, through my involvement with people from all walks of life, I was aware of political interference: for example, why a certain person had not been given a particular role or option. It was much wiser not to argue or discuss political issues at any given time.

On arrival for work at the theatre, we were required to sign in and to sign out, in a book at a window manned by a worker at the stage door. We all had pigeonholes for messages behind this window. One day I found a message in my pigeonhole instructing me to meet somebody at a particular time at a certain place just a few days later. Curious, I wondered who and why someone wanted to contact me. I met him on my own, late in the afternoon after rehearsal, nearly at dusk. I ended up in a car with three men, abducted, although they were quite friendly but firm in their manner.

One of the men said, 'We will take you to a place about twenty minutes from here, where we will explain our reason for meeting you.'

They were dressed in normal clothes, not uniformed.

I said, 'Who are you?'

They gave me their 'names' – they would not have been their real names. We drove through the forest for about twenty minutes, along the lakes, it grew dark and we stopped at a bungalow. It was a very plain cabin and we sat at the table.

They were very straightforward and said to me, 'We want to tell you who we really are and we're wondering if you would be interested in becoming more politically involved. We believe you are very well known and you are a well respected member of the theatre. We are not from the theatre at all.'

Their faces were not familiar to me.

'Look, I've only been recently asked again if I'm interested in becoming a party member, and I'm not. I've said no. I don't want to be involved in anything more, I have no time for anything else.'

'Have you ever heard of Staatsicherheit? Stasi? State Security, that's who we are.'

'Not really,' I lied. 'I know we have State Security, but I'm an artist, I'm not political.'

They spoke very nicely to me, slowly and with well spoken voices,

'Are you aware that if you perhaps become more involved…with this kind of work…that you could have more benefits in your life?'

I said politely, 'I'm quite happy with my life.' I wondered why they had asked me and wondered if they'd asked my colleagues, friends and family.

'Do you see yourself working for us?'

'Working for you? In what way?'

'Working for the Staatsicherheit, State Security. We know everything about you. We need to know everything about everyone. You need to be aware that you can never tell anybody about our meeting here tonight. Never.' He said sternly, 'No matter what the outcome is here, you must never speak of this. To anyone. Do you understand?'

I started to become scared, and nodded. 'Okay,' I asked, 'what would I do?'

'You can do a lot, if you sign an agreement confirming that you are willing to work with us. You can decide that now, tonight, and we can sign it here and give you your instructions afterwards. Keep in mind you can never talk to anyone about this. You won't keep your real name for your work with us. If you sign tonight, we will give you a different name, a code name. So what do you think?'

More information was gradually forthcoming as the conversation continued. I thought that they were much cleverer than the kind of party people who had approached me. Deep inside I knew they had approached the wrong person. I was really scared, my head was spinning, and I felt the men already had power over me. I was frightened about my responses and did not want to say a wrong word.

Altogether, this meeting possibly took twenty minutes, but, because of the intensity, I felt as though it had taken hours. I started to wonder how I would get out of the room and away from the men. Would I be allowed to leave? Would they shoot me? I was petrified. I tried as hard as I could to remain brave and friendly.

'So,' the man said, 'what have you decided?'

'No. I have so much work, I couldn't possibly do anything more.'

The man passed me a sheet of paper. 'Just read it,' he said, 'It explains what's required of you.'

It was a declaration stating that I wanted to work with 'so and so', the code name of a person.

I said, as pleasantly as I could, 'No. I don't think this is for me. Maybe you can find somebody much more suitable than me.'

They were becoming more and more serious and I was becoming more and more frightened. My heart was racing. Would they take me safely back to the theatre? Although I was tempted to panic, I said to myself, 'Come on, Heidi, don't give up. Be strong.'

I said, 'No, I'm happy with my life as it is. I don't need to have more benefits.'

They persisted. One man said, 'Don't worry! Nobody would ever know. We won't ask much time of you. We will just tell you who we want you to work for, and who we want you to find out more about.'

I said, 'What do you mean, "find out more about"?'

They mentioned a ballet director's name, and asked if we had a good relationship. I said we did. They suggested that I could give them information about him.

I said, 'Why would I? Work against him? He's my friend.'

The man said, 'That's why we need people like you. You have lots of friends. We need to find out more about people. We need to find out about their contact with Westerners and West German family members.'

I said, 'He's doing awesome work. Why should it be up to me to find out anything like this about him? I definitely do not want to do this. It has nothing to do with me.'

He said, 'Of course it has nothing to do with you, and he would never find out. Nobody ever will find out.'

'No. I don't want to do this.'

'Are you sure?' Firmly, unfriendly.

'One hundred per cent.'

'You could have so many benefits. A better flat, a two-room flat in a modern building.'

'Oh, is that where they all live?' I said. 'I understand.'

'You can get a pass to go to West Germany whenever you like, you won't have to wait until you're a pensioner.'

'No. I've got no reason to go there anyhow. I don't know anybody in West Germany. I'm happy here.'

'All types of people do this work, ordinary people who nobody would ever expect. Are you sure?' he asked more forcefully.

I felt pushed and answered a bit angrily, 'I'm not interested.' I wanted to get out of there. It was clear to them now. I could feel that they were upset, and I felt blackmailed.

Suddenly, one of the men said, 'Okay, that's all for tonight, but I warn you it won't be the last time we see you.'

I made no comment. I just hoped they would take me back to the theatre. They packed up very quickly and I said I needed to be back in time for rehearsal.

'We'd better hurry up,' I said, shaking inside.

While we were sitting in the car, driving in the dark, one of the men gave me a piece of paper and said, 'I'm giving you this and you must put it in your pocket and make sure that nobody ever sees it. You will read it when you get out of the car. Read it, memorise it and then destroy it.'

The paper said a date and time – two p.m. the following day – and the address of a building where I was to attend, and my code name.

'Yes, I'll be there.' I thought I should agree to everything, I just wanted to be able to get out of the car. Please let me go, I thought. I would deal with it later.

'Think about it overnight. When you arrive at the building, say your code name, and we hope that you'll sign with us tomorrow.'

We were getting closer to the theatre when one of the men said, 'You will probably sometimes see one of us around, even in the theatre. But we will not talk to you.'

I think it meant that if I saw them, I was to look the other way and pretend that I hadn't. This gave me an awareness that perhaps they were almost part of the furniture at the theatre, but that I had never known that previously. From that moment on, I was too scared to ever even look for them.

They dropped me off near the theatre, but not at the main entrance, and I walked back shaking with fear, wondering what was happening to me. Who has been talking about me? Who of my colleagues is suspicious of me? Who else have they asked? More importantly, who has said yes? There were plenty of 'ordinary, simple people' at the theatre who might have been approached. I started to think with a different head from this day on. I was suspicious of everybody. I knew I needed to be very careful now. I started to treat my social life with a more wary attitude. I was more conscious of who I was talking to and what we were talking about. I was not as open any more, more diplomatic.

I never, ever wanted to see those men again. They could have offered me a million dollars, I wouldn't have taken it. I felt very threatened by them but understood that I needed to follow their instructions and report at two p.m. the next day to a building in the centre of Schwerin. I was too scared to speak to anybody about it.

I made sure I was on time. It looked like a block of flats, but the room I went to was fitted out as an office. I introduced myself by the code name, thinking what a liar I was, and simply stated that I didn't know what I was doing there.

The man and woman in the office asked me, 'What have you decided?'

I said, 'What do you mean?' I wasn't sure who these people were. What should I tell them? What did they know?

They said, 'Have you decided, is it yes or is it no?'

'If that's why I had to come here, it's all no!'

'Are you sure?'

'Definitely. I don't know what I'm actually doing here.'

'Right. From now on, you must think that you have never been to this building, you remember nothing at all about this, no code name, just go back to your normal life. Get it out of your mind, out of your life.'

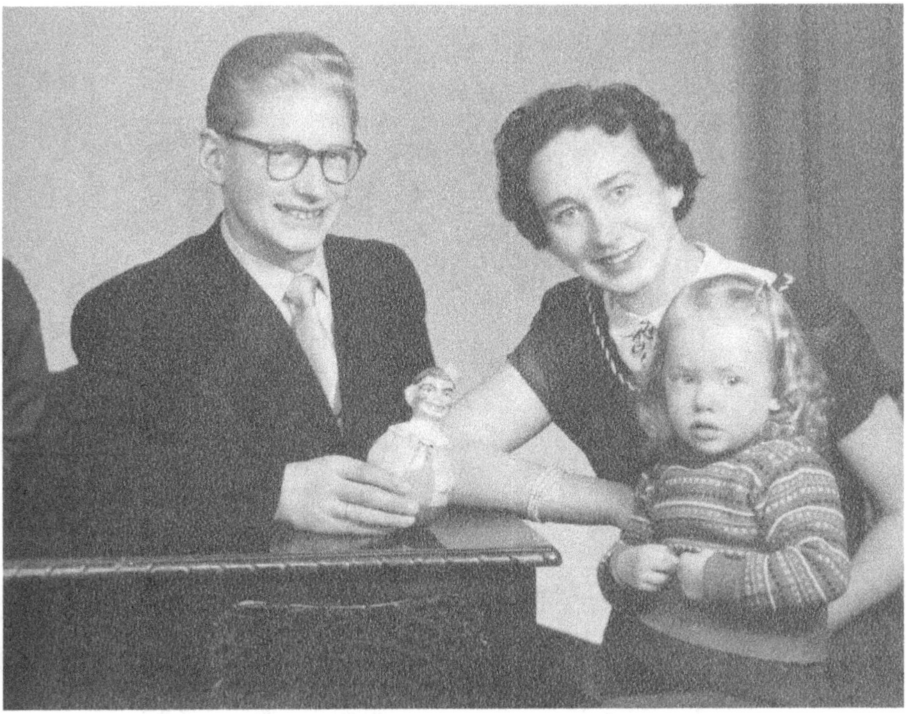

With my mother and father. I am three. East Berlin.

Berlin Lichtenberg, the world where I lived as a little girl. It had hardly changed when this photo was taken in 2001.

On my first day of school. We were all given a cardboard cone filled with sweets.

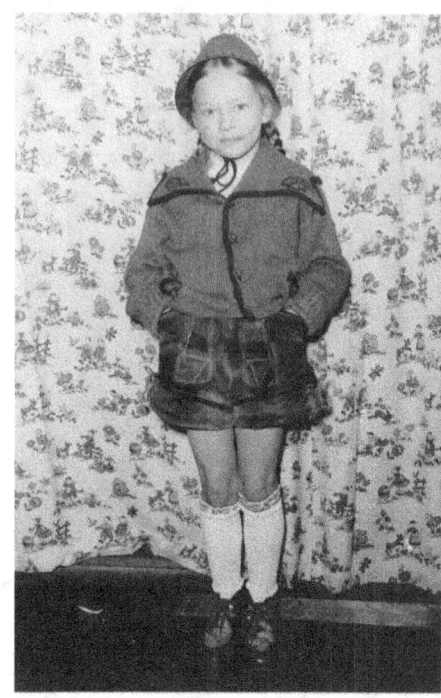

Aged 8 – before the ballet world.

With young friends in our first pointe shoes at Staatliche Ballettschule, Berlin, 1965. I am on the left.

Rehearsing for traditional folk dance at ballet school. I am second from left.

Classical ballet training: 'with blisters on my feet'. I am front left.

Final ballet school exam – 'Pas de trois', Swan Lake. Berlin, 1970.

Enjoying performing in Wir Machen Eine Oper. I am in the centre.

Dancing the 'Love Pas de deux' Carmen suite at Staatstheater Schwerin.

World premiere of Tambari. I am in the centre.

As Eva in the world premiere of contemporary ballet La Creation du Monde.

Three Musketeers pas de deux as Constance with Staatstheatre Schwerin.

Lead role as Anna 2 in The Seven Deadly Sins.

My first flat, when I was 17, was in this building in Schwerin.

As presenter of the art union Gengre Dance at a national conference in Berlin, 1977. I am on the far left.

Rehearsing with Professor Tom Schilling at the Komische Oper Berlin, 1979. I am on the far left. (Photo courtesy photographer © Arwid Lagenpusch, Theaterfotografie)

Ensemble scene of 'Pasdorale' with Komische Oper Berlin, 1979. I am in the second row, far left. (Photo courtesy photographer © Arwid Lagenpusch, Theaterfotografie)

Photo shoot for the Australian Women's Weekly at Melbourne bayside beach celebrating granting of my political asylum. (Photo courtesy photographer Kimbal Baker and Bauer Media Pty Ltd)

Performing at the Sydney Opera House, Sequenza VII, Sydney Dance Company, with Janet Vernon (left) and Graeme Murphy (centre). (Photographer unknown)

In my new working world at the Hofbrauhaus, Melbourne, 1983.

My final day of wearing pointe shoes, 1985.

At my daughter Schatzi's christening, 1986.

Visiting East Berlin for the first time since the fall of the Berlin Wall, 1994. I am next to my mother, with family.

Reunited with my lifetime friend Gerhard in 1994.

Visiting my family in Berlin, 2019.

'Okay.'

They gave me a sealed envelope. 'If you ever change your mind, you open it. If not, you keep it closed and hide it. You never, ever tell anybody about anything.'

'Okay.'

'Make sure you never speak about it. Make sure nobody ever finds this letter. Never, ever in your life. Otherwise, it will have consequences. Go now.'

Consequences… What on earth could happen? What would I do with the letter? Nothing about it all made sense to me. I left the building, talking to myself. Perhaps inwardly I was becoming hysterical, close to having a nervous breakdown.

'Nothing has happened? So much has happened! I hope nobody has seen me… I'm walking out of the building… Is somebody following me? I have a bloody secret letter in my pocket… I must keep it but never open it… I don't know where to go with it… I don't know what's inside it… How do I deal with this? Am I going nuts? Nothing has happened…'

I decided to follow what they said and would not open the letter because I would not change my mind. How strange for me. I have huge natural curiosity. But I was so sure that I never wanted to have anything to do with these idiots that I wanted to hide the letter for ever. Where should I hide it? Who could I trust completely in my life? Only one person. Mum.

The next time I had a chance to go to Mum's in Berlin, I took the letter with me and I said, 'Mum, I have to tell you the biggest secret of all time.' I decided to give her the envelope. She always had so many papers at home and so many books required for her teaching work, she would be able to hide it.

'Hide it safely, Mum, somewhere nobody would find it even if they came looking for it. Never ask me why I'm giving it to you. Never think about what might be in the letter, as I don't even know myself. It's very important. It's life-threatening, Mum. Unless I ask you one day to give it back to me or to open it, keep it hidden.'

'Okay, where do you want me to put it, Heidrun?'

'I don't know. Don't tell me. I don't want to know.'

The experience filled my mind completely for weeks. How come that connection ever happened? I thought about the people I knew and, after a great deal of consideration, decided to approach a colleague. I suggested that we went for a walk, just the two of us. Then, while walking, I explained a little of what had happened to me and said that I felt he was somehow involved. He didn't know that I'd been approached. His brother was an officer in the army. Every boy at eighteen had to undertake compulsory military service in the East German army, although neither of my brothers were required to as both had medical conditions which exempted them. Ballet boys were considered to be serving the state with their art, so they did not have to do any army service. Those who were good soldiers were invited to stay for three years and then to become career officers and stay on. This young man's brother was an officer. When I told him what I wondered, without giving him the details, he said he'd been approached too. I appreciated his honesty and we agreed we'd never discuss it again. We were both shit-scared. It had to remain our secret. Years later, I had a feeling this colleague had actually joined the Stasi, but I never wanted to find out for sure, it would have made me too angry.

From that day on, I felt more watched, under surveillance, *unter Beobachtung*. It was a huge turning point that had a large impact on me for my future life, about who you can trust and who you can't. I had been an open book, a happy, care-free Berliner girl with nothing to hide. Now I knew there was more to life. My life could have been over, my career could have been finished. Horrifying as that experience was, later on in life I realised it gave me a great benefit. I learnt so much from that day. It confirmed that the Stasi really did want to know everything about everyone. I knew how to shut up and how to keep a secret. This was to be a vital aspect of my subsequent defection, so, strangely, my terribly frightening experience with the Stasi was in retrospect a gift. It enabled me to protect myself and others.

I couldn't close the curtain and stop being noticed, but how did I see myself positioned in this society? I didn't want to change and I didn't want to change anything around me. I stayed involved in the union – the union was not party and it certainly was not State Security. I started to more consciously form relationships, sussing people out rather than just being friendly to everyone. For the next few years, my career progressed well as the reputation of the whole ensemble became increasingly well-known. My pain continued, sometimes getting better, sometimes worse, but I had a holistic experience of the ballet world and pain was only one part of it.

After four years in Schwerin, I decided that with all the work I did and my other responsibilities, I deserved better accommodation and was cheeky and brave enough to apply for it. I was allowed to have a bigger room, a little further away from the theatre, a lovely fifteen-minute walk along the lake. My career was predominant but I wanted to have a beautiful and harmonious home environment as well, a balance. I lived with my boyfriend, who was also a dancer.

I got to know the family of a very close friend of mine quite well during this time and became very fond of them. This family was originally from West Germany, and the night the Wall went up, they were visiting East Germany. They were not allowed to return home, although they tried many times, and deep inside they remained hurt and unhappy people. They tried to make a life in East Germany and did the best they could. My friend's two older brothers both tried to escape a number of times. They were both caught and one spent time in jail and the other experienced other severe consequences.

The older brother who had tried to escape over the Wall had been jailed for two years and then eventually I found out that he had joined the Stasi. I could understand how this happened to him; perhaps he couldn't get out of it. I didn't want to judge him. He lived in a house which was so unusual, so privileged. He was a manager of a factory and I never saw much of him. He had a family and I couldn't imagine him trying to get to the West again.

This family had their crises. Their lifestyle and their opinions were very different from my own. They had grown up in the Western world and been forced to live in the East without choice. Even my friend spoke about returning home to West Germany one day and suggested that I should go too, or join him later. I appreciated they had a different perspective to mine.

He was more experienced about the specific details of what permits you could apply to the government for, which I didn't understand. He said to me, 'Would you go to West Germany if you could?'

My answer was, 'No. Why?'

He found it difficult to understand that even if I had a chance to leave East Germany I wouldn't take it.

I couldn't understand why, after all these years, they still had this urge to leave: it was dangerous, it was difficult. I felt that there was a fundamental difference in our thinking and I felt uncomfortable that they would ask me such questions. I didn't know anybody in West Germany. My family and friends, home and work were all in the East. It was irrelevant to me, but I could understand their frustration and I hoped their dreams would come true one day. It would never have occurred to me that the Wall would eventually come down, but I hoped that perhaps one day laws would change and those people who so wanted to return home could do so and be happy.

We often visited one of my friend's brothers, who with his wife and young family, lived in a beautiful unit, right up near the Ostsee. Their unit was modern, they had fine furniture – much lovelier than most people's. They sometimes received parcels from the west, *Westpakete*, containing treats like toothpaste that tasted nicer than ours, and yogurt, other food and chocolate that we couldn't get in the east. They were more worldly than I was in the way they talked and the way they dressed. The men wanted to talk more about politics while the wife and I loved to laugh and enjoyed each other's company. I adored their beautiful children. Eventually, we received news that one of the brothers, with his family, had officially applied in writing to the government for an exit visa to leave East Germany.

My friend and I actually bought a car, an old burgundy Opel, from another theatre friend. It cost five hundred marks and was an old bomb. We spent more time pushing the car than driving it! We were such crazy artists – flamboyant, curious, and bit more daring than other people. We would have had to wait twenty years for a car after applying for it, so it gave us a bit of fun in the meantime. Mopeds and motorbikes were more common, and they were great fun to ride around on.

We visited this family regularly in the old car. They planned to leave. When would they leave? 'Whenever they let us go.' People had no idea when, or if, permission would be granted. They waited five years before they eventually returned to West Germany and in the meantime I had already begun my new life in Australia. Their life changed enormously once they lodged their application and the five years were immensely difficult for them – horrifying, scary, intimidating and sad.

They told us, 'You can't come and visit us so often any more. The authorities have told us they will be watching everybody who comes to our door. Our neighbours are not allowed to talk to us any more, nobody can come and visit us any more, and if they do come, we have to tell them not to. Our kids can't go to the same school any more. Neither of us can work any more. We have had our jobs taken away from us.'

The husband still had to make money to support the family and he found ways and means. He was a driver. Until then I did not know there was a blackmarket in East Germany. He had no choice: how else could he look after his family? The government was paying them some money, but not enough. It seemed to me that they were being punished. They were no longer allowed to make contact with, and receive parcels from, their relatives in the West. They became more stressed, the children cried, their frustration was terrible. I could feel their pain.

We could no longer talk freely in their home. We always had to go for a walk if we wanted to talk.

They whispered, 'We can't talk at home, we might be bugged.' They talked about *Wanzen*, bugs in the wall. They had a phone in their apartment and they unscrewed it and showed me a bug.

It was unbelievable to me. 'You mean they can hear anything you talk about?'

Even when we were walking in the street, they always looked around, wondering if they were being followed or watched. They'd been in trouble many times and the authorities came and told them, 'One more time and you'll face consequences.' I realised that this was an on-going example of the Stasi mission to know everything about everyone.

It became common knowledge that applying for an exit visa to leave East Germany was actually a recipe for a horrendous experience. Those who applied would never know if or when they'd be allowed to go. It took many months or even years for the visa to be granted. Some people ended up in jail because they did not follow all the instructions that they were told to. It was such an immense pressure. I would never have applied for an exit visa because I knew it would be a horrifying time for me after making the application. Although everybody was treated differently, I think I would have ended up in prison if I'd applied. I was known as a person who respected fairness, I didn't like degrading people. I would never have walked across the frozen Ostsee and risked being shot. For the same reason, I would never have attempted to climb the Wall and run.

I believe that those who climbed the Berlin Wall were very brave and that it was commonly attempted but not reported in the news. However, news of such things filtered down through the people as well as other matters such as the need for more control on our guidelines if we were being seen not to be operating within the proper limits. The emphasis was to keep control and make us feel that we lived in a good and safe place.

The nature of the theatre world has always been that you take notice, and talk about, what is going on beyond your own borders. News travels fast. We always heard about ballet dancers and other artists from Berlin who'd stayed in the West. Sometimes we heard rumours of artists who were found dead and the conjecture was left to us. There were no explanations. It was a society of mystery and silence.

Of course, defections were not publicised in the newspaper. For arts, sports and military, East Germany was strong, even compared with much larger communist countries, and wanted to shine. The government sent artists and sports people overseas to showcase their talents, not just to communist countries, but also to Western countries. Artists sometimes travelled solo as representatives to the West and the authorities knew all about the history of each person, whether they were married or involved in a relationship, whether they'd be a risk. To travel as an artist to the West, you had to be 'clean', the type of person who was proud to represent your country, the sort of person who would definitely return home. If a person defected, I always felt *leben und leben lassen*, live and let live. I didn't know what I would do if I was them. I was not in their position. I did not judge them, but I certainly had no sense of yearning to leave East Germany.

Our ballet company was the first in East Germany to propose and implement the idea to educate children from kinder age and throughout schools to experience live performances in state theatres. The Education Department arranged in conjunction with the art union for schools to come and experience a ballet performance at Schwerin and to learn about ballet as an art form. Teaching these young students about expressing stories through dance began a new era of educating children about culture and the arts. We created productions especially for child audiences and presented special afternoon performances and Sunday matinees.

It was a huge mission and led me to establish my own children's ballet group, as not only were theatres looking for children to perform in plays, musicals and ballets but, with growing awareness about the arts, children wanted to participate. I applied to the theatre union to develop my own little group of thirty kids aged eight to fourteen and taught the children on Saturday afternoons. Some of the kids became involved in shows and it was important that those who didn't were acknowledged for their hard work. The children's classes were not designed to be competitive. At Christmas time, I invited all the parents and relatives to a performance followed by a party. They were just performing for fun; some played recorder, some read a poem, others acted, and so I created a form of entertainment that included each child.

I was always too busy, finding time just for fun became increasingly difficult and I was exhausted. My dear friend Gerhard decided I needed a few days' holiday and he invited me down south to a beautiful mountainous area where there was plenty of snow. It was minus thirty degrees. One day we hired a toboggan and used it to go down the slope of an eight-hundred-metre high mountain. This slope was too steep for tobogganing! It was so much fun we didn't care. Before we left, we drank a few glasses of *Glühwein*, hot spiced red wine. Neither of us would usually drink alcohol, but all the water pipes were frozen, so it was reasonable to have something yummy before we left. It was very dangerous and people had to dodge us. We yelled, screamed and sung like naughty children as we sped down the icy slope.

I was twenty-five and experiencing more success in my work. One of the musical directors asked me, 'If you had a choice, would you prefer to be a ballerina or a musical theatre performer? What do you love most?'

My ballet career would not last much longer. My back pain still bothered me at times. I needed to look towards my future. A career in musicals would lengthen the time I could perform on stage. I loved the work and the variety and didn't want to leave the theatre world. His was an interesting question. I felt at this time that I could express myself more fully in musical theatre, where singing and acting were as much required as dancing. It didn't hurt so much either. I could work in musical theatre until I was sixty or older.

Then, with my best friend Gerhard and our two ballet directors, we talked about combining our talents in the future. We dreamed of creating a little cabaret theatre where we could dance and sing and do whatever type of show we wanted. Between us, we could cover the skills of choreographers, directors and producers, but we could not make our dream happen in Schwerin. I realised that if we stayed in Schwerin, we'd stagnate. Things were nearly too perfect at Schwerin and when things are too good, something has to change. I was at the peak of my career and with a wonderful life, but knew it was time to leave Schwerin. I planned to return to Berlin to be in the centre of art and culture, where other opportunities were available.

I didn't want to go to the Staatsoper Berlin because it was mostly known as a classical ballet company. Professor Tom Schilling, artistic director and choreographer of the Komische Oper Berlin, had wanted to contract me seven years ago. Now it was the right place and the right time for me to request an audition with him at the Komische Oper. I was successful, offered a contract and planned to start soon after.

In walking distance from the Komische Oper, the Metropol Theatre staged operettas, and my director and choreographer from Schwerin applied for contracts there, where Gerhard also secured a position as a dancer. We'd all be in Berlin together.

Our plan was to commit to our contracts, get to know Berlin again, and work towards our future goal to create in the Metropol Theatre, whose operetta work was at this time a bit old-fashioned, a new focus on contemporary musicals. I'd devote myself to dancing with the Komische Oper and join my three friends at the appropriate time. Everyone in Schwerin was sad to say goodbye to us, but I was too excited about the plans for Berlin to be sad. It was time to move on.

We were excited about our new lives back in Berlin. It was lovely to meet up with old friends and acquaintances at the Komische Oper. My accommodation was a very old place and it was the worst I had experienced – I hated it. It was small, it was not in a nice area, it was dark and old and freaky for me. I never saw any other people around there.

Coming up to Christmas, I thought about Mum. Her dream for many years was to have a bicycle, which neither of us had ever owned. I planned that I would save enough money to buy Mum a pushbike for Christmas. I walked from home to the tram stop and passed a bike shop and a bike in the window caught my eye. It cost over seven hundred marks. I asked the shopkeepers if they always had bikes available. They said yes, there'd always be a few ready for sale.

I saved from my monthly pay all the money required and one day, a week before Christmas, I planned to pay for it. I would pick it up on my way home from rehearsals in the afternoon and keep it at my place until Christmas.

There was no bike in the shop window! I hoped it was inside. I went into the shop and there was not one bike left. They all were gone. I was so upset and asked if they would be getting more delivered later that week and they said no. I was devastated.

'I've been calling in here and asking if you would have one for me and you told me that you would, that there'd be no problem.'

'They've all been sold.'

I was so disappointed that I couldn't make Mum's wish come true.

Some shops in East Berlin, such as a linen shop that sold sheets, were completely empty at times and had nothing to sell at all. The employees still had to work at the shops, even if the shelves were empty. This I found very depressing. East Berlin was a city of many cafés, different from other East German cities. Most of the people in these cafés were visitors from West Berlin. Often, if I wanted to go to a café, I had to stand in a queue waiting because they were so packed. Sometimes, when it was my turn, I was asked, 'Are you from the West or the East?'

When that happened the first time, I said, 'What do you mean?'

He said, 'It means are you from East Berlin or West Berlin?'

I thought it was an extraordinary question. I said, 'I'm from here!'

He said, 'I'm sorry, but you'll have to come back tomorrow.'

'I beg your pardon? I want coffee now.'

It became the talk of the town and later with friends we figured out that they would rather take west marks for the coffee than east marks because waiters got tipped with west marks, but they wouldn't ever get tips from East Germans, we had such little money, so they preferred West Germans as customers. This was not an officially sanctioned way of doing business. It made me frustrated and upset me and I hated it when we'd be sent away. Who could we complain to? Nobody. Here, where the West and the East were side by side, everything was now political, even buying a coffee.

In East Berlin Intershops sold Western products not normally available to East Germans, but the goods had to be paid for with west marks. So these waiters would then be able to purchase from these shops with the west marks they were given by their café customers. There was no bank or money exchange where we could just swap east marks for west marks, unless we were granted permission to travel to West Germany. Only pensioners could apply to travel at this stage, or officials, sports delegates and artists with proof of their travel. The East German age for pensions was sixty for women and sixty-five for men. There is an old saying, *Einen alten Bauern verpflanzt man nicht*, an old tree cannot be transplanted into new ground. The East German authorities believed that older people would always return from a trip to the West, that it was human nature to return to their familiar homes and to their children and grandchildren. It was not unusual for pensioners to be given permission to travel to the West to visit family members if they had clean records.

Returning to East Berlin after being away for eight years was a strange experience. The whole of East Berlin seemed to be a more political environment. It felt like I was walking on ice, slippery. Nothing was clear, it was rather weird. In Schwerin, it was just the East and although we were conscious of the presence of the Russian army there for security, East and West politics didn't impose into our everyday lives. Now I found that even if I had a chance to get a seat at a table in a café, and asked if I could join people already sitting there, they would say, 'Why do you ask? No, you can't sit at our table.' In Schwerin, I was used to sharing tables. Here in East Berlin people said, 'No.' People were whispering. People were outcast. I wasn't used to that.

Here in East Berlin, where I could see the Brandenburg Gate in the distance from the window of my change room, I felt my life was imposed upon by politics that interfered with my everyday life. I couldn't buy a bike; I couldn't buy a coffee; shops were often empty; people whispered about things. That's not fair. That stinks. And I can't even talk about it without getting into trouble.

The Komische Oper asked me if I wanted to be involved with the union as I had been in Schwerin.

Due to the whole weird atmosphere I felt around me, I said, 'No, I'm not interested, thank you. I've done it for so many years at Schwerin that now I want to have a rest from it and just concentrate on my artistic work. I don't want to be involved in anything at all political for some time.'

I felt this might have been held against me. Basically, I was saying, 'Just leave me alone, I don't want to have anything to do with all this weird stuff. I don't like what I see. Piss off.' I didn't quite know my place in this environment and needed time to branch out on my own to find out how I fitted in. I know that people were spying on me when I was at the Komische Oper. It's hard to explain how I knew it at the time; it was more than intuition. I could sense what I call a 'vibration' from specific people. Those who I suspected were over-friendly to me, and that seemed to be a sign for me to be wary. It has been estimated that at this time in East Germany, one in six adults were Stasi members and informers.

My boyfriend in Schwerin had stayed on there when I returned to Berlin. Our relationship was gradually unfolding. Eventually, he came to Berlin to join another dance company and as his accommodation was much better than mine, I shared his place in Berlin with him. We knew that eventually we would go our separate ways and we did not plan a future together.

I did not tell the Komische Oper officials that I had auditioned at the Metropol Theatre and signed a contract to start there in September 1980, with good payment, including free singing and acting lessons. My friends and I couldn't wait to proceed with our plans.

I had been at the Komische Oper for not quite two years when the proposed trip to Australia was announced. The Komische Opera had travelled to the West before, but this would be the first trip to Australia, so far away on the other side of the world. We all worked hard on the four ballets we planned to take, and had information meetings about Australia, where we were told there would be good weather and kangaroos. Seven weeks on tour – such an extensive trip was quite unheard of.

Although we were told everybody would be going with no exclusions, a few weeks before we left I was sitting in the canteen after rehearsal and someone asked me, 'Heidi, are you coming too?'

I thought that was a weird question and felt a bit intimidated. It indicated that there must be people who were not going to be part of the tour. Someone mentioned that a list of names would be displayed on our information board of those who would be taking part in the tour. It was a sensitive subject, so we didn't talk about it.

When the list came out, my name was not on it. I felt weird. Why not me? I wouldn't ask, I didn't want to rock the boat. We'd all been required to have a full medical and dental check-up. It was discovered that I had a medical condition – maybe that was why I wasn't listed to go. As I didn't feel that the tour would change my life in any particular way, I wasn't particular excited about going or not. Then, in the last few days, it was announced that everyone was going.

For the few days before, I'd been wondering who else would be on the final blacklist. You'd never find out why you'd been blacklisted, you'd never challenge it, and just be left to wonder if it was health or politics. The whole company travelled – some musicians, the make-up artists, our wardrobe assistants. There were about eighty of us going on tour.

Before leaving for Australia, I visited a close friend, Fine, who loved fashion and gave me some lovely clothes to take. She was rather like a big sister to me.

When we said goodbye late at night, she said, 'Don't you even think about not coming back!'

I said, 'Why would you say such a thing? I have no intention not to come back.' I have thought about this moment many, many times since defecting.

We left from Berlin-Schönefeld, our only airport. Our passports and tickets were collected by an organiser. It was snowing and freezing cold on the day we left for the incredibly long flight. It was uncomfortable, I was hungry and thirsty. We arrived in Perth and it took us several hours to take off again on our flight to Melbourne. All I wanted was to get to Melbourne and have some food, I was so hungry. We travelled with a small group of ballet school students and a couple of teachers in our troupe. One of the teachers had some cheese sticks and she shared them with me.

We landed at Tullamarine Airport, Melbourne, and my first impression of Australia was sunshine, blue sky, space, warmth, food. We were taken by bus to our accommodation at the Diplomat Motor Inn in Acland Street, St Kilda. We all stayed at the same motel. We were to rehearse at the National Theatre on the corner of Barkly Street and Carlisle Street in St Kilda, and to perform at the Palais Theatre on the Esplanade, near Luna Park, in St Kilda. The Palais Theatre was, at the time, the cultural centre in Melbourne, as the Victorian Arts Centre had not been completed.

The view from the theatre down to the sea was just awesome. It felt like a wonderful holiday destination, not a place for work. We were told we shouldn't walk around by ourselves, that we should have somebody with us at all times for security.

Our first breakfast was white, square bread toasted. We never had square, white bread or toast at home, so toast was nice. Strawberry jam and honey was available. So I spread my toast with butter and jam, which I loved. I took one mouthful of the toast and said, 'Oh yuck, the butter is off.' It wasn't of course, but I'd never tasted salted butter before, so it was strange to me.

We spent about three weeks in Melbourne, busy rehearsing every day, preparing several ballets for our performances. After Melbourne, we were to perform at the first Adelaide Arts Festival for about five days and then for a week in Canberra and finally two weeks in Sydney.

In Melbourne, I loved wandering around the open market on the

Esplanade in St Kilda, with stalls selling all hand-made crafts. I planned to buy some sheepskin Ugg boots to take home as souvenirs, but wondered how I'd fit them in my suitcase. Although we had different training and rehearsal times, I had two good friends who I spent most of my time with when I was exploring St Kilda.

We had our own staff with us, but local Melbourne staff also assisted. A young woman helped me dress for the performances. She was such a friendly person and we tried to communicate by body language, smiles and giggles. On opening night, all the performers give each other a hug and we say *toi-toi-toi* to each other, with three kisses alternating on the cheeks. This is a good luck tradition in theatre life. I hugged her and said *toi-toi-toi*. She wished me luck and gave me a book. What an unexpected surprise it was to be given an English–German dictionary. I was delighted at her thoughtfulness and that she felt such a connection to me that she really wanted to communicate with me. Although it was time-consuming, from then on we used the dictionary to look up many words and I was so grateful to her. That is how I started to learn English. I kept the book for twenty-five years, until it was completely worn out.

On the third day in Melbourne I had finished my training and rehearsal and thought I'd walk back to the motel and stay there for a few hours until I needed to return for the next rehearsal session. It was a beautiful sunny day, the temperature was in the mid-twenties. I walked along the promenade of St Kilda beach to find my way back to Acland Street. Although it was fine and warm, not many people were on the beach.

I stood there, looking out over the sea, and said to myself, 'Wow, how beautiful is that view!' All of a sudden I consciously heard for the first time in my life an inner voice. I heard it say, 'This is the place you dreamed about when you were little.' Blue big water, white waves, blue sky, lots of space.

I thought, 'This is it, I'm here now, this is the place I so often dreamed about. I'm not a sailor but I've travelled across the world and now I am here at that place of my dreams.'

At that moment, a large white ship came into my view.

I was alone. Hardly anyone was around. I thought, 'How beautiful is that.' I so enjoyed being alone, experiencing this wonderful sight. The water was turquoise, the sky was a different wonderful shade of blue, the clean sand of St Kilda beach was golden. I was completely lost in the beauty of it all. I opened my arms to the sky and took a deep breath and said, 'Oh wow.' I was overcome by a feeling of incredible huge space and freedom. It was an overwhelming sense of complete happiness and harmony.

This is it. This is it. This is the place I want to live, this is the place I want to be. I want to stay here. I will stay here. I will stay here forever. Where am I? Australia. Melbourne. St Kilda. This is the place I want to live my life. This is my new home.

I started to giggle to myself, saying to myself, 'Thank you, God.' It was a profound realisation. I had made the decision. Me, Heidi, who would never have applied for an exit visa. Me, Heidi, who would never have walked away from East Germany over the Ostsee. Me, Heidi, who never would have attempted to climb the Berlin Wall. I was now in an awesome position. I was thinking of 'freedom', but I didn't know what it meant.

If anybody was near me, I did not notice them. Okay, how was I going to do this? I'd never wanted to defect. I'd never wanted to leave home for good. I had a feeling of urgency. I had seven weeks to plan this and I must not tell anybody. Nobody was to find out that I was even contemplating staying. I was certain I would do it, but I didn't know how. All would be fine, all would be okay.

I felt like a little girl with a wonderful secret. Then I looked at my watch, saw the time and realised I had to hurry to get back to the motel to prepare again for rehearsal. From then on, twenty-four-seven, if I didn't have to concentrate on my work, my thoughts were on how I would stay in Australia. Somehow I had a certain trust in myself, I felt no panic about how I would do this. I just hoped none of my colleagues could read my mind. If anybody wondered about how I felt, or suspected my plan, I'd only say 'Australia? It's quite nice.' I knew I would never say to them, 'I love Australia and I would love to stay here.' I would not let anyone know that I planned to defect.

To defect had to be a secret. It was a political crime to defect from a communist country and I did not want to be caught planning my defection. I knew that I would do it on the planned day of departure in Australia, because I didn't want to let my ballet company down. After all, no matter what, the show must go on. There would be no sense running away before the tour was completed, because the East German authorities would try to find me.

A few days after our arrival in Melbourne, we were invited to an official dinner at a well-known restaurant in Acland Street called the Black Rose. Various dishes were served and the food was fantastic! I loved the lasagne, which I'd never had before in my life, and we ate plenty. It was a happy atmosphere. Traditional mouth-watering dishes like *Rouladen* – rolled beef filled with cucumber, mustard and ham, served with boiled potatoes, lots of gravy and cabbage – featured on the menu.

My friends and I decided that we'd return one lunchtime and order the *Rouladen*. We had saved our own pocket money. The German co-owner Ernst, who spoke our language, came over and took our orders. When our meals arrived, they were served with only half a potato accompanying the *Rouladen*. Half a potato! It was a joke! In East Germany, we'd grown up with potatoes, potatoes, potatoes. They were the main part of every meal. It must be a mistake: here we were served a huge piece of *Rouladen* but only half a potato. We signalled to the English-speaking co-owner that we'd like more potatoes, but he didn't understand us so he called Ernst to assist.

I explained to him in German, 'We are very hungry, and we were wondering if we could have more potatoes?'

He said 'Hmm…I usually serve half a potato…'

'But we're from East Germany and usually eat lots of potatoes and we're really hungry. Could we have some more please?'

He was very nice and said, 'No problem.'

Within a few minutes, we were served lots of potatoes with our meals.

His business partner, who was from South Africa, later told me he never would forget taking our plates back to the kitchen with our request for more potatoes. He realised we were from the ballet company and had said to Ernst, 'That good-looking girl is so tiny, but I think she's saying she wants more food. I don't understand it. Where would she put it?'

Ernst said, 'I'd better check it out.'

We enjoyed our time at the Black Rose and said to Ernst that we'd like to come back again.

He encouraged us, saying, 'Come back any time. I'll charge you half price. It looks like you guys need a lot of food!'

Our performances were well received in Melbourne. I danced in *Jugend Simfonie, Youth Symphony*, choreographed by Tom Schilling, with music written by Mozart when he was only seventeen, one of the three ballets the company presented on the tour. I know ballet enthusiasts in Australia talked about us but we didn't have time to really enjoy the success of it. Ballet is just hard work. My two special friends and I wanted to make the whole tour an experience to remember. I remained cautious about my responses when I was in their company, all the time knowing it would be the last time I would ever see my friends.

I wanted to have fun, enjoy something new and make the whole experience an interesting adventure. So I was the one always planning to do fun things together, such as going to Luna Park. Luna Park, a playground for rides next to the beach in St Kilda, has the roller coaster, ghost train and many other fun rides and was open very late at night, so we'd go there after our performance finished at eleven o'clock. It was such fun. This was paradise.

Several of us went to St Kilda beach one afternoon to sunbake and rest. Some young guys started to talk to us. They wanted to know who we were and where we had come from. They spoke no German and we spoke no English but with gestures and drawings we communicated. We walked back to the hotel together and one of them wanted to meet me again after our performance that night and to show me the city. I said, 'Okay.'

We travelled by tram and went to Young and Jacksons Hotel, opposite Flinders Street Station. I'd never been to a hotel before in my life. It was late at night; hardly anyone else was there. On every wooden table was a little music box. It cost twenty cents to play any song of our choice that was listed on the box. I'd never seen such a music machine before and I thought it was terrific.

So, a few days later, I found time to go back into Melbourne by tram to explore the city with my friends. Fortunately, I had great stamina and could get up in the mornings even if we'd been out late at night. Surprisingly, we'd been given the space to do these things. Everything was fine so long as we worked hard and were on time for rehearsals and performances. In the city, we felt like little kids in the strange big, wide world. The shops looked so bright to us, full of colourful goodies. Such a contrast to shops at home, where at this time, other than for basic foods, many were empty.

There was a large supermarket in the city and I loved the smell of it as I wandered through the aisles. I could hardly believe all the different foods and goods on the shelves. Yoghurt, cheeses and packaged ice creams… Plastic bags given away even if only one item was purchased. At home, we either brought our own bags to the shops or items were wrapped in plain paper. How extravagantly wonderful! Everything smelt gorgeous – the toothpaste and the soaps were scented, at home they were not fragranced. Colours, scents, flavours, plenty of everything… what a wonderful place I was in.

On my twenty-seventh birthday, on 21 March, I had a lovely surprise. We all had our own place in the change room at the Palais Theatre, and on my spot sat a bunch of flowers and a card. I was thrilled, my first thoughts were, 'Who knows that it's my birthday?' I opened the card and it was from a former teacher of mine from the ballet school who was travelling with the tour and responsible for the students. I was so far away from home and family and it was lovely that she thought of me. I realised that although she was the wife of the director of the ballet school, she was an awesome woman who not only remembered my birthday but also cared enough to make my birthday special.

During the day, my two friends suggested that we would go out that night to celebrate my birthday.

I said, 'Where are we going?' and the two of them decided it would be a surprise.

'Tell me, tell me, where are we going?'

'It's a surprise! We'll take you and we'll pay for you.'

'Okay!'

They had organised a surprise birthday party for me with forty members of the ballet company upstairs in the beautiful private party room at the Black Rose Restaurant. I'd never had a big birthday party in my life and this was very significant for me. I was the only one who knew it would be the last time with my colleagues and friends, so it was extra special. One of my friends made a speech for me and I felt rather suspicious, thinking I hoped none of them had any idea of my plans. A beautiful birthday cake and a little wrapped gift were placed on a table. Presents and a cake! The icing on the cake said Ich liebe dich, I love you.

I'd never seen a cake decorated like this before and asked my friends, 'Who is that from?'

They were all smiling and looking at me. They encouraged me to open the presents and it was perfume and talc labelled 'The Black Rose'. Who was it from?

It was a great night of music and dancing and the two owners of the restaurant joined us. All the time, I was totally aware of the necessity to enjoy this time with everybody. I did not want to hurt any of my friends or other colleagues, and I was so grateful for this wonderful occasion.

We danced until early in the morning and then my friends asked me, 'What do you think, Heidi? Who has given you the cake and the present?'

I said, 'Well, they weren't from you!'

They said, 'Come on, Heidi, you know. Somebody's in love with you.'

'Don't be silly.' I really didn't guess. Falling in love was not on my mind. 'Tell me who it is.'

They said that the cake and the gifts were from Ernst, the co-owner of the restaurant.

'Why?' I asked.

'He told us when we went for lunch together that he has fallen in love with you.'

'Come on…' I felt rather shy. Ernst was friendly to everyone. Was I really special to him?

A few nights later, my two friends said, 'Let's go to the Black Rose, Ernst has organised a *Kartoffelpuffer*, potato cake, night.' Ernst had heard me say I loved *Kartoffelpuffer* and this evening was just for the four of us. 'Ernst said it's especially for you, Heidi.'

'I can't resist *Kartoffelpuffer*, but you two stay beside me!'

We sat in an alcove decorated with candles, and I certainly could feel that Ernst had arranged all this especially for me. We had a wonderful night.

A fruit shop in Barkly Street on the corner of Acland Street fascinated me. It wasn't a particularly big shop, it had aisles, and the vegetables and fruit were arranged beautifully. The polished apples were arranged in rows and shone. All the vegetables were clean, large and perfect, brightly coloured. It looked so different to fruit shops at home. Our vegetables were covered with dirt. I often visited this shop during our stay in Melbourne, mostly just to look, sometimes to enjoy the experience of having such a wide range of choices – an apple, a pear, a banana – what would I have today?

The lady and gentleman who ran the shop looked European, but although we tried to communicate, I didn't understand English and they didn't speak German. We became fond of each other and I looked forward to visiting their shop. After a little while, they gave me a free apple or a pear. How sweet of them. I was most grateful. I knew I would come back to St Kilda, that it would be where my new life would start, and I knew I would have to work and earn money. As I loved this fruit and vegetable shop and the owners were so friendly to me, I concocted a plan in my head that perhaps I could work at the back of the shop, preparing the fruit and vegetables for the display and gradually learning English at the same time. I thought it was an excellent idea.

There was a German-speaking girl working in a photo shop in Acland Street. My two friends and I enjoyed looking at the pictures in the shop. She said she wanted to take a picture of us together, with a Polaroid camera that produced instant prints. We had never seen cameras like this before. The image appeared before our eyes and it was fantastic. She took three photos of us, and gave one to each of us. We hadn't asked for her to do it; it was so nice of her. We met such friendly people.

One afternoon, I took a stroll on my own down Fitzroy Street, St Kilda. I knew we were only supposed to walk around with a friend, not alone, but that didn't always work. I was attracted to a shop that had various prepared salads displayed in the window. They looked beautiful. How colourful and attractive! I simply loved food, as I still do, and would like to have tried something. The guy working inside waved to me. I thought, 'How friendly!' and waved back. He waved at me again, and I waved back again. Then he gestured for me to enter. So I did. He started talking to me in English, and I gestured to him that I couldn't understand. He asked where I was from and as we tried to communicate he began spooning salad onto a plate for me. I said, 'No, no, no...' knowing I didn't have money to spend. I had to watch every cent. I wasn't really hungry, just enjoying window shopping, but he insisted and I thanked him for his generosity. More friendly people.

It was our last night in Melbourne when Ernst suggested that with my two best friends we go to a dance along the beach. It was fun and became clear to me that he was interested in me. He wanted to keep in contact with me. It was nice to feel special. He wanted me to give him the phone numbers of the hotels that we were to stay in after leaving Melbourne. I was able to find out the information and gave it to him and wondered if I would ever hear from him again.

We left Melbourne by plane for Adelaide and had to wait so long to get on stage at the Arts Festival. We waited on sofas in the bistro, and while waiting, I talked with my director-choreographer, Tom Schilling. He asked me how I liked Australia.

'It's good, it's interesting.' Why is he asking me? Can he read my mind? We seldom spoke about anything other than work.

He was famous in East Germany and had built a wonderful reputation for his work so had often travelled as an arts representative beyond our borders.

'I've travelled quite a lot and it's all interesting. But never in my dreams would I have thought that our company would tour to Australia,' he said.

Please don't ask me questions. I knew he'd had previous experience of dancers defecting. People had gone to jail related to such things before the time I joined the company. If you knew that somebody planned to defect, you were responsible for telling the authorities of their intentions, so that the authorities could take control of the situation, otherwise you were likely to be sent to jail. You would be a good citizen by telling the authorities of course, because nobody should defect.

I did not want anybody to find out my intentions, I did not want anybody to go to jail. I was very aware that if I truly wanted to stay in Australia, it was impossible for me to tell anyone. I had to keep it a secret to make it possible so nothing could happen to me or anyone else. My life was my responsibility, nobody else's.

My director continued, 'I've seen the world, and I'm happy with my life. But I do understand that people can be confused. And I do understand that some people are not happy with where they live.'

I felt uncomfortable. I hadn't been a member of the company for very long and touring and excursions were always a great way to get to know each other better. Had I received too much attention? Did my colleagues see that I had fallen in love with Australia? Did my director recognise something in me, a dissatisfaction with home that perhaps other defectors had exhibited? I was relieved when we were called onto the stage for rehearsal.

I gave myself an important message. 'Heidi, be careful what you say, who you go with, where you go, how you look. Pretend all is fine.'

From Adelaide, we continued our tour to Canberra, where we stayed in another hotel. By this stage, we noticed that the conditions of our changing rooms, of the places where we rehearsed and even the theatres did not meet the same standards as at home. Unfortunately, we felt that in Australia there was less emphasis on culture and theatre than in East Germany. We made the best of it but it was interesting, because my preconception was that in a Western country everything would be better than at home and I realised it was not necessarily so. In Canberra, we did not even have a theatre to perform in, it was just a town hall. We were used to lavish theatres and always packed houses back at home.

In Canberra, I received a phone call, passed on from reception to the room I was sharing. How exciting. Who could be ringing me? It was Ernst, calling from Melbourne. He wanted to come up to Canberra to see the performance and spend time with me.

'I haven't got time, Ernst. We're really busy. It's all work, work, work. We would have no time together. You must be crazy!'

He was determined. I sneaked off after a performance to meet him and he gave me a single rose. I thought, 'How cute is that?' We spent some hours together. It was romantic and lovely. I was aware that he had left his family because he wanted to be with me. However, my intention was not about falling in love with this man. Nobody was meant to see us together and nobody did. He had to leave again to be back at his restaurant the next day and at around lunchtime I received another phone call from him, telling me he'd nearly had an accident because he was so tired. I thought this was crazy – he was risking his life for me.

Days later, I received a long love letter from Ernst. I had not told him my plans to defect. This was interesting.

The company had been booked to dance at the Regent Theatre in Sydney, which was within walking distance from our hotel, the Chevron, near Kings Cross, although sometimes we took the underground train to the theatre. We'd been told to be aware we were staying in the red light district and not to talk to anyone. But I wanted to experience this red light district and find out about it. I'd never heard of anything like it in East Berlin. Walking down the street with my friends, we saw shops, restaurants and cafés, there was nothing particularly unusual... but what was going on here? Muscly men outside different premises with flickering lights, encouraged us to come in to see the show.

'What sort of a show is it?' Curiosity got the better of us.

We entered what appeared to be a little theatre. There was music for a few minutes and then a woman came on stage and began to perform a striptease.

I shrank in my seat and said to my friends, 'I think I'm in the wrong place here!'

It wasn't really our scene, but now we knew a bit more about the red light district.

One night, we went to a performance of *Les Girls*. What an awesome show! I'd never seen such a thing as this crazy show starring transvestites, but I loved it. What amazing performers those divas were! I thought it was hilarious and felt it was a spectacularly professional show where they involved the whole audience.

There were only two weeks to go before the end of the tour.

How am I going to do this? What am I doing? These thoughts came more frequently. How am I going to stay here? Where will I hide?

Sydney was so picturesque, the harbour scenery was spectacular and the Opera House a wonderful sight.

When I left our hotel in Sydney, I met the young fellow who'd taken me to Young and Jacksons in Melbourne. He visited me with his very good friend, an older man, who was a teacher. They showed me all the tourist sights of Sydney. Perhaps the young man was a bit infatutated with me, but as far as I was concerned he was just lovely and thoughtful and I enjoyed thinking that Australian people were very friendly.

While staying at Kings Cross, we sometimes went around the corner from the hotel to visit a Greek restaurant. Owned by a family, the restaurant had private little niches where I enjoyed dining with my two best friends. Sometimes I went alone. The mother and father ran the restaurant with their two sons and they were interested to know about us: where we were from, why we were in Sydney. I liked communicating with these people who knew about Germany and the Berlin Wall.

Over the final few days in Sydney, I had to make my plan. These people showed me affection, they hugged me when I visited them. I felt like I was home with a family when I went there. Perhaps they could hide me? Perhaps my friend and his teacher could help me? What about Ernst, he had tried to contact me many times in Sydney, but he was married and I didn't really want to rock the boat. I thought that it was dangerous of him to ring me all the time and leave messages for me at reception. I didn't ring back. I certainly did not want to ring back from the hotel, in case anyone paid too much attention to my behaviour.

In Sydney, I received more letters from Ernst, proclaiming his affection for me, explaining that he had told his wife he had met someone else, and that he had moved out of their home. He wrote that he wanted me to stay in Australia, although there'd been not a word spoken about my plans to stay. If I didn't want to stay, Ernst claimed he would follow me to East Germany. He wanted to marry me. It was full on, and in a way that scared me. I didn't really want to have a full on relationship when I was making such a huge important decision about my life. My head needed to be clear. I consciously stepped back a bit and did not return his calls. I was busy with my work.

Eventually, I thought I must reply to Ernst. It would be rude to ignore him. I called him from a public phone in the street. He said he needed to see me. He said I should come to Melbourne.

'Are you crazy, Ernst? I can't do that! We're not allowed to get on planes on our own and just go wherever we like. You remember your conversations with my colleagues about what we're allowed to do. I can't do that. You aren't aware how dangerous that could be for me.'

'Oh, come on. I'll order you a ticket. There are planes from Sydney to Melbourne every hour. Just come for a few hours and then you can go back.'

Two or three girls from the ballet school who travelled with us had talked too much with the receptionist at the motel in Melbourne and they were removed from our company and were being held in the East German embassy in Canberra. Those girls would stay at the embassy until we left. It was explained to us that we were not to get close to anyone in Australia. We were warned not to have any deep contact with anyone, that there would be consequences.

I didn't want to end up at the East German embassy. But Ernst really wanted me to come to Melbourne. I thought if I saw him I could encourage him not to give up his family just for me. A one-on-one conversation could be good and I decided to risk it. I was to leave early in the morning, before Sydney woke up. I shared the hotel room with a young girl from the school. I was ten years older than her, so I thought I could handle any questions she could have asked me. Our rehearsal times were different and I hardly slept for the seven weeks anyway, packing as much into each day as I could. So, my room-mate and I came and went at different hours. I didn't sleep and sneaked out to a taxi at about four in the morning. Ernst had arranged a ticket for me to collect from the airport counter. He was to pick me up from Melbourne airport. It was my only full day off. I thought that I'd be pretty safe. As long as I was back late in the afternoon, nobody would have any concerns.

I told Karl, my best friend, I was going to Melbourne, that he must keep it a secret and that I would be reachable on a particular phone number.

'Ah, you're going to the Black Rose,' he guessed.

I said if he needed to get in touch with me he was to do so, otherwise, if anyone asked him where I was, he was to say I was sightseeing in Sydney. We always needed to be prepared for the unexpected. If one person fell sick, then changes had to be put in place so that the performance could still go ahead. That was my concern: if I was needed, Karl had to be able to contact me. We swore we could trust each other.

About two o'clock in the afternoon, Karl rang me at the restaurant in St Kilda to tell me one of the dancers had taken ill and I would be performing that evening. He said everyone was looking for me, asking him, 'Where's the Gierschen?' He explained that our director, Tom Schilling, was going bananas. Karl said, 'You have to come back, otherwise you'll be in terrible trouble.'

I knew he was right. This was panic! I had to get back to Sydney. I was scared I would be late. We rushed to the airport, I caught a plane and arrived back in Sydney later in the afternoon. I would be on time for rehearsal. I probably should have found some of the company officials who were searching for me and apologised, but feared their questions. My instinct was that the best thing for me to do was to go straight away to Schilling's room and simply tell him myself that I was here now and available. His door was slightly ajar. I felt nervous as I knocked and he called for me to enter.

'Tom, I'm here...'

I could tell by the look on his face that he was relieved to see me.

'Yes, you're here! Great! Go and get ready for rehearsal.' He asked me no questions.

Had I spoken to any of the officials, I am sure they would have interrogated me about my day.

When I did see them, they said, 'Where have you been? What have you been doing?'

I said, 'I'm here now. I've told Tom I'm here. That's all that matters, isn't it?'

That was too close. I'd created too much attention towards me. I said to myself, 'Heidi, be careful.' I was scared. I felt somebody had clues now. Keep silent and focus on your work. No more distractions.

Over the next week, I made sure there'd be no further suspicions about me. I was early to rehearsal, early to breakfast. Look at me, everyone, I'm here!

Tomorrow is the last day of the tour. *Scheisse*, shit. How am I going to do this? I will just disappear. Australia is so big, I will just walk out of Sydney into the bush and disappear. I could hide under trees and on beaches for days. Nobody would find me in this huge country. I don't know… Hide… Be gone.

The next day was to be our final performance. Afterwards, I will pack up quickly without showing I'm in a hurry. I will be first out of the building and back to the hotel. I will not be there to board the bus taking us to the airport the following morning at eight o'clock. I have to be gone.

This is my plan. I've timed that I can run back to the hotel from the theatre in twelve minutes. Running will be quicker than going on the underground train. I will grab my blue bag from under the bed. I have to be out of the hotel first before anybody else returns. If I can do that, then I can be gone. I need courage to be calm, to be in control. Nobody must see me hurrying as I leave the hotel. I will just be a young, anonymous woman walking towards the beaches, away from the centre of Sydney. When they count up in the morning and find I'm not there, how long will they look for me? I have no idea. I just know I can disappear.

During the day, we had rehearsals and at about lunchtime I became a bit emotional. I was thinking of my two dear friends, who knew nothing of my plans. I would never see them again. What am I doing? What about my mum?

Mum was on my mind all the time since I made my decision to defect. What will Mum say? I may never, ever see her again. Why do I want to be so far away from her? No, I don't want to be away from Mum, or anyone else at home who I care about. I just want to have freedom.

I went to the Greek restaurant, my head filled with serious thoughts.

Mum was alone, but she had a friend, a man, who she'd only recently met. After so many years alone since her separation from Dad, she never wanted to have any involvement with a man as she devoted herself to us and her work. I used to say to her that I didn't want to see her growing old by herself and that I was sure she'd meet a terrific man one day. I met him a couple of times before coming to Australia. Mum had asked me what I thought of him and I said, 'Mum, he's a good man. Don't let him go.' I had to think about him deeply while I contemplated my decision. If he really is a good man, as I thought he was, Mum will be okay. She won't be angry with me. She will understand some day. Somehow, I will be able to contact her one day and we will talk and I can explain everything to her. Mum was my major concern, but I felt she was not on her own.

How and where will I ever explain my decision to my very dear friend Gerhard? Somehow I felt optimistic and thought one day we would see each other again, although I couldn't imagine how it might happen. I wasn't thinking politically. It would have been impossible for me to consider that one day the Berlin Wall would come down, yet I just had a strong feeling we'd meet again. Perhaps one day I could travel to Germany – West Germany – and when they were old enough and pensioners, they could travel from East to West to visit me. It might take many years, but it was possible. I had a sense that I would not see them for a long time, but it would not be forever.

I didn't want to think about bad outcomes, but it was possible that I would be caught, something would happen to me. Maybe somebody is aware of my intentions and will speak up and the authorities will find out I have this idea and they will catch me and I will go to jail.

I needed to tell somebody. I'd been suspicious of the phones in the hotel we were staying at, to the extent that when my room-mate was out of the room one day, I tried to open up the phone to see if any listening devices – bugs – were inside it. I really wasn't too sure what sort of a thing I was looking for, but decided it might not be safe to talk there.

I went to another Sydney hotel, the Gazebo, to use a public phone. A public phone surely wouldn't be bugged? I asked in reception how much money was needed to make an overseas phone call to Germany and what the numbers were to make the call. I tried to be very casual. The people working there certainly did not know me. I rang my older brother in Germany. I wanted to get a message to Mum, who did not have a phone. He was strong, he could tell Mum, I thought. It had been bothering me that either my brother, my mum or Gerhard might have plans to pick me up from the airport, although it hadn't been arranged and I wasn't expecting it. I didn't want that to happen. I knew that if they did go to the airport, they'd be taken away for questioning about my disappearance immediately and perhaps sent to jail. I did not want anybody connected with me to be at the airport when the ballet company arrived home in East Germany.

I hoped my brother understood from the little I said what I planned. I felt I couldn't say too much. It might have been dangerous for him and for me, and the call was costly.

'It's me. Please tell Mum not to go to the airport when we come back. Nobody should go to the airport. I'm not coming back. You'll hear from me whenever I can.'

'Okay.'

I hung up. That was done. I'd let him know. I felt it was safe. Then I became worried – just in case he didn't get it, or couldn't get the message to Mum. Under no circumstances must Mum go to the airport. It was too dangerous for her.

I decided to tell Karl of my plan. Perhaps he would decide to stay in Australia too, I thought. Surely I couldn't be the only one who wanted to stay in Australia. I would be prepared for us to stay together, that would be fine. I knew where to find him at the hotel, resting before rehearsal

'Can you come for a coffee with me?'

Karl didn't seem to be particularly keen.

'Come on, I really want to spend this last afternoon with you.'

We went to the Greek restaurant and sat in one of the private nooks.

'Are you okay, Heidi?'

'I'm okay. But I have something very important I want to share with you. Can you keep a secret?' I asked quietly.

I knew his answer would be yes.

'Are you sure? One hundred per cent? There has to be no doubt.'

'For you I can.'

I could trust Karl completely. 'You have to keep this secret for as long as I tell you to keep it. Can you do that?'

'Yes.'

'You might know already what I'm about to tell you.'

'You want to stay, don't you?' he guessed.

'Yes, I do.'

'Really? Wow. Can I stay too?'

'Yes, we can stay together!'

He was much younger than me. His ballet career had only really just begun.

'Do you really want to stay?' I asked him. 'There will be tough times.'

'How are you going to do it, Heidi?'

'I'm just going to disappear after tonight's performance. You can come with me, but you have to make up your mind now. I don't want to talk about it further. Make up your mind. Yes or no.'

'No.' He had a partner back at home who he did not want to leave.

We agreed that once everything had settled down after he returned home, perhaps two or three weeks later, he would go to my mum's, memorising her address as I would not write anything down for him. He would explain to Mum that he was a colleague of mine and a dear friend and that as soon as I possibly could, I would contact her. Somehow. He was to tell her I was fine.

We knew that in the morning, when it was clear that I was missing, he'd be the first to be asked about me. He just had to say, 'I don't know anything… I don't know anything… I don't know anything.' There was nothing else he could say.

We shook hands; we'd made a pact. We arranged that he would stay at reception at about ten past eight in the morning, and I'd ring reception and ask for him, just to find out what was going on. Karl was to answer with only one word 'Okay' or 'Bad' – that was all.

We both had tears in our eyes when we parted at about three o'clock in the afternoon.

He said, 'Heidi, you really don't know where you're going. Why don't you contact Ernst? He would help you.' I had to make a decision now. We both felt we'd see each other again one day, but perhaps it was just wishful thinking.

Right, Mum is looked after. Now, who will help me? Who will hide me? Perhaps this Greek family? Maybe, maybe not. What if they dob me in? What about the young man I met on the beach and his teacher who visited me in Sydney? No, that doesn't feel like the right thing to do. Karl is right. Yes, Ernst would help me. He loves me and even talks about coming to Germany, which is somehow ridiculous – he doesn't even know yet that I'm not going back there. There's no doubt in my mind about that. I will tell him my plan and see what he says.

I returned to the Gazebo to make another call on the public phone. This time, it was an interstate call to Melbourne. I wanted to make the conversation short. I didn't expect anything from him, but I just wanted to let him know I would stay in Australia.

Ernst answered the phone, surprised and pleased to hear from me. 'Heidi, oh, so you're all leaving tomorrow morning, aren't you?'

'Yes. But I'm not.'

'What? Are you staying?'

'Yes.'

'Where?'

'I don't know!'

'Wait for me, I'm coming.'

'What do you mean?'

'I'm leaving now.'

'What? You can't just leave now!'

'Yes, I am. It will take me several hours, but around about the time your performance finishes tonight, I'll be there.'

'You'll never make it. I have to be gone as soon as the show's over. I can't wait for you to be here.'

Ernst was confident it would take him about seven hours, speeding most of the way to Sydney, and convinced me it was possible. We arranged to meet near the theatre.

'Where?' he asked.

'Listen carefully, Ernst. Around the corner from the theatre, in the little side street, there's a church. It's a dark little street. I'll hide behind the church. But I'll only wait five minutes. You must be there, otherwise I'll just have to go. Somewhere.'

He was serious. 'No, Heidi. You wait. I will be there.'

I went to our hotel, back to my room, and my young room-mate was about to leave.

'What are you doing tonight after the last performance?' I asked her.

'I'm going out.'

'Me too. We could actually pack our suitcases now before we go to dance for the last time on stage in Australia. Yippie!' I sounded full of enthusiasm.

'Do you think that's a good idea, Heidi?'

'Yes. If we pack together, we can leave our suitcases ready for tomorrow morning at the foot of our beds.'

While we were both busy packing, and my room-mate was too busy to notice what I was doing, I stuffed a few things into a blue sea-sack which I'd borrowed from a friend back in East Berlin. It was a quite large, home-made, cotton bag. I used it as my everyday bag while we were on tour. I put some toiletries in it, as I hardly had any money left and knew I wouldn't be able to buy any, and a few clothes: a pair of jeans, a blue skirt and yellow top, a white blouse, a red dress, a beige dress, my favourite black and white cotton top from Fine, the white souvenir tour T-shirt naming the sponsors AGC Australian Guarantee and David Frost, the pale blue leotard, black woollen long-legged warm-up leotard and olive-green sweatpants. I'd bought a tiny little teddy bear with me to Australia as a mascot, and put it, too, in my sea-sack escape bag. I put it under the bed where my room-mate could not see it. My *pointe* shoes and the rest of my training clothes were to go into our huge bag that had separate bags in it for each of us, with our names on it, after the last performance. That would be returned on the flight separately.

I needed to leave after my room-mate so that I could keep our hotel room key. I said I wanted time alone, to have a little rest. I checked my sea-sack. I lay back on my bed. Right, Mum is okay. Mum will know not to go to the airport. I trust she will not panic. My brother and my friend…taken care of.

This is my grand plan: If Ernst is coming, then he will pick me up from the church and I'll get him to drive me to the hotel and park the car in the dark opposite the hotel where I can't be seen. He can take the room key and go into the hotel and get my sea-sack from under the bed. I can't return to the hotel and risk being seen by anyone. He can grab my bag then just pop the key in the key-return so my room-mate is not inconvenienced. Then we drive out of Sydney as far away as we can back to Melbourne. Perhaps we can stay overnight in the bush somewhere until the company has left.

I had no plan for what would happen after the dance company had left the country.

Everything will be all right. I hope Ernst is on time.

The final performance is over. Everybody's hectic and excited. There's plenty of talking, singing and shouting in the change-room. Nobody is taking particular notice of anyone. Everyone is too busy packing up for the last time in Australia and we are all getting ready to go out for our final night in this wonderful city. I remove my stage make-up with baby oil as quickly as I can. No time for a shower, I have to be first out of the building. I must be first to leave the building.

I'm running down the corridors, looking for the exit. Stop running, Heidi. Walk fast. Stay calm. I get to the stage door. Four colleagues are outside having a smoke.

'How come you're leaving already, Heidi? We've only just finished.'

'Oh well, I want to go out…'

I keep walking away from them. *Scheisse*, they are watching me. I'm hurrying across the bluestone cobblestones. I need to be around the corner in two minutes. I feel their eyes on me.

They call out, 'Where are you going?'

Two of these colleagues I believe are Stasi members. Perhaps they have been following me all the time. That's it now, I'm busted. I put a fake smile on my face, pretending to be very casual. Now is the most important moment in my life. I can stop walking and change my mind. No, that could be deadly. I must follow my dream.

I continue walking. I see the archway ahead that I need to walk through, and then turn left at, to go to the church and meet Ernst. I look up. A car has stopped, parked right in front of me. It is a blue Mazda. It is Ernst's blue Mazda! I am only ten metres from my colleagues. He gets out of the car, to go to the passenger side and opens the door for me. I gesture to him, 'Are you nuts!' Now they will recognise his car! They will recognise Ernst. They will see me get into the car. That's it, I'm busted. I jump into the car.

'You bloody idiot! *Du Idiot!*' I am hysterical, screaming. 'What do you think you're doing? Didn't we plan that you would park out of sight around the corner? They're watching us. They've seen you.'

'Heidi, don't worry.' Ernst is so calm. 'Who are they?'

I tell him their names.

'Don't worry. They know me, that's all right. I'm just taking you out for your last night in Sydney. They have no idea what we're doing.'

'But you don't understand the danger! Maybe they suspect me. Maybe they've been following me all the time.'

'If that was so, you'd know by now. They wouldn't have just let you go like that.'

'But you don't know, maybe somebody's waiting to get us…'

'Heidi, stop. You're just making up something that's not there.'

'You haven't got a clue, Ernst. Do you know anything at all about the Stasi? No, you don't, do you? Just drive as fast as you can. We need to be gone as far from Sydney as we can.' My plan, my plan. 'No, stop, stop, turn round. We need to go back to the hotel quickly.'

'Where is it? I don't know where I am.'

We find the hotel, park in a dark street. I cover myself with a blanket.

I instruct Ernst on the room number, give him the key and tell him to bring my bag from under the bed. 'Make sure nobody sees you.'

'Don't worry about it,' he says calmly.

Within a few minutes, he is back with my bag. 'I took the back fire exit because I saw somebody coming.'

'That was good thinking. Great. Let's go now.'

Ernst says, 'Heidi, I'm so hungry.'

I say, 'I don't care. Let's get going.'

'Let's celebrate!' Ernst announces happily.

'WHAT!'

'Let's celebrate a new life together.'

I think he must be crazy. 'You're mad! *Du bist verrückt!* You are absolutely mad! *Du bist wirklich verrückt!* Can you please drive out of Sydney now.'

'I'm so hungry. I'm going to take you to the best seafood restaurant in Sydney. Heidi, we're going out tonight, it's celebration time.'

I am utterly flabbergasted. 'Can we do that maybe next year, not now?'

'But it is today, it's now that we have to celebrate!'

I can't believe what he is saying. Ernst was not the reason I decided to stay in Australia. As far as I was concerned, we had just got to know each other. 'Maybe for you but not for me! Please go.' I start crying.

'Calm down,' he says reassuringly.

'How can we possibly go out to eat? What if somebody sees us? I couldn't eat anyway. You can go out. I'll wait in the car, under the blanket. Park the car in a dark back street. And you go out to eat.'

'Heidi, no.' Ernst is so calm. 'We will go out together. If somebody sees us, that's fine, I'm just taking you out on your last night in Sydney.'

'But if we're seen, they will get suspicious.'

'No, they won't. And where I'm taking you they can't go anyhow because it's far too expensive for them.'

'Where is it?' I am completely overwhelmed.

'Down on the harbour, overlooking the Opera House. It's a beautiful big restaurant.'

'I can't believe this. I feel sick. I think I need to vomit. You don't understand. I think you've fucked it up.' I never swear. I am in total turmoil. 'You just don't understand. Let me out. I'm going to walk away by myself. I should have known better than to trust you. You are an absolute idiot.' I am completely exhausted.

Ernst keeps on driving.

'Please stop the car. Let me out. I'm walking as far as I can out of Sydney. I don't want to be caught. I don't want to be seen with you. I don't care what you think. I'm sorry I told you, I should never have told you.'

Ernst says calmly, 'We're here.'

We are right outside the large, flash seafood restaurant on the Harbour, overlooking the Opera House. 'Come on, let's enjoy the beautiful evening.'

I feel like I am lost in space, a zombie, numb. I cannot think any more. I am in shock. My head feels like it is spinning.

We sit opposite each other at a huge table and near large tanks of live lobsters for the diners to choose from.

'Look at that big one,' Ernst says enthusiastically. 'Lobster is a delicacy. I'll order it and we'll share it. This will be the best meal you have ever eaten in your life!'

'I don't care. I am not eating these animals. They're still alive! I don't eat live animals.' I feel sick. I want to disappear in a flash from Ernst. I hate him terribly. 'Eat quickly and then we can go.'

Before long, we are presented with *two* meals at the table. Lobster mornay. Ernst is expecting me to eat this lobster. I don't care about eating, I am escaping! I am running away! I am not celebrating anything – *yet*. I am furious.

I whisper to Ernst, 'Don't you get it? I don't want this *Scheiss* meal.

I don't want this animal.'

He says, 'Just relax.'

I'm watching him eating his bloody lobster mornay. I am thinking that Ernst is the weirdest and most stupid person I have ever met in my life. I am breathing, I am just sitting still. There is nothing else I can think any more.

'I am going to have a nervous breakdown if you don't hurry now. I have to go. If you don't get it right now, I'm just going to run. I'm leaving now.' I stand, ready to flee.

'Just calm down. Stay. I'm nearly finished. I had to eat something. If we drive during the night, we don't know what will be open and when we can get something to eat again.'

Ernst finishes his meal. He pays the ridiculously high bill.

We walk back to the car. I am so scared.

'Can we drive away from Sydney now…please?' I beg.

I see and hear helicopters and planes in the sky overhead. Perhaps they are looking for me? No, they don't even know yet that I have gone.

After that night, I hated lobster for many, many years.

Act Two

Freedom, choreographed by Lothar Hanff and Eva Reinthaller for the Schwerin Theatre Ballet Company

We drove until about five in the morning, taking the long way, the coast road from Sydney back to Melbourne. Stopping at a motel in Eden, we rang the doorbell, then we were shown to a room. Ernst collapsed on the bed and straight away fell asleep.

After a few minutes, I shook him and said, 'Excuse me, what are we doing now? How long do you want to sleep here?'

I didn't want to sleep. He said he was exhausted and to let him sleep, I stayed awake, anxious and furious.

I woke Ernst at about six o'clock in the morning and asked, 'Do you have any idea what we do now?'

'I don't know. I think I should ring Paul, my solicitor.'

Running a business, Ernst used the services of a solicitor from time to time. Where I came from nobody had a solicitor unless it was to settle a divorce.

'What are you talking about? I haven't even done anything yet and you want to talk to a solicitor?'

Ernst explained that his solicitor would have some idea of what we should do. I didn't want him to know anything yet, because the ballet company wasn't to leave from the Chevron hotel for the airport until eight o'clock in the morning, so before that nobody should talk about anything.

I explained it to Ernst. 'You understand, Ernst? Nobody should talk about anything before that. Can't we just hide?'

'No, Heidi.'

'Do you have a better idea?'

'I'll call the Australian tour manager and ask him what he suggests can be done. I had several conversations with him when he came for dinner to the Black Rose and he seems to be a nice guy. He gave me his phone number.'

'No way,' I said. 'He would be responsible to report any clue to find me. Just because you think he's a nice guy doesn't mean you can trust him.'

Ernst needed more sleep. He was exhausted.

I just sat up and waited for…what? Time passing by, thinking about everyone and everything, about what would happen at eight a.m. in the foyer of the hotel when they realised that I was missing. I hoped that nobody would suffer from any consequences and that they would leave to go home from Sydney without further delay.

It is ten past eight. I am to call Karl, who will be waiting at the reception desk, as we arranged. I have butterflies in my tummy. I dial the number, a woman's voice answers, I ask to speak to Karl.

He answers, calmly, one word only. 'Okay.'

I am relieved. I can think of only one thing now – trust. Still with my eyes wide open, I have had no sleep yet.

I wake Ernst at about ten-thirty to tell him of the phone call and I'm wondering, what next?

Ernst suggests he call the tour manager now, without mentioning my name, simply to ask what would he do when he found out that a member of the ballet company had defected.

Mr Nice Guy said he had a responsibility to make an effort to ensure that everyone was on the plane flying back to East Germany. I thought that was fair enough, that was his job. I really didn't expect him to be able to do anything to help me.

Ernst was a bit disappointed. 'The best idea is to ring Paul now. Trust me. I won't mention your name. I'll just say something like, if there was a member from a visiting ballet company from a communist country who wanted to stay in Australia and not return home, what should they do?'

Ernst rang Paul at home and asked if he wanted to take on my case and Paul agreed. Ernst explained, 'Paul said as soon as we are in Melbourne we should go to his office. As simple as that.'

'Is it? Simple?' I didn't know what to think.

'Don't worry. He'll take it all in his hands.'

Ernst slept some more, I was still too nervous to sleep.

Later, we left the motel to go to Melbourne, with a blanket mostly covering me. We were on the road, far away from Sydney. I was exhausted and a feeling I can only describe as 'nothingness' overcame me. At that point, I just had to trust Ernst. He was driving, knew where we were, knew where to go and who to meet.

As we continued driving to Melbourne, Ernst listened to the radio and eventually a news reporter stated, 'An East German ballerina is missing…' Then, much later in the day, another news bulletin announced, 'Ballet company leaves the airport after a six-hour flight delay because one member is missing…' No name was mentioned in the report. Members of the dance company would have been interviewed about my escape before the plane left Sydney. My absence could not stop a plane and I was happy to know that the Komische Oper company had flown out of Australia.

We heard a few days later from Ernst's business partner that all the media had been at the airport. Reporters were chasing reports from the East German authorities and the Australian government.

Early on the Monday morning, driving in Melbourne, we saw news headline posters from *The Age* displayed on sandwich boards outside milk bars: 'Ballet Dancer Defects – Melbourne Hideout'. That really freaked me out. *Scheisse*, now they will catch me. I was so distraught that Ernst had to stop the car in a laneway and I climbed into the boot of his car to hide until we reached a car park at the back of a building very close to Paul's office.

When we met Paul in his upstairs office in Brunswick Street, Fitzroy,

I thought, 'What? He's a solicitor?' I'd never seen any solicitors before, but imagined that they'd wear a suit and a tie and look like intellectual businessmen. Paul had longish curly hair like a hippy, a beard, two big round eyes in wire-framed glasses, and he dressed in casual clothes. To my mind, he looked like a farmer, sitting at his desk full of papers. Later, when I met more Australians, I could see that Paul was a real dinky-di Aussie with an Aussie accent like many others.

Finally, we sat together in one room. I realised now I was on the run. Paul remembers so much more than I do. It is very hard for me to make sense of what happened when we met, as I could not understand English. Could I trust this solicitor? I started to feel sorry for Ernst, realising that this was more complicated than I could have imagined.

I admired Ernst for being able to talk in English and communicate with Paul, as I couldn't understand a word they were saying, and kept asking him to translate.

Ernst explained, 'You must trust me here, Heidi, and you must trust Paul. I can't do it alone.'

Paul asked him lots of questions about me. It was a strange experience knowing that these two men were talking about my predicament and I had not a clue what was being said. Used to talking for myself, I felt fearful and insecure. I was exhausted. Paul took notes of the discussion and asked, if I was permitted to stay, would Ernst support me. I didn't want to be a burden to anyone. Ernst agreed. It hadn't occurred to me that such an arrangement would be necessary, as I had always been independent. I explained that I thought I'd ask the people at the fruit shop in St Kilda if I could work there, that I'd have my own money and could support myself. But, as Paul and Ernst said, at that moment I had no job, no money and no family to support me. Ernst agreed to do so. It was very kind of him.

I had no idea of the likelihood of the Australian government deciding to let me stay. I was entirely politically naive about the situation, but I trusted Paul to make it happen. By the time we'd met, Paul's initial response was encouraging. He'd already spoken with officials, although he was concerned that I could be found not just by the press, but also by East German officials, before the Australian government's decision was made. Until something was authorised by the Australian government, I could certainly have been captured and sent home by my own countrymen. Paul made it very clear that we had to hide – but where?

Paul prepared me for the interview which was to take place late Monday night, and prompted me to say that it would be dangerous for me if I was made to return to East Germany. Perhaps I might go to jail or be killed. I felt that I couldn't really make such claims. I'd heard stories about people who'd defected over the Berlin Wall and were shot or jailed, but what I was doing was entirely different and I had no idea of the consequences. I really didn't want to say that I would be in terrible danger if I had to return. Ernst was to translate for me.

When we arrived at the interview I felt like a criminal surrounded by eight to ten men in black suits whose looks frightened me. Sitting at a large, round table, I was asked if I would be hurt, or if my family members could be in danger or suffer because of my actions.

I said, 'Yes.' I was so bloody scared and I don't even know what I was scared of. My brain could hardly function, I was completely exhausted. I didn't understand the significance of what I thought were complicated questions that the officials asked me.

I said to Ernst, 'Can you tell them I'm a simple person, I love Australia, I love the people, I love Melbourne. I don't want to go back to East Germany, I want to have freedom, I want to travel. I want to live in Melbourne and be the best I can be and I won't be a burden to anyone.'

'Not now. Ssh…'

Then we were asked to leave.

Ernst found out from his business partner that during the day he'd had to shut the restaurant for three hours because the press had taken over. There were about fifty men and women in the dining room, waiting for us. When he entered through the back door, the press were all on their feet taking photos of him. He had no idea what was going on, as Ernst hadn't been in touch with him over the last few days and Brian didn't know where he was. The media did not believe him – he and Ernst were business partners, surely he must know where Ernst was?

We stayed at a flat that Ernst had access to, where nobody would know where to find us. The only ones who knew we were there were Ernst's brother and Paul. On the first night there, although I was incredibly tired, I couldn't sleep. Ernst slept like a rock, exhausted.

The next morning, on the way to Paul's office again, with me hiding in the boot of the car, Ernst heard a radio announcement that I'd been granted political asylum. Paul confirmed the report and was ecstatic. He explained that not only was I allowed to stay in Australia, I would be protected.

I still wondered if a stranger could physically capture me and what might eventuate, so was very happy to lie low and to keep away from Acland Street. I needed to be confident that the East German authorities knew that I'd formally been granted political asylum; only then would I be entirely safe. Paul said that I would have other people by my side, just in case anything happened. I would be followed all the time for protection, but I wouldn't realise who was following me. That freaked me out. He told me this information to assure me that I was safe. I felt I was in a lonely place. I really didn't understand the decisions and didn't know what it all meant.

Who is behind me, following me? Is it someone who is keeping me secure or is it someone who wants to capture me? What a weird feeling.

I was familiar with dealing with the media as a well-known dancer in East Germany. It was all about being on time; appointments were made, the expectations were clear and it was exciting. I was never shy. But I was to learn that in my role as a person making news in Australia, the media was a very different machine.

After the announcement that I had been granted political asylum, Paul explained that we needed to attend a press conference. 'People from Australia know that you can officially stay here. Australia wants to know who you are and to hear you say thank you to Australia for allowing you to stay. And there are people who are little bit jealous of you, who may want their family members to come or to stay in Australia who have been refused – they want to hear from you.'

I was reluctant. 'I love Australia but I don't understand anything about Australian politics and do not want to have anything to do with it.'

However, the press conference took place in the Park Royal Motel in Melbourne. I wore a light blue skirt and a sparkly yellow top which were the dressiest clothes I had in my sea-sack. Paul explained that I was the topic of international news, reported in the UK, definitely in West Germany and the USA. I wondered if my mum's sister in Canada had heard about me. He said there'd be media representatives from all over the world present at the press conference.

'Do I really have to go through with this?' I wondered why I had to explain to everyone; there wasn't much to explain.

'Yes, you must. And there will be political questions asked of you.'

'You know I can't answer political questions, Paul. Don't you get it? If they ask me what it was like in East Germany – Was it really so bad there? How are your mother, your brothers, your friends? – What can I say? How do I know? I won't be able to be in touch with any of them for a long time, until pension age. I need to talk with them first before I say anything else.'

This was so hard for anyone to understand. I bombarded Ernst and Paul with questions all the time, they must have been sick of me, trying to understand my emotions. I felt so frustrated and suffered terrible headaches which I'd never experienced in my life.

'Paul, I won't even understand what they ask me!' I protested.

He explained that there could be over a hundred people at the press conference.

'Really? It sounds like what happens for a Hollywood star.'

'Yes, it will be like that.' He explained I needed to smile and be friendly and to say that I loved Australia and I loved its people, so that people would feel welcoming towards me.

'I don't feel like smiling, I'm so terribly tired.'

'Come on, you can do that. You're an artist, you can do it.'

I was scared what I'd be asked and I was scared what I would answer. I said to Paul that I would only answer yes and no.

He explained I'd have an interpreter behind me, and that it wouldn't be Ernst. They wanted to keep Ernst out of it. 'Heidi, you will have to say something.'

We came into the hotel and there were plenty of people waiting there. As soon as we entered, the photo flashes started. Somebody gave me an enormous umbrella to carry, I have no idea why. I had to walk and smile, carrying this big umbrella, like some big movie star. I thought, 'How stupid is this!' I felt utterly ridiculous. A rope barrier sectioned off a stage area, I was mindful of smiling, the cameras continued to click and eventually several reporters began calling out their questions. They were directed to ask one at a time. Each question was translated, and I simply answered yes or no as I'd planned.

The only question I actually remember came from a German-speaking reporter, in a sweet-talking way.

'Heidi, what would you say if you were approached to be a model for *Playboy* magazine for a fee of million dollars?'

I'd been told to keep smiling! How degrading was this question! I had to have an answer, so, smiling, I said, 'Definitely no.'

I hoped none of the other reporters understood the question. But one journalist asked for it to be repeated in English. The German-speaking reporter repeated it and I answered firmly again, 'No.'

That was it, the press conference was over. I felt very weak at the knees and close to collapse.

In the days to come, I went to the Black Rose restaurant with Ernst, entering through the back door, and sat out in the alcove, as much out of sight as possible. He was forever on the phone. Every day, people from the media phoned to make appointments with me, or else just visited the restaurant looking for me, wanting to talk to me. It was totally overwhelming – everything was about me, me, me. How he managed to concentrate on his business responsibilities and duties as chef at that time, I will never understand. What an experience for both of us.

Over the next few weeks, the media was full of stories about me. I felt intimidated about all the news in every paper. On the radio and television, they were constantly talking about me. I didn't understand the language, but I was everywhere. Ernst tried to translate every word for me. I felt immensely frustrated. He must have found it very hard. Newspaper cartoonists drew jokes about me and I felt insulted. Now they were making fun of me, making me look ridiculous, and it certainly was not funny. I cried so much.

Initially, I was the topic of many stories in the newspapers but I wondered how they could write about me without interviewing me. They had pictures of me and even some photos were published of other dancers who the media claimed were me. They never got my story from me, had never met me, but they made assumptions about me, wrote details that were not true, and created a false perception of me in their articles. This made me very mistrusting and cynical about newspapers and I decided then never to take any notice of news reports ever again.

The first weekend after I defected, Paul took Ernst and me to his family's weekender in the bush at Yarra Glen. I was introduced to his lovely wife, Helen, and we all enjoyed a Chinese banquet at their favourite Chinese restaurant at Healesville. We had a fantastic time. They were so very friendly and supportive and we have remained close friends all these years.

Paul recognised a journalist from a local newspaper at the restaurant and said to her, 'Would you like a scoop?' and introduced me to her for a special impromptu interview.

During those first weeks, we spent so much time at Paul's office. There was no way I could have predicted the media interest in my story and Paul negotiated their proposed financial offers on my behalf. I remember speaking with Derryn Hinch on the radio and Jana Wendt on TV. Don Lane wanted me on his popular television show for a live-to-air interview. It was agreed that I'd appear on the show, but that the questions needed to be provided to me in advance. I could not have coped with on-the-spot questions about politics or life in East Germany that I could not or would not answer, aware of my priority not to say anything because of my family, friends and colleagues back at home. I believed that they'd be spied on, interviewed and questioned relentlessly about what they had to do with my defection until the authorities were satisfied. None of them had anything at all to do with it. Don Lane gave me the questions and Ernst translated them for me before the show. I memorised my prepared answers in English.

At the hotel room before the show, the room was full of dresses, handbags, earrings and shoes, even Christian Dior make-up. I was told it had all been given to me and that I could choose whatever I liked or keep it all if I liked. There was not much I fancied; it all looked too posh – all gold, silver and bronze, not my style at all. I just wanted to be me. I decided to wear a burgundy dress, which wasn't too over the top, and to carry a little wine-red coloured handbag which I still have today. Somebody wanted to dress me and do my hair and make-up. I said to Ernst to tell them I would do it myself. I wanted to be as natural as I was. I wanted to be me. It was clear that they weren't used to their guests being so insistent, particularly when they tried to advise me how to do my make-up, and I just did it the way I wanted and felt confident.

Don Lane was a nice gentleman – he stuck to his questions and it all went okay – but I was pleased when it was over.

We stayed in the hideaway accommodation for a couple of weeks, then Ernst organised a flat in a bayside suburb, not far from St Kilda. I asked him why he didn't try to get one in St Kilda at a big block that had a great view of the sea. He explained to me that they were Housing Commission flats, for people who were poor. I said, 'Well I'm poor and they look awesome! I couldn't live in a big building like that back at home even though I'd have loved to.' His views were definitely very different to mine.

Paul received offers of big money for my story – people wanted to know who I really was. Already I was being encouraged to write a book about my life and my defection, but at that time I had no interest in putting my story down on paper. He advised me to sign a contract with Consolidated Press, involving a feature interview with the *Australian Women's Weekly*, the most popular magazine in Australia at the time. Paul said that then the curiosity about me would come to an end and people would leave me alone and wish me good luck. He persuaded me to agree.

The journalist, David Richards, came to the restaurant to meet me. I thought he was crazy; he moved so fast and talked so fast and seemed so intense I wondered how I would ever cope with that, as I felt tense enough myself without his input.

When I was introduced to him and told he would be taking me to the beach and taking photos of me there, I said, 'I'm not going with a man I don't know!' But it was arranged, and that was it.

David took me to a women's dress shop somewhere in South Melbourne. He chose various clothes off the racks and held them up to me as he conferred with the lady working in the shop. He indicated that I should try the clothes on. They were all brown and beige and dark wintry clothes: a heavy skirt, a funny blouse with a bow, a huge jacket. I looked three times as big as I was. I hated the clothes, although they told me I looked absolutely stunning. We went to the Kerferd Road pier, and I had to walk up and down the pier while the photographer took pictures of me. Then I had to change in the car into a blue and red all-in-one tracksuit. He told me to do ballet in the sand on the beach. I argued – you can't do ballet in the sand! I thought I would make a fool of myself. We argued heatedly, but I finally cooperated and just did the best possible.

The interview took place after the photo shoot at the Black Rose, with Ernst as translator. I insisted that it was not to be published unless I approved of what was written. Consolidated Press flew us to Sydney to meet Ita Buttrose, who was the editor and a very important woman in Australia at that time. Our appointment was for only half an hour and she wanted to meet me. She was very nice and polite and allowed us to read the draft, rather under pressure, as Ernst translated it to me while we were there. As I refused to talk politics and wanted only to say the least possible about my family and life in East Germany, the journalist put the emphasis more on the romance between me and Ernst.

The feature article, published in May 1980, ran over several pages and I was the cover girl of the issue. After it was published, many people recognised me and stopped me in the street. They were friendly but I just wanted to be left alone. The media pressure and attention was completely unexpected. I sometimes felt like I was having a nervous breakdown. Can I do this? Can I manage it? It was too overwhelming. My migraine headaches continued and worsened. Paul and Helen introduced me to a doctor who understood the stress I was going through and recommended that I needed to take it easy. I wasn't interested in medication. The doctor helped me to understand that for any human being going through the pressure that I was under it would be expected that they'd have headaches. At times, I felt I couldn't cope any more.

I was just hoping that the fuss would finish soon. I wanted to start living my life. But I was also grateful. My experience was unique, it was all extraordinary. I was a normal person. I had left nothing behind me to hide. I just loved Australia, loved its people, and Melbourne was the realisation of my dream to travel the world. I was in a country where I could have that freedom to decide what I could do. I wanted to start a new life without anyone or anything expected of me any more, although the way it eventuated was unexpectedly different.

I'm grateful for the whole experience and say 'Thank you' to the people of Australia, but it was sometimes too much for me. I know that there were two or three phone calls taken in the restaurant where the caller claimed that they would throw a bomb in the restaurant so that we would all blow up. Paul explained that there were people who were upset because members of their family had not been permitted to stay in Australia and they thought why should I be allowed to, that it wasn't fair. I felt great fear and believed that the threats were genuine. It was scary, but I was advised not to put too much emphasis on it. I wonder if anybody else has ever understood how I felt when sometimes I thought they were haunting me. At times, I had nightmares. But nobody could steal my dream.

A letter from my mum arrived, written on 14 May 1980 and sent via my Aunty Dora in Canada, whose comments throughout I understood and appreciated. It reached me on 11 July, saying that Mum had the opportunity to come to Australia on a free ticket, which I suspect was offered by the Stasi, if she would attempt to bring me back to East Germany. But she didn't take up the offer because she believed that I knew what I was doing. Here is part of that letter:

> On the evening of Sunday 20 April 1980 we all were excited you were coming home, and prepared a wonderful display with eleven beautiful long-stemmed roses for your belated birthday. On Monday afternoon we had the most horrible experience. It was an anonymous telephone call ordering us not to go to the airport, which made us wondering and nervous. We were all hoping that the return flight was cancelled due to bad weather. All of a sudden, I remembered the strange dream in every detail I had some weeks ago, where you appeared and said your goodbye to me. It made me feel very uneasy. Days later, I heard that you will not return home. It was one and a half weeks later when I heard you again over the phone and confirmed that you are happy and healthy. I was happy to hear from you but at the same time very sad because we all might not see you again for a very long time – and some other reasons.
>
> I'm well aware, dear Heidrun, that whatever you do is your decision. But I am also aware of the fact that you can be at times quite vulnerable and easily influenced. Since I do know you so well, I urge you to thoroughly reconsider your decision. Gossip here tells us that you have stayed over there because you fell in love with a man. Please be assured that I have great understanding for the deep feeling of love. Bear in mind that one can't be happy with just one person in the long run. [Why not, actually – Aunty Dora] For real happiness you need people next to you and here you have a huge circle of friends, let alone your mother and your two

brothers. Do you really think down there is the world you belong to? [It's surely better than the other one – Aunty Dora]

For nearly ten years, you have entertained so many people and brought enjoyment into their lives here with your art of dance. At the age of ten, you stopped being a child and dedicated yourself to intensive training. Perhaps the glamour and glitter of this for you in this so unfamiliar world has impressed you so much that you became overwhelmed by it. Yet, what do you think might happen once you can't dance any more? That time is coming closer. How will your life be then down there? Here you would be entitled to an artist's pension, you would have sufficient money, time and support to prepare for a new profession. With all my heart I urge you to please consider once more your decision.

I have made thorough enquiries, to find out what would happen to you if you would return. I have been assured that you would be able to commence your new work with the Metropol Theatre as you desired so much without any prejudice and negative *Nachteile*, consequences. Most of all, we – Kalli, Wolli and I – would be so glad to have you close to us again. [Don't believe a word, Heidi. You would be lost forever – love Aunty Dora]

I look forward to your next phone call as that seems to be the only lifeline we currently have. When I hear your voice, I feel a lump in my throat and I'm barely capable of talking to you [Surely it wouldn't be that bad – Aunty Dora], which might sound quite stupid. Dear Heidrun, it is to be hoped that you will receive this letter via Aunty Dora and I expect you to answer me very soon, even if you can't give a final decision. [Heidi, be careful – Aunty Dora] In the hope of receiving a few lines handwritten from you very soon, I send you my love and many kisses,

Your mournful Mum.

[Heidrun, please be very, very careful. If you want to write an answer, send it to me and I will pass it on from here. Don't write anything that has the potential to harm you in any way. Your mum has written her letter in a quite incautious manner. They could have opened her letter and read it. It happens all the time. Again, best of luck, Your Aunty Dora]

Act Three

Carmen, choreographed by Lothar Hanff and Eva Reinthaller for the Schwerin Theatre Ballet Company

The official meetings and requirements and all the attention from the media were totally unknown territory in every way for me. All I knew was that I had found love: love for Australia, love for its people and, most importantly, love of freedom. I was starting a new life, a transformation in every way. I was being reborn, I was a new me.

Our flat was just simple and small with one bedroom, but to me it was luxury. I felt as though I was on holiday. It had a servery between the kitchen and the dining room, which I thought was really cool. We had no furniture. We bought our first furniture dirt cheap from people who were planning to travel around Australia for a year or two. I thought it was really classy furniture – we had the fabulous couch for many years and a lovely antique trunk which I have kept.

Ernst had to go to work. He then decided that as he was receiving so many phone calls at the restaurant, calls all to do with me and organising my life, I needed to be there. Meetings, decisions, who to speak to, who would pick me up, they were an ongoing distraction and as I felt lonely and scared at home anyway I was happier to go with him each day.

His partner was kind and friendly to me and we became great friends. He helped me learn English. During the hour or two in the afternoon that the restaurant closed, he patiently taught me by speaking very slowly to me and introducing new words, and encouraging me to write things down. I'd write down the English term and next to it the

German. I'm a very visual person, and need to see words written, so it was not so hard then for me to learn. I was building up my vocabulary day by day.

From the first few days after my defection, Paul received several phone calls from ballet companies from all around Australia offering me contracts. He asked me what I wanted to do. I felt I was in no position to do anything. With all the other distractions, I wasn't thinking of signing contracts at all.

Firstly, I had not been able to maintain my training. I would need to practise long hours every day to rebuild my fitness and technique. Secondly, I wanted to stay in Melbourne. Although I had an offer from the Australian Ballet Company in Melbourne, I didn't take it. I didn't feel it was the right company for me in terms of the style of dance it was performing, which was mostly classical. The Ballet School at the Victorian College of the Arts was announcing its opening, and they kindly invited me to be an official guest and to make a little speech. When I visited it, the ballet school was nothing like what I expected. It was smaller than our ballet school in Berlin and didn't compare well with what I was familiar. So, thirdly, I wondered if being involved in ballet in Australia might be a step backwards in my career. As an experienced theatre performer from East Berlin, I felt I was at my peak. I'd had an awesome experience of the theatre world. I felt that there was nothing more exciting that anybody could have offered me here in Australia that I hadn't already done. I didn't want to go backwards. I had decided to make a new life here and that meant I didn't have to retain my career from my old life.

The media were at a stage where they'd covered my arrival, then that I was safe to stay in Australia, starting a new life in Melbourne. The next 'news' they pestered me for was how I would earn money.

I told Paul that my idea was not to have anything to do with ballet, that I wanted to go and work in the fruit and vegie shop in Acland Street. I wanted to learn English first and be around quiet people where I attracted no attention. I said I wanted to work at the back of that shop washing and counting carrots and then displaying them very creatively. I still had not approached the lady and gentleman at the shop with my idea. I didn't care about wealth, all I needed was enough money to buy food. Essentially, I wanted to remove myself from the public eye, to be embraced into the Australian way of life now that I was officially a resident here and nobody could send me back home. I wanted time to think about what I would do with my life. The fruit shop would be my refuge – not far to the water, not far to the Black Rose, the Palais Theatre, Luna Park and the flat. All within walking distance. Ernst could go on with his life and work and do what he had to do and I could start my own life.

Paul thought it might be rather an unambitious type of job for me, but I said, 'Why not? I'm starting a new life. I need to earn money. It would be a lovely place for me to work.'

He said, 'Heidi, the Australian people want to see you dance. Come on, Heidi. All these offers are there.'

I said, 'I don't really care.'

Had I returned to East Berlin, I'd already signed a contract with the Metropol Theatre as a musical performer, already determined that my ballet days were coming to an end. Ballet was not what I wanted to do any more. I explained that I had much more enthusiasm now for musical theatre and that it was clear to me that there was no company at that time for me to go to in Australia that was dedicated to musical theatre.

Paul urged me, 'Heidi, say yes, please, to something. Start working, otherwise the media won't stop pressuring you.'

Although I didn't really want to be in Sydney, eventually I decided to take the offer from the Sydney Dance Company. I was flown to Sydney to meet Graeme Murphy, the artistic director, and Janet Vernon, assistant to the director. It was a young contemporary dance company about the size of the Komische Oper Ballet Company. On my visit to audition and sign the contract, I was smuggled into the rear entrance of the building, through the wardrobe and scenery workshops, and upstairs to the studios, to avoid further unwelcome attention from the press or anyone else. How could I know if the East German authorities had given up on me?

Graeme Murphy had a big smile and was very vigorous and energetic. I loved his body movements. There was a sense of competition between the Melbourne and Sydney companies and as it's in my nature to always support the new, I wanted to support the Sydney Dance Company. I loved what they were doing, I loved Graeme and Janet. Although I couldn't understand much language-wise, I felt their passion for their profession and I met people with a warm heart.

My contract as a guest artist was presented to me written in German and English from Dick Allen, the administrative director of the Sydney Dance Company, who had been seconded there from the Immigration Department for some time. Included in my contract was the offer to perform with the Sydney Dance Company overseas. I said, 'Oh, wow!' But I wanted to settle in Melbourne. Although it sounded attractive, I wanted to settle down. Dick is a wonderful man. He had an understanding of the issues I faced, and welcomed me into his family. His approach instilled in me a feeling of some control at last about my life. Dick and his wife and little children became like a family to me. I enjoyed the most wonderful home-cooked Asian dinners with them.

My accommodation in Sydney for the duration of the contract was in a motel not far from the theatre, just a short trip on the underground train. I lived on Continental tomato soup.

I went to Sydney alone and was made very welcome by the whole company. Graeme Murphy choreographed a special piece for me called *Dance to the Guitar*. It was very difficult and contemporary and represented the growing body of work from Graeme, who was really at the beginning of what developed into an outstanding career. I was so impressed and challenged and really wanted to do it well. What a privilege I had – I was going to dance on opening night of the season at the Sydney Opera House. The whole world knows about the Sydney Opera House. I felt as though the quality of my work was appreciated by every member; each one offered me real friendship and respect and I had no sense that I was being used as some kind of political statement, which was a wonderful relief. I was a dancer, back in my profession, doing what a dancer does, the best every moment. I was happy and satisfied.

When I began working with the company, I experienced severe back pain. I didn't want to tell anyone and had no money for a doctor. I didn't know how the health system worked here or how to communicate about it. In East Germany, free medical and hospital treatment were provided by the government. The pain was another indication to me that my days as a ballerina needed to come to an end. What would happen later on in life if I kept dancing? Could it be dangerous to my health? My body was saying 'enough'. On opening night, I thought I could not actually go on stage. At the end of my performance, my body jammed – I had to be helped to move from the stage.

My life was about work. The media scrutiny diminished and I had a private life at last. Making new friends, I felt more settled but maintained the idea to return to live in Melbourne as soon as my contract was over. Some weekends when I didn't have rehearsals, I flew to Melbourne to see Ernst. I met his family and friends and became increasingly involved with his circle of people. St Kilda is to this day a sort of multicultural village community on the doorstep of the city of Melbourne and I got to know all the shopkeepers and other German-speaking people. I learned that lots of foreigners organised their own clubs in Melbourne – German clubs, Greek clubs, Italian clubs. So, on my few days off when I returned to Melbourne, I met more people and more diverse people than I did living in Sydney, where those I met were members or associates of the dance company only.

I danced with the Sydney Dance Company for one season, part of which included performances in Melbourne. How could I thank Graeme and Janet? I went to Woolworths in Kings Cross and bought a teddy bear for them. I had always collected teddy bears, all shapes and sizes; collecting them made me happy. Using my dictionary, I wrote sincere words to them on a card expressing my gratitude and affection. After the final curtain fell, I said to Graeme and Janet that I needed to talk with them. All the dancers were surrounding me in a circle on stage. I gave them the teddy bear and stumbled some words of thanks, explaining that I wanted to leave and wishing them all the best of luck. They were stunned.

'I'm sorry. I want to go to Melbourne. I want to start a new life.'

We were all crying. It was hard for me to explain why I needed to leave. I could speak a bit of English, just to communicate factual things, but couldn't express myself from my heart. I felt sad, but it was what I had to do. Graeme somehow understood and wished me good luck. They invited me to every opening night of the Sydney Dance Company in Melbourne and to their after-parties. He and Janet are still my friends today.

I had such a strong urge to return to live in Melbourne. I wanted to work in that fruit and vegetable shop and think about me. I still wanted to find my new me.

Back in Melbourne, the next few months were all about meeting people, learning the language and being independent. It was important to learn the language as quickly as possible. My new life in Melbourne was expanding.

The shop owners in St Kilda all recognised me and were welcoming and pleased to see me. I talked to them all. I went to a dry cleaner who was German and asked him if he knew of a German–English school where I could learn the language. I felt like I needed to learn to drive a car and asked if he knew of a German-speaking driving school. This couple guided me, giving me some phone numbers and names. At that time, I couldn't find a government program for me to learn English, but there were evening classes available in St Kilda.

I went to a few classes and then one night the teacher said to me, 'Heidi, are you sure you want to come back?'

'Yes!'

'You've probably realised this class may not be right for you. It's a bit slow for you. You are a very fast language learner.'

'Do you think my time is wasted here?'

'Not wasted, but it's too slow for you.'

'Can't we do it faster?'

'No, I have to take everybody else into consideration. I suggest you just get out there and talk to people.'

'I can do that. But I wish you could explain to me why we spell usually u-s-u-a-l-l-y. The English language doesn't make sense.'

'Heidi, in English, you can't explain everything exactly.'

'When I went to school, we were taught all the rules of German, how and why things are spelt and sound as they do. I find English very challenging.'

'Heidi, I have no problems with you learning the language, but I think you'll learn it much faster out there in the real world than you will in a classroom.'

That was the last time I went.

How could I learn the language faster? I could work in the restaurant as a waitress. I'd seen the waiters take orders in their notebooks. I could do that, talk to people and learn the language all at the same time. If ever I wanted to know something, I could ask the front-of-house host. I was forever going to him with a notebook, writing things down.

Ernst sent me to the supermarket to get some toothpaste. I couldn't find anything that had the word toothpaste on the packet. Eventually, I thought I'd found it. Walking back down Acland Street, I stopped at my favourite fruit and vegie shop and greeted those dear shopkeepers, who gave me a kiss and a hug.

I said casually. 'Tomorrow I'll come back and see you. Maybe I'll come to work for you.'

They seemed pleased and gave me an apple.

When I returned to the Black Rose, Ernst and his partner laughed their heads off.

'That's not toothpaste. It's shoe polish.'

'No! It looks like toothpaste.' It was in a tube. I felt frustrated with myself. This was not a good day. I hadn't accomplished anything. Later in the day, I decided to ask if I could work in the restaurant.

'Me…work here…asking people…serve food…me,' I stumbled.

'Okay.'

'Really?'

'Tonight.'

'I'm working tonight?' Fantastic.

'I'll help you,' he offered.

Completely excited, I went to the kitchen and told Ernst my news. He said, 'Heidi, you can't do that.'

'Why not?'

'No. You can't really write English. I won't understand your orders.'

'It will be okay. I'll take my little notebook and just say, "Please order," and ask the customers to point to what they want on the menu and copy it exactly. I'll write it down nicely and neatly for you. It will be fine. I'll be talking to people and learning more words. Sauce and potatoes and crêpes, mushrooms…and I'll ask the staff to come to the kitchen to show me what each of the foods and ingredients are.'

I don't think Ernst was very impressed with the idea. I thought that he might have almost had enough of me, but I wanted to give it a go. It would have to be better than doing nothing.

By pointing, smiling, writing, concentrating and saying 'Thank you very much' and 'Enjoy', I felt as though I managed my first night's work at the restaurant rather well and then when I was paid at the end of it I was delighted and suggested that I'd work again the next day. 'I'll do tomorrow lunch?'

Ernst asked if I was sure I wanted to work at the restaurant, and I said that for the time being it was fine: I'd get more confident, I could start talking to people, I no longer had to hide out the back as I was officially allowed to be there and people loved to recognise me and ask how my life was going.

After a little while, I had regular customers who came particularly because I was working there. I had to be aware that I didn't end up talking more than I worked.

The daytime clientele were mostly local business people. The Black Rose Restaurant had been very well known and highly regarded for several years. It was European, a lively place and famous for its pre-theatre dinners at five o'clock and after-theatre supper, as it was frequented by many patrons and performers of the Palais Theatre. The alcove area was set-up for larger groups of customers and decorated with ballet posters. International artists who came to St Kilda to perform at the Palais Theatre often dined at the restaurant. I felt at home surrounded by theatre-loving people.

BYO – bring your own drinks - was a completely new concept for me. People brought their own alcohol with them to the restaurant to drink while they had their meals. I think this practice is unique to Australian restaurants and I thought it was crazy.

'Corkage? What's that?'

Ernst explained that customers were charged for him to take the top off the bottle and pour the drinks for them. I thought it was hilarious – people bring their own drinks to save money and have to pay to have them poured.

'Surely you can't charge them just to open a bottle!' I protested.

'We do! We supply clean glasses. It's a cost to us.'

'Oh no! I'll do it. I'll pour their drinks and clean the glasses.' I was sure that they were not capable of running a proper business if this was what they did. I soon discovered it was a common practice in the restaurant industry.

One of the waiters was most helpful to me. One night he took me out with him to a Mexican restaurant in Fitzroy Street, St Kilda. I'd never been to a Mexican restaurant before and thought it was fantastic. He knew Don Lane, who'd interviewed me on his show. I felt Don Lane and Bert Newton were very special people in the media; they'd been very kind and understanding to me. Ian organised for us to visit Don Lane at his wonderful home in Brighton, near the beach, one afternoon for afternoon tea. It was very special. What an eye-opener Brighton was – it was first time I'd seen such mansions.

I kept working at the restaurant, learnt the language, became more independent, then I thought that driving a car would be a good idea and had driving lessons with a German instructor. He put me behind the wheel immediately, I was terrified. Fortunately he had dual controls.

We drove around Beach Road. I was too nervous to learn to drive a manual and I thought learning in an automatic was much less nerve-racking. After six lessons, I went for my learner's permit, which at that time was a straightforward multiple choice answer test. Back in East Germany, it took learners two years to get their licence, which included lessons in car mechanics and maintenance. It seemed incredible to me that in Australia I would be able to get a licence without having a clue about how cars actually worked.

On the day of my driving test, I was turning left but had not judged cautiously the distance between the car and a truck coming down the road. I proceeded, and was criticised by the licence testers. I always drove a bit too fast and my instructor had to remind me to keep an eye on the speedometer. I really didn't think I'd been successful with the driving test, but, to my surprise, I was given my licence. In the first trip I ever made driving home from the restaurant in Ernst's car to our flat, which was only about two minutes away, again, turning left, I should have waited for a vehicle to pass before making my turn. Understandably, Ernst was temperamental.

On the following Sunday, I drove down Beach Road into North Road. A police car with a siren ringing drove alongside us and indicated that I should pull over. I didn't think I'd done anything wrong. Ernst had taken a nap as my passenger and woke up when he heard the siren. He translated that the policeman said I'd been driving too fast. I'd been doing eighty in a sixty zone. Usually, that would have resulted in cancellation of my probationary licence.

The policeman recognised me. 'Heidi! You're the famous ballerina! Do you love Australia?'

'Oh yes, I love it,' I assured him enthusiastically.

He let me go with a warning to drive more slowly.

Ernst explained to me that I'd been very lucky. As time went on, I became a better driver.

Eventually, Ernst told me we needed to leave our flat, that somebody had bought it. I couldn't imagine what he meant.

'How can somebody buy it while we're living here? They can't just throw us out.' This was something completely different to East Germany, where, once you rented a flat, you stayed there always unless you, the tenant, wanted to leave. 'I'm happy here. I'm not moving out of here, I'm settled. We'll stay,' I said to Ernst. We'd been living there for about a year, the flat was a comfortable little home. I didn't want to leave.

'No, Heidi, we have another four weeks here and in that time we have to find somewhere else to rent.'

We found another first-floor flat available in the bayside area, on the Esplanade, the main road, with a balcony overlooking the beach and the foreshore. I thought it was paradise. Having such a view was like living on a holiday.

Sunday was the day for going places with people I met. It was our 'sleeping-in' day, meeting friends and family day, a day for exploring Melbourne, enjoying home and getting to know our great neighbours, and driving around Victoria. I realised so many Australian people lived in houses with their own gardens and wondered why they would want all that extra work. I had a huge garden in front of me – the Elwood foreshore where I loved to lie on the grass in the sun. I loved taking photos of the sunrise and sunset and seascape. I just adored it.

As Christmas time approached, I explained to Ernst that I wanted to have a real live traditional East German Christmas tree and he said that they weren't available in Australia. He took me to a Christmas tree farm, where we chose our pine tree. I bought loose branches from which to make a traditional Advent wreath and made a stand for it which I painted red and placed in the middle of the table exactly like Mum did. I wondered how I'd attach real candles to the tree and from where I'd get my traditional Christmas balls and other decorations. I asked the couple at the dry-cleaners for advice and they suggested I contact a German man, Fritz Schwaab, from St Albans, who imported traditional Christmas ornaments from Germany. Fritz Schwaab was well known and respected in the German-Australian community in Melbourne. We went there before the beginning of Advent and we met a nice, elderly man who had lots of interesting stock, including traditional Christmas chocolates and biscuits.

He explained that he was an ex-Berliner, and had come to Australia in the 1950s by ship, as had many other Germans. At that time, Australia was seeking lots of professional and trades people and he was one of thousands who migrated from Europe, to build a new life in a new country after the ravages of the Second World War. He talked to us about arriving in Australia, the 'kangaroo land', and having no electricity in St Albans in those days.

The Australia he remembered and talked about so interestingly had changed greatly by 1980. He made us coffee and cake. Again I thought, 'Gee, Australian people are nice!' I always seemed to meet great people. I felt this elderly man and I had a similar mentality and I really appreciated meeting him. The little shop in their home smelt like Christmas back in Berlin. We enjoyed talking about the old traditions like Nikolaus and I began to feel a bit nostalgic and sentimental. The weather was warm and getting hotter. There'd be no snow in Melbourne in December. But I'd still have my wax candles on the tree. Fritz advised that the candles wouldn't last in the heat.

I said, 'Rubbish!' I felt sure he was joking. 'Of course they'll last.'

As we organised our purchases and were about to leave, this lovely man said, 'Heidi, I'll send you a little parcel for Nikolaus. Just from me to you.'

I really didn't think he would remember, but on 5 December, I received a parcel from him – lovely biscuits from Nürnberg in West Germany called *Nürnberger Oblaten*. The biscuits were famous in Germany, the factory existed for hundreds of years and everyone knew of it, but I had never had the opportunity to actually try them ever in the past as they were not available in the East. They were in a beautifully decorated tin. I cried. I was so far away from home and he had thought to do this for me to make me feel like home. How sweet. He made my day.

Inside our flat it looked just like Christmas at home in Germany, but it didn't smell the same, as the pine tree had a different fragrance.

The St Kilda bakeries didn't smell like Christmas at home. I learned that in Australia, Christmas was celebrated on Christmas Day. However, Ernst's family was following the German tradition and got together on Christmas Eve. West Germans go to midnight Mass, which was new to me of course. We spent Christmas Eve with Ernst's family and I thought about Mum and felt and hoped she was all right. I knew she was thinking of me too.

On Christmas Day, the Black Rose Restaurant was open and very busy. Ernst and Brian were passionate about decorating the Black Rose with live pine branches in a traditional German way. Their customers loved the atmosphere they created. There were sittings for Christmas lunch and then dinner at night. Going to a restaurant to celebrate Christmas, that was a weird custom to me, but I thought why not – other countries, other traditions.

Fritz was right about the candles on my Christmas tree. When we came home to our flat on Christmas Day, the candles looked like walking sticks, all curled over at the top. The tree had dried out and didn't look so nice. I had no spare candles and had wanted to light them. I was so disappointed, I cried. I went to bed still crying, it was probably a build-up of emotion. I planned that the following Christmas I'd put the tree in a bucket full of sand pinched from the beach and water it like a plant. That should help to keep it fresher longer. I thought that if I closed the blinds, the tree and the candles would last longer and look fresher. I was determined that Christmas would be happy from now on.

In 1981, the Victorian Arts Centre had opened. Business at the Black Rose would be affected, as ballet productions would relocate from the Palais to the Arts Centre in the city. It was time to rethink the business situation and the decision was made to sell it. Everybody was sad. We had so many farewell parties for the Black Rose that it seemed we celebrated all the time. Brian decided to move with his family to Sydney and Ernst told me of his ambition to buy a restaurant in the city called the Hofbräuhaus, where he had worked when he first came to Australia. Ernst took me to Market Lane, in the heart of Melbourne's Chinatown, but the Hofbräuhaus was no longer there. A Greek restaurant was operating in its place. Ernst spoke to the owners, who said they'd be happy to sell.

With two other partners, Ernst bought it and they wanted me to be involved. I enjoyed the restaurant business by now – at the Black Rose, I'd met lots of artists and other clients, loved being involved with food, had great admiration for Ernst's skills as a chef and appreciated that there are many factors to running a successful restaurant. But I was sad to be leaving St Kilda. After this time, business in St Kilda declined for quite some years, so perhaps it was the right time to move.

Ernst and his two new business partners and I went out to a business dinner at a wonderful Melbourne Chinese restaurant called the Supper Inn (which even today makes the best lemon chicken), to make decisions about re-establishing the Hofbräuhaus Restaurant. The Hofbräuhaus was originally opened in the sixties by three Australians who went to the Hofbräuhaus in Munich and decided to establish such a place in Melbourne which served Bavarian-style southern German food, drink and entertainment.

Two hundred patrons dined at the Hofbräuhaus on its reopening night in 1981. Even the mayor of Melbourne was invited to the auspicious occasion. As I was a celebrity, I was a drawcard and promoted in the advertising. The Hofbräuhaus operated as a licensed restaurant, not BYO. By now, I was confident with taking food orders and handling dinner plates and loved meeting the diners. We wore uniforms – the girls wore authentic dirndls. Mine was red with a fitted bodice, low neck, full skirt, frilly white blouse underneath, and a green apron. Long white knee socks and a red *Seppel* hat completed the outfit. Later, the girls and guys at front of house wore traditional *Lederhosen*, leather shorts, knee-length socks and comfortable shoes with a white shirt or blouse.

We had a floor show and the band played mainly Bavarian folk music all night. This was one particular type of folk music that I hadn't been exposed to in my youth. After the main course was over, patrons were invited to come up onto the dance floor and join in the variety of fun. They could ring the traditional cowbells; men joined in the slap dancing (traditionally it's not something that women do); and they wanted me to dance a solo to something special. What to choose? Ah... people love the cancan! I love being crazy and just put on some fancy frilly underpants under my dirndl uniform and danced the cancan from the famous operetta *Orpheus in the Underworld* by Jacques Offenbach. I had always loved this popular operetta and its catchy music. I had danced the cancan many times. It was such a wonderful contrast to my professional classical background. Here I could just let my hair down and go crazy. It's a dance of letting go.

Even contemporary dance and other folk dancing didn't come close to the crazy, wild exuberance of dancing the cancan, where I screamed with the joy of it. Full of fiery energy, I was the best cancan dancer! It was such fun to get others up onto the dance floor and have the men and women around me joining in with the flirting and screaming. The floor show changed from time to time but I stuck to my cancan from day one and did it every night until we finished running the Hofbräuhaus. People loved it and it was hilarious, lots of fun. Most nights, we invited patrons to dance the conga out in the street. It was a place with a cosy atmosphere of wine, dine, beer, music, dancing, singing, meeting people and fun – to celebrate the joy of life.

I was a good sales person and understood every traditional dish on the menu so that I could explain clearly to people what each one was like. Rouladen, Wiener schnitzel, boiled pork hocks called *Eisbein*, sauerkraut, red cabbage, potato or bread dumplings, herrings in a mayonnaise sauce – these were not necessarily the meals I had back in East Germany but I learnt about these meals from the West Germans.

I eventually learnt about all drinks and bar service and soon mastered pulling a beer. Mixed drinks were popular in the early eighties. When somebody asked for a drink that I'd never before heard of, such as a Harvey Wallbanger, I'd always say, 'Can you tell me what is actually in it? It's my first night tonight, I'm really a ballerina, can you please help me…' I used that line for months! I was astonished the first time somebody ordered an 'orgasm'.

Have I heard correctly? This cannot be what he said.

'Um, what do you mean?'

'Don't you know what an orgasm is?'

Warily I said, 'No, yes…well, I know what it means, but you want to drink it? Can you tell me what it is?'

Some of these experiences were hilarious. I definitely had much more to learn about cocktails.

My work days were incredibly long. We had to set up the restaurant, and moving heavy, long wooden tables and chairs was hard work. We cleaned the restaurant every night, decorated it, set the tables and folded the serviettes ready for the next day. Early mornings and very late nights with just a few hours' sleep became the pattern of my life. Unlike my theatre work. which finished at about eleven o'clock after an evening performance, restaurant hours were much longer because there was so much to do after the last patrons left. Cleaning and preparation took an extra couple of hours. Initially. we opened seven days a week but after some time decided we just could not do that any more – we needed one day off. I worked many hours, so it paid well and I started saving, which was a brand-new experience for me.

It didn't take long for the Hofbräuhaus to build a good reputation and a regular, loyal clientele. It was the only German-themed restaurant in the heart of Melbourne and our patrons loved to see us in our costumes. We enjoyed having many tourists from other countries visit, people speaking so many different languages, and many of them recognised me and wanted to know about my life story. I was often asked if I was from Russia. People in Australia did not understand much about communism in Eastern European countries at the time and many thought that communism in Europe only referred to Russia. People of my own age had no idea that Germany was divided into East and West.

I loved to hear other people's life stories. Life in the restaurant was very educational. I felt very worldly and the diversity was fantastic. I loved it all, serving people, giving my best, learning something new every day, and ensuring that our guests had a great day or night out suited me perfectly. It seemed as though I had a maternal instinct that could be directed to the staff and patrons I met at my work. I thrived in this multicultural environment. Even our staff came from different countries; some spoke very little English, and I understood how they felt and their desire to communicate. Located in the middle of Chinatown, I was able to learn so much more about Asian culture, and people, and neighbours, and business. I felt very global.

'*Zicke-zacke, zicke-zacke, hoi, hoi, ho*i' is a German cheer called out when friends are having fun and a drink with friends. We used it often at the restaurant. Australian travel industry professionals dined regularly with us and were fascinated by this happy salute. However, they couldn't pronounce it, so, to join in the fun they called out, 'Aussie, Aussie, Aussie, oi, oi, oi.' I've often wondered if this great Aussie cheer now recognised worldwide began with those travel agent guys at the Hofbräuhaus in Melbourne.

Over the fifteen years that I was involved in the Hofbräuhaus, I developed a certain routine. Up at seven in the morning, I had breakfast and planned my day for the first hour. We drove to the restaurant by nine o'clock and started preparing for our lunchtime clients. There were always phone calls to make and to take, tables to set, meetings with salesmen, writing letters, planning and writing new menus, meetings with staff, drink fridges to be filled. Much needed to be done so that when the doors opened for our patrons, everything was ready for one hundred per cent service. Then I'd change from my day clothes and into my work uniform. It was just the same as in theatre when the curtain opens, so it was a discipline that I was comfortable with. There was no floor show during the daytime.

After lunches were completely finished, we closed the doors for a couple of hours, and then at six o'clock we opened for evening meals. I tried to fit in an evening meal for myself just before the doors opened, but finding time to eat was actually quite a challenge and often it was at supper time rather than dinner that I had something. We opened until about one o'clock in the morning, or whatever time licensing laws permitted over that time, and at the end of the night the staff unwound as we sat together for a drink or a coffee and a chat at the end of the night. I enjoyed the quietness of folding the serviettes in preparation for the following day, sometimes in companionable silence with other tired staff. I don't remember ever going to bed before two in the morning.

In 1982, Ernst and I took five days off work and I had my first overseas trip. We travelled to Hong Kong and I loved its different languages, different culture, different sights and smells. The desire to continue to travel has always stayed with me. It's part of me.

By 1983, I felt more settled. I was living in a place where I felt content and happy. I never had any doubt about my decision to defect to Australia. My life was so busy – working hard, earning money, dealing with all the demands of my life, there was no time for regrets. People asked me often if I was homesick. The honest answer was always no. I had no time to be homesick. I had my family in my heart and just knew that I was always in their hearts. That would never change. I always longed for a family life with children, and Ernst and I married at the Liszt Restaurant in Elsternwick on 19 June 1983. It was difficult to fit a wedding into our busy working lives.

I didn't want to dress as a traditional bride in a long white dress. I chose a lovely soft silver grey dress, with a frilled scooped neckline, just below knee-length, and wore a garland of little red rosebuds in my hair. I wore a red rose corsage and carried a bouquet of white roses. It was a lovely celebration, I was very happy and felt great. Our marriage celebrant was the editor of the *Australian Dance* magazine, which was first released in 1981. The next day, we worked at the Hofbräuhaus and then took all our staff out for supper at Monroes, a well-known restaurant in Fitzroy Street in St Kilda at the time. We had become friendly with the owners of Monroes when they came to our restaurant one night before establishing their own. We enjoyed talking to them and exchanged experiences and advice about the industry. We left on our honeymoon to Europe the next day.

Could anyone possibly imagine how I felt to be going to Europe – Italy and Switzerland, France and West Germany and West Berlin? Through my best friend, Gerhard, it was possible to connect with another very dear friend in East Berlin. We'd been friends since I was nine years old. How I missed her laughter and her wisdom. I believed that the officials had not found out that she and I were still in contact. She was like a sister to me. A Melbourne friend suggested we visit his brother, who lived in West Berlin, to drive us around and to take us to a watchtower near the Berlin Wall which we could climb to look over the Wall into the East. I had no idea such watchtowers existed.

So, leading up to our trip, I had written some letters and sent them to Gerhard's cousin in West Berlin. He then sent my letters on to Gerhard, who made sure that they would get to Mum or my dear friend. Gerhard's cousin was our middle man. My dear friend had the wonderful idea that we could see each other in the distance from the tower. She arranged the day and time she'd be walking at a certain spot in East Berlin while I organised for us to be at a particular watchtower and, although we could not attract any attention and wave to each other, as uniformed guards with binoculars would see us, at least perhaps we could see each other. She really was bit of a rebel. The soldiers walked through the boundary zone with their German Shepherds, and jeeps drove up and down the no-man's-land zone. This sounded dangerous to me, but Ernst said not to worry and that it would be exciting.

'No, Ernst, we'd better forget about the whole idea. I know that East Berliners are not allowed to do that.'

Nobody was allowed to walk in the streets adjacent to the Wall unless they lived there. It would create suspicion to be seen walking there. It would be obvious to the guards that they were trying to make contact or communicate with someone on the other side. However, against my better judgement, I was persuaded to go along with the plan. My dear friend organised both my brothers to be 'walking' near the Wall at the arranged time. We wouldn't be able to touch, we wouldn't be able to hug, we wouldn't be able to talk to each other, so what did this grand plan aim to achieve? Just to experience the wonderful feeling of connection with each other was sufficient for me to decide that although the risks were real, they were worth it.

I had never been really close to the wall in East Berlin. From the distance that I was familiar with looking at it, it looked solid, plain and grey, bland, ugly and boring, topped with coiled barbed wire. As we approached the tower in West Berlin, I felt very nervous. We climbed up the steps of the watchtower and could see that there was actually a row of towers on both the East side and the West. Ernst and I were alone on it. From the West Berlin side, I was surprised to see that the wall was covered in coloured graffiti. I thought it looked mad. I thought maybe it was what free expression and freedom was all about, but to me it just looked as if all the graffiti artists wanted to paint like Picasso. I recognised we were close to the area where I lived and worked with the Komische Oper. We could see in the distance the buildings and blocks of flats near where I once lived. It was the middle of the day, most people would be at work, and there was hardly anyone walking near the Wall. Any people we could see were so far away. It looked deadly to me.

'I'm scared,' I whispered. 'I'm sure somebody is watching us. I'm sure somebody is recognising me right here and now.' I shyly pointed to a building near the Wall. 'I'm sure there are Stasi people living in that building. I can feel them looking at us and they're probably...'

'Don't be so silly, Heidi.' Ernst found the scene interesting but I felt increasingly paranoid.

I was completely beside myself. 'Maybe the Stasi will come and catch us. Maybe the secret police from West Germany are working with them.' My head was full of confusion. 'When is Wolle supposed to be coming?'

'Now.'

'I can't wait any longer. I'm too scared. Let's go now.'

'Wait, there's somebody coming.'

We peered into the distance. Far away walking alone on a long road, a young man came into our view.

Ernst was very excited. 'Is it your brother?'

'Don't talk to me,' I whispered. 'Maybe they have bugs on the tower and they can hear us.' I knew my mum had been given strict instructions that I was never, ever allowed to be in touch with my brothers again, under any circumstances.

The figure in the distance gradually comes closer and I become more and more confident that it is Wolle. 'Oh my God, he's wearing bright yellow trousers.'

Ernst starts waving madly.

'Are you crazy? Put your arm down. If they're watching us, they'll know what we're doing. Just look.'

Ernst keeps waving and I try to hold his arm down.

Here's my brother, in bright yellow unmissable pants, waving shyly, looking at the tower, walking faster now. I hope nobody sees him or us – it's so bloody obvious. My heart is beating madly. This is my little brother. My heart... My brother goes around the corner. He can't just turn around and walk up and down in front of us, so he takes the corner, but I have a strange feeling. He's gone. Our moment of distant connection is over.

'Something's happened,' I know it.

'Don't be so negative, don't be so suspicious.'

'I can feel it. I know it. Something's happened. He would not have gone around that corner and disappeared so quickly. That's not what Wolle would do. Somebody has pulled him around the corner, too suddenly. He won't come back.'

'Heidi, he'll just go round the block. He'll come back.'

'We'll see. I know you don't believe me. I know something has happened to him.'

We wait and wait. He does not return. I wish we had never come. I should have said no to the whole idea. Perhaps Wolle has been captured. Perhaps he is going to jail. They will want to know why he is wearing those bloody yellow pants. Whose attention is he trying to attract. Oh God, how I regret it all. I am ready to go. I want to go down the tower stairs, now. Get away from here.

Ernst tries to calm me. 'Now we're here, we'll wait another five minutes for Kalli.'

That is the plan. We will see Kalli and my dear friend walking in the distance in a few minutes. The wait is killing me.

We see two people coming together. They stop in the middle of the street, stand there, looking towards us. It is them, we agree.

'They're talking to me.' I can feel it. They are too far away to see their faces or eyes. 'Can you see, Ernst, something has happened. Why are they just staring at us? They want to tell us something has happened.' I whisper. I can tell that they are talking to each other. With the greatest concentration, I can see Kalli is trying to gesture to us with his hands. It's something about his watch, or his wrist… What is he saying? I can see his fingers, sticking up… How many…three?… four?… Two hands….six…seven. It's so frustrating.

The two figures walk slowly along the road, calmly, and eventually go around the same corner where Wolle disappeared, but they just walk round the corner slowly. Somehow, they move differently to the way Wolle did.

'I have a feeling this is it. Let's go now. We've seen them.' I have to leave this place now.

We go to a pub in West Berlin for something to eat. Ernst and our driving friend are busy talking about the world and politics while I am absorbed in my own thoughts of my family and concerned about my younger brother. How can I contact someone to find out if things are okay? I am trying to make sense of Kalli's hand signals. Could he have been trying to tell me to phone him at seven o'clock? Maybe. Kalli has a phone in his home. That is what I want to do. Our movements could easily have been followed. I am scared. I will ring Kalli from a public phone. I won't say much.

The phone is ringing and someone has taken the call. There is a moment of silence.

'Is it you?' I say to my brother, who I haven't spoken to for three years.

'Mh,' Kalli answers.

'Is everybody okay?'

'Mh mh,' he murmurs.

'Is there a problem?'

No answer from him.

Scheisse. I had better shut up. 'Okay, bye bye. All the best.'

Something is seriously wrong. My holiday is ruined. What can I do? I will ring my dear friend, much later tonight, I have her number.

We stayed at the pub for hours and I felt safe there. I didn't want us to be alone. I didn't want to return to the home of our driver, where we were staying. If we were being followed, I felt safer in a public place surrounded by many people.

I called my dear friend from a public phone. I could talk more easily to her.

'Is it you?'

'Yes, it's me,' she answered excitedly.

We had not spoken a word to each other since the night long ago when she loaned me some clothes and told me not to think about staying in Australia. She started talking straight away.

'Is it okay for us to talk?' I was unsure.

'Yes.'

'What's happened?'

'They took Wolle in a car.'

'Who?'

'Stasi, police…don't know. They bundled him into a private car around the corner. We saw it but came too late.'

Stuff it! My brother has done nothing wrong. He is not a criminal. How can anyone tell me not to see my brothers for the rest of my life? How ridiculous is that. I want to stand up for our rights.

Apparently, Kalli went from one police station in Berlin to another until he finally found Wolle, who had been kept for several hours until he agreed to tell them what he was doing walking near the Wall when he didn't live near there. He looked so suspicious in his bright yellow pants – that was not a good idea. The police wouldn't let him go until he told them and, as he did not want to go to prison, he had no option.

'I wanted just to see my sister in the distance.'

This could have had severe consequences. Poor Wolle, they eventually let him go. They must have had his personal file already checked out.

I found out later that my defection had affected others. At the time of my defection in 1980, someone close to me was going out with a girl who was an elite athlete, educated at an East German sports school. She was chosen to compete at the upcoming Moscow Olympics, and it was considered she could be world champion. After I defected, she was told to attend an interview and was asked if she was still in that relationship. When she said, 'Yes,' she was asked if she was aware of my defection, and that I was a *Verräter*, traitor.

This girl I had never met was given a choice – either to end her relationship and continue to be supported in her career, or, if she chose to stay in the relationship, her sports career would be finished. She couldn't believe it, and was offered no further explanation. She answered that her decision was to stay in her relationship. At that moment, she said goodbye to her career forever. She became one of my best friends.

Our visit to West Berlin was an eye opener. It was sad, frightening, tense and discouraging. Lives had been put in danger. I didn't want to ever return to this place. I was happy to leave West Berlin after three days.

For the next few weeks, we travelled Europe and I absolutely loved the rest of the trip. Most importantly of all, it was secretly arranged through our middle man that we would meet somebody very special. My mum.

My mother was given an early pension because of health issues, which permitted her to travel when she was only sixty-two years of age. She had brothers and sisters in West Germany and after retiring from teaching had a valid reason to apply for a permit to visit her youngest sister in Stuttgart, West Germany. Mum certainly could not have put on her application that she was planning to meet me

We travelled by hire car to Stuttgart and planned to drive Mum to visit her other brothers and sisters in other parts of West Germany. We arrived at my aunt's small flat and we were all so excited. From the moment I saw my mum, we hugged. There were no tears, we were just thrilled to meet. She looked great. I couldn't believe she had been able to create this opportunity. My aunts and Mum had set up a little table for Ernst and me, decorated with fresh flowers, with some small wedding gifts on it and a beige teddy bear. How thoughtful! One of my uncles was a *Bäckermeister* and he'd made a huge strawberry cake filled with cream, about thirty centimetres high – what a treat. It was his wedding gift to us.

Mum and I loved walking around Stuttgart. It was lovely to visit such a beautiful city, but what made it so special was just having so much time together. We had never in our busy lives had much time to spend with each other. We talked about what had happened to everyone as a result of my defection. We were open and honest with each other. Nothing she told me came as a great surprise. The Stasi had believed that Mum must have known I had plans to defect. They questioned her many times. She was put under heaps of emotional stress. They pressured her and used all the tactics they had, but there was nothing that Mum could tell them. The Stasi were well trained in identifying 'mistakes' but we made none. It took them a while to investigate all they could and they had to give up in the end. Mum knew nothing, and that was the truth.

The Stasi had interrogated my brothers about whether they knew of my plans. They knew nothing – I'd lived away from home for so many years. Nobody knew about my plan of escape but me, and that was the beauty of it. I knew that was my triumph: I'd kept everybody out of it completely. I had only shared my secret with Karl, just hours before I escaped, knowing that I could trust him.

With Mum, Ernst and I visited the famous Hofbräuhaus in Munich out of interest, and we stayed in the famous posh hotel Die Vier Jahreszeiten, the Four Seasons. We took Mum there for dinner and ate so much! Mum adored the salted herrings in mayonnaise with onion rings, her favourite dish. Our tummies were swollen after the fabulous dinner and afterwards we went to the foyer and sat on the couches, just enjoying each other's company, being together.

Mum said, 'Heidrun, you really look happy now.'

And I was.

There were tears when I said goodbye to Mum on our return to Stuttgart. When would we see each other again? Who could possibly know?

'Mum, next time, you come to Australia, okay? Believe in it. We'll find a way.'

The authorities never found out that we had met in West Germany.

In 1984, we needed to leave our flat and I although I did not want to move again, Ernst suggested we buy a house. Why would I have wanted a house? I'd never thought of living in a house in my whole life. It would be bigger, yes, but that would mean more housework. More work, but no more time to do it. I did not even have time to enjoy my little flat!

House hunting was hysterical. I'm sure we inspected forty houses before we found one to buy in the bayside area. To me, it was far too big, but it was a new adventure. Borrowing money to buy a house seemed absurd to me, but I understood from people I talked to that it was 'the great Australian dream' to own a house. Borrowing, to me, meant that you couldn't afford to buy. Why then should we buy a house? It was a foreign mindset to me. Owning 'property'? Borrowing money? Saving money for living expenses was all I knew.

I began to feel my life was not in a good balance. It was just work, work, work, and I've always known that there is more to life than work.

Thoughts of a family started to fill my mind and my desire to have a child. As I'd turned thirty, it seemed the right time for me. How would I fit it into my mad, busy restaurant life? Could I ever have a 'normal' life?

When we moved in to our house, I felt a bit weird in such a big space, I was used to cosy little spaces. As time went on, I loved it and made it into a comfortable home for us. I wanted to have a big fence surrounding the home, for privacy, security and to reduce noise, as the house was on a main road. The idea of people on the street being able to look in to my home, through my windows, was unsettling. I'd never had this problem living in my first-floor flats. The two-metre-high brick wall required a council permit. How would we get the wall built?

Then I was pregnant. It was not a surprise. We were both excited about the baby, although I had health issues that concerned my doctors. I had to go every month for a scan at the Royal Womens Hospital in Melbourne. At four months, my doctor was amazed at the activity of my baby. It was doing somersaults and my doctor said he'd never seen anything like it before – at that age the baby is usually quiet. I felt absolutely great, so that allayed his worries. I continued to work at the restaurant, wearing a red jacket over the neat little 'baby bump' in my lederhosen. Another dream of mine was on the way to becoming reality. I adore kids.

In 1985, I was introduced to spiritually minded people, through an apprentice at the restaurant. It was something completely new to me. There were many conversations about the meaning of dreams. It was my introduction to meditation, the concept of past lives, different spheres of life. Although it was rather weird, it was incredibly interesting. As time went on, I incorporated some of these spiritual ideas and practices into my life. I began to understand that whatever happens in life, the good and the bad, all is fine. I developed an understanding of the importance of peace of mind, a kind of an acceptance of whatever life experience I was confronted with. This attitude was helpful for me with the pressure of working such long hours, on top of the stress associated with perhaps all businesses. Perhaps it gave me more energy. I always looked well, I never looked tired, I always laughed and enjoyed myself even if I was dead on my feet and had serious concerns about the business. I'm grateful I was introduced to the universal laws and was thirsty to learn more. I began to develop my belief that we are all connected throughout the universe.

In 1986, a clairvoyant told me that one day I would be sitting with my mum and all my family back at my mother's home in East Berlin, together, around the dinner table, celebrating. It sounded ridiculous.

'Do you know where I come from? I'm from East Germany. Do you know anything about East Germany? It's impossible. There's the Wall. I never can go back home.'

'That's interesting. You will go home. Something happens in about three years' time.'

He'd lost me now. 'That's a joke.'

'I tell you what I see.'

He did not know me at all, yet he told me several significant things about my past, present and future life that, absolutely astonishingly, were or have since come true.

In my eighth month of pregnancy, my doctor became very concerned. Something was seriously wrong. He instructed me to return the next day. On my way back to work, I felt very nervous and cried. I had an unusual medical condition. My baby's life was in jeopardy. My doctor's face showed his concern for me. My dream child was due in January 1986, but the situation was dangerous. My doctor had to decide on a date for my baby's birth: 24 December.

'No way,' I said. 'That's Christmas Eve. I'm not going to hospital!'

'Believe me, Heidi, it has to be a Caesarean, as your baby is also breech. We have to do it on that date at the very latest.'

'Are you working on Christmas Eve?' I asked him.

'If I have to, yes. Heidi, I'm booking you in now.'

'But it's my decision!'

'Heidi, do you want to have that baby that you take home and raise or…?'

'I'll have my child, but not on the twenty-fourth. It's our family

Christmas celebration at my place and my mum is coming for the first time to Australia. I'm not coming to hospital at Christmas, I'll come after Christmas.'

'Heidi, I don't know whether I should laugh or cry. Please sign this.'

'No.'

'If you don't sign, I'm not responsible for the birth of your baby. You'll have to find somebody else.'

I signed. We had health insurance. I'd been advised we should pay for this type of hospital cover. It was another responsibility that East German people did not have to concern themselves with, where all health matters were funded by the state. I did not want to go to hospital on the twenty-fourth.

It was planned that Mum was to arrive in Melbourne on 4 January. She hoped to be present when her first grandchild was due to be born. That was a sufficiently important reason for her to apply for a visiting visa to Australia. Surely the East German authorities would have no problems about her visiting her daughter for such a special event. She had two sons living back home in East Germany, so she would definitely return home if she was permitted to travel to Australia. I had decided that if the East German authorities refused her application, I would use the Australian press to make a big fuss about it and then I was sure she'd be permitted. The Australian media had used me for their purposes; this time I would ask the press to help me. Mum was so enthusiastic about coming to see us that she returned to evening school to refresh her English language skills. She did not want to have to rely on me to be her interpreter at all times. At home, Ernst and I spoke a mixture of German and English and I learnt that if you don't speak your native language regularly, you begin to lose it. As the years have gone by, sometimes I have had to look up the English–German dictionary because words just slipped from my mind. 'If you don't use it, you lose it,' as the saying goes.

Mum's application was accepted. She had decided that if she was coming such a long way, with such a long flight, she wanted to stay with us for four months. We undertook renovations to our home, as I wanted it to be as beautiful and comfortable as possible for her visit and for the new baby. The whole house was turned upside down with builders and dust, I hadn't bought one nappy in preparation for our baby's birth, and now instead of expecting my baby in January, she was due in a fortnight. I decided it was really time to finish working at the restaurant. There were many other things I needed to organise as well as taking care of myself.

'I'm sorry, guys, but I need to stop working now.'

'You can't do that. This is the most busy time of the year,' said Ernst.

'I know that. Don't you think it's time to look after me and our baby now?'

Christmas lasted for one and a half months in our industry. Every night there were restaurant bookings for Christmas break-up parties. The restaurant was festooned with Christmas decorations; we went to a great deal of effort to make it lovely, very much like a German Christmas atmosphere. New Year's Eve was also a big night in the restaurant. Staffing was difficult as everyone wanted to spend special time with their families and friends, and now I was suggesting I would not be available to work.

'I know that, but I'm expecting a baby and I think I've worked long enough. I'm sorry. And I'm inviting some friends to come to the Hofbräuhaus tonight because I don't think we'll have a Christmas party at home.'

My husband of course was focused on the business, and as I did not have any family members or friends around me as support during the pregnancy, I felt at times very lonely. I wanted to share my joy and concerns with my mum and family.

Twenty friends arrived at the restaurant after our diners had left for a lovely, spontaneous Christmas party. At one o'clock in the morning, the band was about to finish, and I still wanted to keep dancing, to celebrate my new life as a soon-to-be mum. I shared fears with the women and laughed with the men, tired and emotionally drained. The last dance was rock and roll, and only I and my dancing partner, Shane, took to the floor.

He was concerned the dance would be too vigorous for me and the baby. 'Heidi, no, I don't want to be responsible for your baby coming early!'

'Shane, please, only one more dance, and it's the last, okay?'

We had so much fun. We eventually went to bed at about four in the morning. I lay awake planning the next couple of weeks, slept a little, then I woke and asked my husband if he'd wet the bed. I'd had no time to go to childbirth classes – I think I went to two. In one session, we were told when the baby was on its way we'd get 'signs', but as I hadn't been to the next session, I must have missed out on hearing what those mysterious signs were. The other session was to show us some exercises to do. I bought the tape and did my Richard Simmons twenty-minute exercise program religiously at six-thirty every morning. I still do the exercises today. It was also the first time I was introduced to the idea and usefulness of resting for a few minutes after working-out while listening to inspirational messages. My doctor hadn't informed me either; perhaps he thought I knew, perhaps he thought there was no need to discuss such things as my pregnancy was now not going to go full-term.

Ernst said, 'Maybe your waters have broken.'

'What do we do now? That wasn't supposed to happen now.'

'Sleep a bit longer,' he mumbled.

But I phoned my GP, my very dear and wise doctor who I love so much, just after six in the morning.

'Heidi, maybe you should get ready to go to hospital by ten o'clock and ring your obstetrician to let him know. He'll meet you there then. It sounds like you don't have to wait until the twenty-fourth!'

'Oh, my God, you mean it could happen today?'

'That's the usual way. Relax, Heidi.'

'Okay, Percy. What's the next sign?'

'Didn't they tell you at the classes?'

'I didn't have time to go!'

'Heidi, you are one in a million.' He made me laugh in all my panic.

In the shower, I experienced my first tiny labour pain – Percy explained contractions would be the next sign. I had another, then another, each one stronger than the previous one. I felt a bit dizzy.

I woke my husband, quickly gathered a few things to take to hospital, including my favourite large soft brown teddy bear that I could use as a cushion. 'Quick, hurry up, it's time to go. I've got labour pains.'

'There's no great hurry, they last for hours.'

'Not with me!' Somehow I knew my body was ready to have the baby.

My husband drives through red lights down St Kilda Road to the hospital because my contractions are so heavy so suddenly.

'Hurry up, I think it's coming! I think it's coming *now*!'

He parks the car in the car park.

I get out of the car and realise I can't walk. 'Ernst, I think it's half… there! Please, carry me. I can't walk!'

'I don't want to take the responsibility,' he says. 'I might drop you.'

'Why would you want to drop me? I've never been horrible to you!'

'I'm not saying I want to drop you, I'm just scared I might, and I'll be responsible. No, you have to walk.' He's terrified.

'I can't…' I am screaming. 'I want to divorce you here and now. You go home. What sort of a father-to-be are you? What sort of a husband are you? Go home, I don't need you. I don't want to see you any more. I can do it myself.' I always do everything myself! I drag myself inside the hospital entrance.

The staff person says, 'You have to fill out these forms.'

'Can't you see I'm having the baby *now*? Please just get me to a doctor… *now*!'

'Just as soon as you fill out these forms.'

I say to my husband in German, 'It sounds like bloody East Germany… We start filling out forms!' I am screaming, 'My baby's coming *now*, nobody wants to help me… Tell her it's coming out *now*! Can you tell her it's half born already?' I'm lying on the waiting room floor.

The woman realises the urgency and says, 'Forget about forms!' Finally she hurries.

We take the lift to the eighth floor. I am transferred to a bed.

A nurse lifts my legs into stirrups, which I remember seeing in a movie. She says, 'Oh, my God, I can see the bum!'

I scream to Ernst, 'I told you it was half born, I knew it, and nobody believed me. What happens now?'

The nurse puts an oxygen mask over my face.

I pull it off. 'I can breathe,' I say, or do I? What language am I speaking or am I just screaming? The mask is back on, I take it off. 'I don't need this bloody mask! Don't wait for my doctor, it's ready now.' I say to Ernst, 'I said I didn't want to be in hospital having this baby at Christmas.'

Ernst can't speak. The poor guy, this is all too much for him. He can't handle seeing me in pain. God bless him.

The sister instructs me, 'Heidi, don't push. Your doctor will be here about eight, to perform the Caesarean. I'll show you how to pull back.'

'Pull back? The baby is coming out, isn't that what we want?' Am I swearing in English or German?

My doctor arrives.

'Oh, my God, I see the bum! There's no time for a Caesarean. It's very dangerous. Heidi, listen carefully. Take the most enormous breath in that you can. I've never done something like this before, so let's do it together. Come on. I'll push the baby back in, turn it around, and try to pull it out gently by the legs. That's when you must push as much as you can, Heidi.'

'Ouch!' I scream, and follow all his instructions. 'I told you yesterday I would not be in hospital on Christmas Eve and I wanted a natural birth!'

My baby is born at five minutes past eight. Our daughter. What a joy. We are a miracle.

I am gently hugging and kissing my baby, who I wished for. She is placed on my chest. She is so beautiful. I whisper, 'Thank you. You are our miracle.' This is the most joyous moment of my life.

Ernst is close to me, sharing all the way the tears of joy and love with us.

For two weeks I stay at the hospital. *Schnulli Pulli* has trouble eating, breathing, sleeping, and cries all the time. The press visit me. I am beginning to wonder about freedom of the press. How did they know I was here? Now they take photos for the newspaper of me and the baby. Is there no end to their interest?

Occasionally, I sneak out of the hospital because I hate it there, and I go to visit the restaurant for a few hours and feel on top of the world. My baby is in special care. The hospital staff think I am crazy. We are discharged from hospital on 24 December, Christmas Eve, and we take *Schnulli Pulli* straight to the Hofbräuhaus to cook and prepare there for a Christmas Eve family dinner at home that evening. I am the happiest person on this planet.

Mum arrived in Australia on 4 January 1986 as planned and we introduced her to her first grandchild at the airport. This was the beginning of a great love affair between Mum and *Schnulli Pulli*. The media came to our home; they took beautiful family photos. Over the first few weeks of Mum's stay with us, she simply loved being with us, immersed in our family life, spending time at home and in our garden with us.

She told me that my dad had visited her at some stage since I'd defected. The doorbell rang one day, and she opened the door and he was standing there. She couldn't believe it. He had hardly changed since the day he left. He arrived carrying a bunch of flowers and a cake.

Mum said, 'What are you doing here?'

He said, 'May I come in?'

She hesitated and then said, 'Only for a few minutes.'

He came inside and Mum said, 'Why have you come?'

'I just wanted to find out where my daughter is.'

Mum was absolutely shocked, because in all those years, she had not heard from him. 'I want to speak to her before I answer that,' she said.

'Why can't you tell me?'

'Maybe she doesn't want you to know.'

He was disappointed. 'Can you at least tell me how she is?'

'She's fine.'

'But where can I find her?'

Mum said, 'She's far away. Thousands and thousands of kilometres away.'

'Really?'

She asked him to leave. Mum felt that she needed my permission to give him information about me because I was now an adult. I thanked Mum when she told me this, with great respect. It was the first time my dad had come back in to my life.

My defection was reported in an art newspaper in East Germany, but this was not the norm. The report stated surprise about my defection. To cross borders, permission – a visa – is always required and I had one. But people are expected to return. By defecting, I had rejected the communist system, I had abandoned my country. This is never publicised in the newspapers, which are of course run by the state. 'Freedom of the press' is an unknown concept under communism. The government controlled the media as they did everything else. To publicise a defection might give others ideas to do the same. I was not only a rebel in the eyes of the East German communist system, I was stamped as a political criminal, someone who had betrayed her country.

One day, I received a phone call in the restaurant from a man named Achi.

'It's Achi here.'

'Who are you, Achi?'

'I'm a Berliner and I want to meet you. I just came to Australia.'

Could he be a Stasi person? Don't tell me they are still looking for me.

Achi explained that he found out about my defection when he was still in Berlin with his family. His family came to Australia after successfully applying for exit visas. I didn't want to talk to him, because I was suspicious of him, but Achi kept ringing back. I asked my husband to take his calls.

Achi, a passionate musician, bought his wife and two children to meet us at the restaurant. Berliners have to know other Berliners, he said. Mum was with us at the restaurant that night and also enjoyed meeting this crazy, open-hearted person. We then invited them to visit our home on the following Sunday. When they came, we explained to Achi our intentions of building a high brick fence, and Achi announced that he could build it. He wasn't a builder, but he had many different skills.

'Don't worry, Heidi, I'll build you your Berlin Wall!'

What a mad idea. How we laughed. Achi did a fantastic job. We called it the Berlin Wall ever since. We have all been friends since that night.

Mum enjoyed walking along the beach with our baby in the pram for hours. I appreciated the time alone to rest and rejuvenate and learnt so much about mothering our new baby from Mum. Mum minded the baby at home of a night, so I was able to return to work at the restaurant almost straight away. I wondered when this opportunity to spend time with her would ever come again.

After four months, it was time to say goodbye and that was a very difficult, sad thing to do. The day before she left Australia, Mum fell at Victoria Market, where she loved to go and had bought some little souvenirs. She broke her foot but refused to let us take her to hospital. My heart was broken, seeing her limping onto the plane. I promised I'd write to her every Wednesday from that day on and I did so for years. When would we see each other again?

She went on the plane with her broken foot, and on her arrival at the airport in East Germany, her whole leg was so swollen that she had to be taken by ambulance from the airport. For months, she had to lie on her couch. The point was clear – she did not want to upset the East German authorities by extending her travel visa. Otherwise, perhaps next time she wanted to travel, her application would not be granted.

During Mum's visit, I told her that I'd written to her many times.

On her return home to East Berlin, she decided to get answers to a question that had been bothering her. She only ever received a few of my letters infrequently. She went to the State Security Office in Berlin to find out what had happened to all my letters and photos. They were all in a file. She was permitted to read them, but not to take them home.

Mum and my stepfather, Opi, visited us in Australia for about three months every two or three years until she was eighty. Although it was all about visiting me and her granddaughter, over the years we were able to take them to see Sydney and Queensland, and they loved Australia. There was never any question of them staying in Australia. She had two sons in Germany, so it was two against one. I understand that completely and have never been upset about that. Their last visit was in 2000.

The restaurant industry in general started to experience hard times in the mid-eighties to the early nineties. Australian taxation rules changed and the rules for claiming the costs of business entertaining were changed. Combined with the recession, this affected our lives and there were times of more hard work and stress associated with financial hardship. We had to learn to make staff cuts wherever possible and do as much as possible ourselves. I found a lovely older woman I could trust to mind our daughter. She was minded for several years as I needed to work even harder to earn money to contribute to our many financial responsibilities. What I'd hoped would be a transition phase from work to motherhood, and a life primarily at home, was not to be. It was a constant juggle and not easy, I often felt totally exhausted and upset at times. I just loved spending time with her on Saturdays before I went to work in the afternoon and on Sundays, which remained our family day.

During school holidays our little girl came with us to work of a day and loved being dressed in a little dirndl, helping as she could. She was so cute. One day, my young daughter asked me for money to buy a hot chocolate at the Pancake Parlour, opposite us in Market Lane, knowing they gave their customers free lollies. The little entrepreneur returned and decided to put the lollies in a breadbasket with our business cards, then stand outside the Hofbräuhaus and sell them for a dollar! We had many people make bookings because of her enthusiasm. She loved being involved with the restaurant.

By the time she was preschool age, I sometimes needed to bring her to work of an evening. She slept on a blanket on the office floor, but often wanted to wander around the restaurant with Mum and Dad, which was not appropriate. To enable us to have a better balance of work and family life, we changed the business location and decided to concentrate on the lunchtime trade, but this wasn't very successful. Times were rather difficult.

Mum's second visit to Australia in 1987 was in time for our daughter's birthday in December. This was my first Christmas Eve with Mum since my defection. It was such a pleasure to organise together the food, decorations and baking. We made it very special and Mum joined with us and my husband's family Christmas Eve celebration. On Christmas Day, we were – as always – booked out at the restaurant for lunch, which was a great treat for our clients. Our German-style Christmas Day lunch included a visit from Father Christmas for the pleasure of the children. On Boxing Day, 26 December, I liked to organise a little Christmas lunch just for all of us at home. I welcomed one of the guys from our staff to visit our home, dressed as Father Christmas.

During Mum's visit, we decided to get a dog. I'd never had a pet in my life before, although growing up in East Germany it was common for people to have a dog. Small dogs were most popular, as everyone lived in flats, and sausage dogs were particular favourites. The beautiful East Berlin Zoo was not far from my childhood home and Mum sometimes took us there on a Sunday afternoon. One day, I wore my good yellow summer coat, and a duck rushed up to me and grabbed the hem of my coat with its beak and pulled me over the fence. Another day, when coming home from the S-Bahn, I was bitten by a little poodle, so I was rather scared of animals. The idea to find a dog for the family was not taken lightly by me. My husband, being a 'yes-sayer' to any ideas that were proposed, simply answered, 'Yes, what sort of dog?' when getting a dog was mentioned.

My very good friend Ulla had a lovely Shetland collie in Schwerin. Daisy would put her head on my lap when I laid on Ulla's couch. I fell in love with her. I was never scared of that beautiful dog and I knew how connected and precious she had become to Ulla and her daughter. I thought that was so special and decided to find a Shetland collie for us. Where would I find such a pet? A salesman frequented the restaurant and one day he showed me some photos of his new dog. 'It's a collie!' After finding out where he'd bought his puppy, we contacted the breeder.

Which one to choose? They were all so beautiful. Willi – one of nine in the litter – was the lightest in colour, took an instant interest in me and nipped me playfully on my ankle, so the choice was made immediately. Willi was *Schnulli Pulli*'s birthday and Christmas present that year and became her constant, loved companion. He was a much-loved family member for sixteen years and taught me about unconditional love which I appreciate to this day. He kept us fit, walking or riding our bikes with him daily. Sometimes we walked him along the beach at two o'clock in the morning after coming home from the restaurant. Having a dog was a fabulous commitment.

For our New Year's Eve celebration, I maintained the old tradition of eating doughnuts after midnight and found two wonderful cake shops in Melbourne that baked authentic Berliner-style doughnuts. I decorated the lounge room with streamers, just like Mum used to do, but fireworks were banned in Melbourne so I could not replicate for my daughter that fun and excitement I enjoyed as a child.

Our life had three definite values: firstly our family, secondly the restaurant and thirdly enjoying the environment – mainly of the Bayside area. Whenever I had the chance, I took our daughter to play in the sand at the beach, buckets and spades, swimming and walking. We enjoyed riding our bikes occasionally along the bike track. We loved our fish and chips from St Kilda, a piece of cake from Acland Street, my daughter playing in the playground near the Stokehouse Restaurant with other little children alongside the picturesque bay. Like a magnet, I have always been drawn back to this fabulous scene of water, space and its personal feeling of significance for me of freedom. I was in love with living here.

Our babysitter stayed overnight and went home each morning after I got up. Late at night when we came home, I always sneaked in to the room where our little girl was sleeping just to enjoy looking at her peacefully. I'd be as quiet as possible, yet most of the time it was as though she was waiting for me, no matter how late it was, and she'd wake up and reach out to me with her little hand and say, 'Mami, please stay.' She would not let go of my hand. How cute! I was touched every time. Night after night, I lay beside her on the floor, still holding her little hand in my hand until my hand and arm became numb. In my heart, I was devoted to my family but the obligations of our business life placed extreme demands on my time. Sometimes I wanted to just run away from all those responsibilities. I needed a rest, time out…for me and my family.

In 1989, on 9 November, I stayed up particularly late as I had tablecloths from the restaurant to wash and hang out to dry. It was four o'clock in the morning when I eventually went to bed, completely exhausted, which was a feature of my life at this stage. The phone beside my bed rang at six o'clock. Half asleep, I answered it.

'Heidi, is that you?' The unfamiliar mature woman's voice speaks in German, excitedly.

'Who is this?' I mumble.

'Heidi, have you heard? The Berlin Wall is down! The Wall is down, the Wall is down!' She's chanting. 'Congratulations!' She's talking nonsense.

'I don't believe what you're saying. Please don't ring me again.' After only two hours' sleep, I'm not in a very good mood. I hang up the phone.

The woman rings back. She's a nutcase.

'Excuse me, I don't know who you are, I've not long come home from work…' I'm trying to get rid of her.

She rings again, again, again. 'Heidi, it's true! Don't you understand? Haven't you heard the news? Turn your television on.'

I wake my husband and pass him the phone. He has more patience than me. Ernst invites the woman to come to the restaurant at lunchtime to meet me.

'Ernst, are you mad? I don't even know her.'

He says, 'She just wants to meet you and talk to you.' My husband rolls over and returns to sleep.

Who am I meeting at twelve o'clock at the restaurant?

An unfamiliar elderly lady arrived at the restaurant at twelve, accompanied by her daughter and a huge bunch of flowers. 'Heidi? Congratulations! I want to share the excitement with you! I have followed your story for years.'

People have followed my life in Australia since knowing of me in 1980. I never sought this inquisitiveness and, actually, over the years became rather tired of it. I did not really appreciate her interruption to my work.

'Are you sure it's true?'

'Don't you watch television, Heidi?'

'No. I have no time.'

'Haven't you listened to the radio this morning? The Berlin Wall is down.'

'I don't believe you.'

My husband turned on the radio and confirmed her news. I just did not believe what I heard and read in the newspapers. We went home early in the afternoon to follow the story on the TV. But why should I trust the media? They'd misreported my story when I defected, why would I rely on their reports now? This news could be just another story. The Berlin Wall was down? No, it was impossible. The media chased me for my response to this news. Politically, there had been nothing reported leading up to such an incredible event, forecasting great change in East Germany. Apparently, social action had taken place for months leading up to the event, but it had not been reported widely in Australia.

For two weeks, I would not believe that the Wall had come down. We watched footage on the television of people in masses walking through the checkpoints at the Wall, and Ernst couldn't understand my resistance to the evidence. Then I decided to phone my mum's neighbour, trying to get in contact with Mum. I rang but when I said it was me, Mum's neighbour hung up on me. I rang again, she hung up on me again. I didn't give up. She was an elderly woman, and must have been scared to speak to me.

'Don't hang up on me, please! I only want to speak to Mum and ask her one question. You don't have to worry.'

'But we don't want you to talk about anything.'

'Please, I just want to ask Mum one question. I want to ask if it's true that the Wall is down.'

'Yes, it is.'

I can not absolutely believe it unless I hear it from Mum. She is the only person I can trust completely.

'Please, please, let me ask my mum.'

'Okay, but only for one minute.'

'It will only take thirty seconds, I promise.'

I wait while they get my mum.

'Heidrun, yes, it's true! Isn't it wonderful? Now you can come home, I can cook for you, we can celebrate together. It is true!'

Then I believed it. The clairvoyant I met in 1986 was spot on. How amazing.

In so many ways, the fall of the Wall was wonderful. It was magnificent to gain freedom without any war or bloodshed for East German people. I believe it was one of the major achievements of the twentieth century. Has there ever been a revolution which has been so peaceful? How unique. I have great pride in the East German people for how they conducted themselves. This had nothing to do with the political powers that controlled Germany – Russia, France, America and England – it was the citizens of East Germany, particularly in the areas of Leipzig and Dresden where the *Arbeiter*, the workers, conducted meetings in their factories and prepared for the historic event. The movement started as a groundswell, simply from the workers' desire to have freedom to travel.

From the moment the announcement was made that people could travel from East to West, the restrictive power of the wall became non-existent. I have seen documentaries of people that night crossing at the famous Checkpoint Charlie and climbing over the Wall, helping each other, standing on top of it celebrating, drinking champagne and singing joyfully. People came with their own tools to help tear down the wall. Pieces of the Wall were kept as mementoes and even sold as tourist souvenirs all over the world. East Germans showed their unbelievable excitement and sense of celebration, but there was no violent behaviour. As soon as my older brother heard the news of the Wall, he took a car full of people and travelled from his home in the north of East Germany down to Berlin. He wanted to be there. Part of history. Anyone who could walk or drive to the famous Brandenburg Gate in the centre of Berlin got themselves there. It was a peaceful revolution. The military did not respond with violence. The time was right. The power of the people acting as one, in unity, was touching and mind-blowing.

However, when the Berlin Wall came down, people all over the world who were relatives of those who originally owned country properties and farms decided to return to East Germany to claim their property. Incredible things have happened there. Some people of course were evicted. Big disasters happened because some people suicided on receiving letters from lawyers saying they'd have to leave what had been their homes all their lives, with no rights. These were terrible situations.

It took me five years after the fall of the Wall to return to what was previously East Berlin. There were many reasons why it took so long. Where were all the Stasi people? They were all still alive. I heard many stories of people returning to their homeland who were never seen again. There were stories that Checkpoint Charlie was not safe, although it was meant to be completely safe. Stories of the Stasi, the bigwigs, rising up again, stories of people going crazy because without communism they had nothing to believe in any more. People were fleeing to the new, free country that had been East Germany from other communist countries, to seek a better place to live, for safety, security, family reunions, food and freedom. Violence was increasing, people searched across borders to find family and friends they hadn't seen for forty years. Many stories told that it was absolute madness over there. I did not want to be in that madness and uncertainty. Security was all-important to me, and when I returned, it would be when it felt safe, and I would only travel with my husband and our child.

I loved writing letters and, before the wall came down, wrote often to Gerhard. Our letters came and went via his cousin in West Berlin. My friend Fine and I communicated too. Fortunately the authorities never seemed to discover our connection. However, I was never able to write to my brothers. Mum had signed a statement prepared by the State Security that she was the only person to have contact with me.

Wolle missed me very much. He applied several times through the FDJ organisation to serve as a volunteer for a year in Vietnam. He thought he would feel more closely connected to me. Finally, his request was granted. While in Vietnam, he took the risk to send me a card. It was a big surprise to hear from him at last. This experience encouraged him to apply later for a visiting visa to Cuba, which, as well, was granted. All he wanted to experience was the sense of freedom.

My older brother had connections through his freelance interpreting in France, and I once received a birthday card from him in 1984, via his contacts in France, saying that everybody was thinking of me and that the Berlin Wall had been built higher. After the Wall came down, we could all write freely at last. It was hard to believe. I laughed.

Mum returned to Australia in 1992 and to our delight she brought my brother Wolle's five-year-old daughter with her. They stayed for five months. Within days, the girls understood each other and loved each other and until today they have a special bond. Mum was doing all she could to bring the family together. The first English word my niece learnt was 'cuddle'.

'*Tante* Heidi, please give me a cuddle.'

From then on, she called us 'the Cuddle family'. Wolle was envious, and became motivated to visit us the following year. That was wonderful. He loved Australia, we loved having him stay with us. He added so much quality into our life. I cried when he left, missing him immediately.

I was not ready to return to what was previously East Germany until June 1994. Our daughter was eight years old and I was no longer frightened, and trusted everything would be okay. My husband had wanted to go earlier, but I felt it was not appropriate. We planned to be away from Melbourne for six weeks. The flight was exciting, I was full of anticipation.

Gerhard and my older brother and my younger brother's daughter met us at the airport, Berlin Tegel, located in the previous West Berlin. Mum stayed home to welcome us by preparing lunch for everyone.

It was fourteen years since my defection. Times had changed. They had cars and drove us through West Berlin then through the Brandenburg Gate and Alexander Platz, previously in East Berlin, and down Karl Marx Allee through several suburbs. The buildings looked much the same as they had fourteen years before, except that many walls were covered with graffiti. There had never been any graffiti in East Germany before I left. As we drove down Karl Marx Allee and Frankfurter Allee, we passed what I remembered to be the first big-screen cinema, where I'd so enjoyed seeing my first ballet movie *Sleeping Beauty* as a child. Then we passed a block of flats where my teacher used to live. Did she still live there? It all looked the same in one way, but it was dull, ugly and dirtyish. The road was busy; various sorts of cars made their way along it, not just the Trabbies, Skodas and Volvos of the past. Memories flooded back. There was the café that Mum used to take us to for ice cream sometimes on Sundays, and on my right, we passed the Karl Marx Buchhandlung, the bookshop where I'd been to so often with her. Everything looked the same, yet completely different. It was surreal. The impression shocked me.

We arrived in Lichtenberg and as we drove into the street of my childhood home, it all looked the same but somehow sadder. I felt like I was watching a movie.

On our arrival at Mum's, I could smell green bean soup, my favourite, and *Kassler*, smoked pork, cooking in her kitchen. We had no sense of tiredness after our long flight; we were far too excited to notice. Mum looked happier than I had ever seen. It was so great to see her. At last, family reunion; the flat was crowded. Our home looked exactly the same, as though I'd only left the day before.

The first thing Mum said to me was 'Take your shoes off and put your house slippers on.'

Some things never change. I thought that was hysterical! When it was time to share the meal, Mum maintained the tradition and served herself first.

Our daughter was delighted to see her special *Omi*, grandmother. We enjoyed many outings and loved spending time with the whole family.

I asked Mum for the secret unopened letter she'd hidden for me that I'd been given by the Stasi men many years previously in Schwerin when they tried to coerce me to become an informer. I opened it and read it without any emotion whatsoever. It had no meaning now. It was not longer relevant in any way. I don't even remember the code name that I'd been designated. It was just a piece of paper, rubbish, which I threw in the bin.

Our family gatherings were lovely and when it eventually came time to leave, we were all sad. I really felt I was leaving home all over again. I had missed my friend Gerhard so much. While we were in Germany, he did so much for us and took me back to the theatres where I used to dance, to the places where I used to live, to meet my old friends, and he was delighted to entertain us in every unforgettable way.

I took a book with me on this trip and kept notes of what I felt, what I saw, who I met. This was to be the beginning of writing my life story. The nineteenth became a special date for me: I defected on the 19th, we married on the 19th, we left for Germany on 19 June 1994 and I started taking notes on that date, the minute we were up in the air, in my special notebook with little white flowers on its dark blue cover.

> 19.6.1994. *Immer ein ganz besonderer Tag*. Always a very special day.
> This day my family and my dearest friends, all of us, have been waiting for so long. We've waited for fourteen years for this experience to fall into each other's arms again in East Germany. A trip back to the past. Whoever would have thought that in '89 the Wall would have come down. Hope and dreams I have had about this, but it was too unbelievable to imagine that this would ever have happened.

It was a wonderful summer in Europe. Did we want to stay? My husband's life, family and business were in Melbourne. But we loved Berlin so much we wondered if perhaps one day we could live half a year in Australia and half a year there. Escaping the winters might be a great way to live. We said our goodbyes.

Our daughter cried on the plane, heartbroken. 'I want to stay with my *Omi*.'

They had a very special bond. She cried and screamed uncontrollably all the way on our one-hour flight from Berlin to Frankfurt. Neither we nor the flight attendants could console her.

Eventually, I whispered in her ear, 'I've got an idea. You know what? We're going back to see *Omi* for Christmas! It's now August, then September, October, November, December…we'll be back!'

'But I don't want to go back,' she sobbed, 'I just want to stay.'

Gradually, she stopped crying. 'Do you promise, Mum?'

The plane was about to land.

'I do.' How could I do it? There were no spare funds but I was determined to keep promises.

On our arrival home, it was customary for us to collect Willi from the farm where he was born. We all loved this outing, it was something special in our busy lives to enjoy the drive out to the countryside. After collecting Willi, we regularly stopped at a café for afternoon tea and made the most of our day out together.

We settled back into work and school life, and I continued to find time to write to my special people back at home; this was most important to me. My husband and I had several conversations about perhaps opening a business in Germany. There were opportunities there at this time that could never have existed before. Perhaps we could open an Aussie pub in Germany? We had been considering selling the business for quite some time.

I worked more hours than ever before to save for our trip back to Germany at Christmas. Our daughter's birthday was the annual celebration for the year. We always hosted a party at home on the nearest Sunday to her birthday for up to about fifty friends and neighbours and business colleagues. It was always a special occasion.

My daughter and I visited Germany later that year as planned, just before Christmas. Ernst was unable to join us; that time of year was impossible for him to be away from the restaurant. It was a perfect, white Christmas with the Kris Kringle markets open as in my childhood. Berlin certainly looked prettier covered in bright, soft, white snow than it had in the summer. We built a big snowman with a carrot for his nose.

Our daughter stayed at home with Mum while I met my dear friend Gerhard alone at last. There'd been no time to spend alone with him on our previous visit. He worked in the Europe Centre in a music store; he was very knowledgeable about music.

We met in the Kris Kringle market and at the first sight of me he looked at what I was wearing, a lovely little silver-grey fur jacket my husband had given me, and said, 'You must be freezing!'

I said, 'No, I'm okay.'

'Come on,' he said, taking me by my hand.

We went to a huge department store and he insisted on buying me a lovely, long woollen dark brown swing coat. 'Wear it now,' he said, 'Put your little jacket in your bag.'

That was very special, particularly because Gerhard had, in a letter, told me that he thought of me as being like the daughter in the show *Fiddler On the Roof*. When the father Tewje farewells his daughter to leave home to follow her lover, who has been banished to Siberia, her father sings words to the effect of 'Oh Lord, please make sure that she always will have enough garments to keep her warm.' Gerhard knew that plenty of warm clothing was not really needed by someone in Australia, but in his mind he felt the feelings of that father towards me.

Although it was five years since the fall of the Wall, it was still like a brand-new world in this free Berlin.

Gerhard and others told me that you could visit what had previously been the offices of State Security headquarters in Lichtenburg to view your personal file and read the records the Stasi had collected about you. Each citizen had an individual file, noting changes in employment, reasons for such changes, and other factual information, as well as any notes added by informers. We all knew that such details existed in our files. I had a strong urge to see my file.

No special permits were required to access my file, I simply had to visit the offices and ask for it. I gave the staff my name and other identifying information, and paid a small fee for them to forward my file to me. It felt so weird for me to do this. In GDR time, this was a building nobody wanted to go near. I was told that if they didn't send me the file within five years, then it meant that they hadn't been able to find it.

We had so many Christmas celebrations that year! Everyone we visited seemed to host another Christmas event. When *Schnulli Pulli* was given her Father Christmas presents, she was expected to perform a little song or dance, as was the old tradition. She was raised as a bilingual child, so she loved it all. I cried tears of joy.

For the first time in my life, I went to church for Christmas in Germany. We drove through the forest to a little village and fifteen of us walked to the church, wearing thick winter jackets and hats and carrying blankets, it was freezing – perhaps minus twenty degrees Celsius – but it was magic. We attended evening Mass in an old wooden church, lit only with candles, and sat close together on cushions on hard, narrow wooden benches. Children of all different ages from the community performed a nativity play. It was so awesome, just beautiful!

I visited the Komische Oper and met old friends and colleagues. I could not believe how happy they were to see me. Many of the dancers, too old for ballet, had left by this time. Others later defected too, but those I saw had no hard feelings at all about my defection. This surprised me in a way, but I think that since the Wall had come down and the political climate had transformed, the timing of my visit was perfect. If I'd been able to return while the Wall was still up, which would have been impossible, I'm sure they would have greeted me rather differently.

We had a wonderful time during our visit, but my daughter announced to me that she would never, ever go away without Papa, her Dad, again. 'Next time we go, Mum, we need to take Dad.'

There was never time to be involved in the community other than in our professional capacity as restaurateurs. I had become a business woman, but deep inside in my heart, family was number one. If there was anything on at our daughter's school that involved parents, I always happily attended.

The school sent home a note at the end of the year, explaining that the music curriculum would not continue. What? This alarmed me. Every child needs to learn and play music, singing, dancing and to experience theatre. I made an appointment to visit the principal and offered my services once a week to teach music lessons to the grade three classes. I wanted the kids to have fun learning. I worked with the children for the whole year and we presented a variety show.

I took the children on public transport to an old people's home to entertain the elderly to brighten up their day. The children were absolutely fantastic. All fifty of them played in two songs on the recorder. I taught them the traditional German song '*Kuckuck*', 'Cuckoo'. My goal was for everyone to participate, not to compete; all were to be included. Some of the kids thought they couldn't sing well and had no confidence. Not many boys and men dance in Australia and I wanted these boys to experience the joy of dancing. Unlike their academic work, it didn't matter if they weren't very good at it, I just wanted them to enjoy artistic self-expression and creativity.

At the Christmas concert, the stage was full of fifty kids singing and dancing to a popular song at the time, 'I like the nightlife, I like to boogie', wearing costumes organised by their parents. The kids received standing ovations. It was such a success and a joy for me to see them having fun.

My daughter came home from school one day in 1995 with the news that she had to write about a famous person. 'Who should I write about, Mum?'

'I don't know. It's up to you. There are many famous people to choose from.'

'I know! I'll write about you. A famous ballerina! I can interview you.'

In the last sentence of her project, my daughter quoted me as saying, 'Now I am writing the book about my life.' It was true – I added to my notes regularly, but 1995 still wasn't the right time for me to complete this major project.

Although I was definitely a business woman, underneath it all I was still an artist – and artists are different to 'normal' people. In Germany, I was not just a *Künstler*, an artist, I was a *Tänzerin*, a ballerina. People used to say to me, 'Wow, I could never do that!' As a well-known, successful artist, others put me on a pedestal but I had worked hard for the applause that came for just a few minutes at the end of a performance. We worked on a ballet all day every day for up to four months. The hours that went into training and rehearsals far surpassed the hours of performing. We received our applause only when the curtain closed. This is not a 'normal' way to work. Our work was almost always of a night, like that of shift workers. I had worked in a factory briefly when I was young. Now I have spent many years working in the restaurant industry, very hard work, and the rewards are completely different to the rewards of a performing artist.

Yes, you have to be a bit weird to be a devoted artist. And you have to be devoted and disciplined to become a successful artist – be an idealist.

Around this time, I received the Stasi file that I'd requested the previous year. It arrived in the mail, in a large envelope. It took me quite some time to read through it and in some ways I was a bit disappointed. It began from when I began my employment in Schwerin, just standard information. I expected my defection to be fully noted, that the whole story would be included. It didn't contain all the details which I had expected, just a summary of the event. The only real names in the files were those of my family. Anybody who'd advised about me, informers for the Stasi, had their code names blacked out. Brief entries were made about my movements – 'Blank' saw me walking down the street, as I was going to some particular place…I was followed. Several different people informed on me.

I'd heard from Mum about this practice of blacking out names. Apparently when the files were first made available, names were not blacked out and people saw in front of them the names of their family members, colleagues, their lovers, and their friends as their informers. I can imagine the devastation of discovering that the people you loved the most may have worked against you. People couldn't cope with the information that confronted them. There were many suicides and killings as a result, a violence in our part of former East Germany that had never been experienced before.

At Christmas, we returned to Germany to re-create with my husband the lovely time we'd enjoyed the previous year. I revisited the former Stasi headquarters to try to access the code names of those who had informed about me. I wanted to know who spied on me. That would have been very interesting to me, but further information could not be found.

Our daughter experienced a traditional New Year's Eve fireworks display for the first time – lighting up every window in Berlin on our way driving back from my brother's house in Schwerin to Mum's flat.

We enjoyed another fantastic visit, and, as the three of us had German citizenship, there'd be no problem for us to resettle in Germany maybe one day. Our thoughts of moving to Germany intensified; we talked about it with more seriousness, but our daughter expressed that she was no longer keen to leave Australia and her friends. So we decided then that as a family our home was Australia, and we would just work hard to enable us to visit Germany regularly and to bring Mum out as often as we could.

Although I like adventure, I love to have a base, a home. I realised that I hadn't been able to establish my life as a family life. The pressures of work had been too many and too time-consuming to allow me to be a really good mother and wife. I decided my life needed to change. The business was sold and Ernst took on other work. Our daughter moved to a Steiner school, which we felt was more suited to her talents and needs. This education system was different and emphasised art and music, craft, nature, participation rather than competition. It was a holistic approach to learning and I enjoyed learning about its philosophies. It felt like home. Through people I met at the school, I was introduced to interesting attitudes to living, such as growing organic food, our toxic environment. I wanted to know more.

Sometimes after taking our daughter to school, I returned home exhausted. Perhaps my life of hard work, long hours and very little sleep had caught up with me as Mum had predicted when I was a child: 'Heidrun, too much hard work has consequences!' The Steiner school offered art classes for parents and I decided to attend. I had missed exploring my creativity in recent years and during this time of change I learnt more about myself. I returned to craftwork, which I'd loved as a child but had not explored for many years. These days, I love to draw. I call them my spiritual drawings, colourful designs inspired by my thoughts about people. I looked after our home, enjoyed a strong and ongoing interest in art and crafts and enjoyed walking on the beach with Willi in the daytime, instead of at three o'clock in the morning. I appreciated silence around me during the day and started meditating at my special bench on the beach. A friend taught me how to master the craft of decorating wooden furniture and wooden utensils. It was beautiful working with my hands. It felt something like dancing.

I started reading. I made some beautiful friends of a family we met through the Steiner school who made a great impression on my life. I loved writing, and I loved learning, but had never taken much interest in reading. There had never been the time. The father of this family encouraged me to read again. He taught me patience, I started with five minutes at a time, and the first book I persevered with was *Personality Plus*. As time went on, I read more and more and enjoyed it greatly. I consciously made time to read, to make it part of my life again. Now, I can read for hours. I began reading newspapers, more interested in life stories of magnificent people than news stories. I loved, and still do, reading about people who make a difference to other people's lives.

I have always loved food, preparing it, arranging it, cooking it… even washing the dishes. I love the whole celebration of food and gathering together in small numbers. Food is a gift. Now I had time to invite guests to our home for a meal, I wanted to cook for them, I'd never want them to bring something to contribute to the meal, that would have been an insult.

I understand that many people in their forties see that age as a time of change. In a way, I took the robot-working machine apart bit by bit and reassembled each section in a different way to make a new me. Where did it all fit together now? I started listening to my body and could not ignore the increasing pain in my feet and legs.

One day, I noticed a huge newspaper ad with a photo of a smiling man advertising a three-hour business seminar. I thought, 'I should go to it. Probably I should have gone to something like it fifteen years ago! There's more I need to research before going into business again one day in the future.' The seminar was fantastic; about three thousand people attended at the Dallas Brooks Hall and filled my head with so much information. The most important message I took home was that the presenter announced that the fastest-growing industry – globally –

in the next ten years would be the health industry. Over the following year, I thought about this idea and embarked on personal study about business rules, strategies, regulations and laws.

I was always told I had healing hands when I massaged. Mum, in particular, who doesn't enjoy personal touch (she has never even been to a hairdresser in her life), suffered headaches when she visited around this time and I encouraged her to let me give her a massage. 'I can achieve miracles, Mum, trust me!' I claimed. Maybe the white-witch of my previous life had left her powers with me – who knows? – but after my five-minute massage, my mother has never had a headache again. I massaged other family members and friends and, although untrained, was able to give them relief. I was looking for some connection to the health industry, talking to people, researching, wondering what next to do with my life. Perhaps I should become a masseur? I was curious about finding my next field of work.

Meanwhile, my foot and leg pain were still bothering me, causing me great frustration. I could hardly walk. The only shoes that I could wear were runners. I needed to get up about two hours before taking my daughter to school, simply to prepare myself for the walk. For the first time in my life, my body was really letting me down. I began seeing a doctor regularly. He wanted me to undergo surgery for bone spurs, the cause of my pain, but I decided that I would simply have to live with this condition. My frustration grew, I felt not too happy.

Soon I was introduced by friends to a major international health and personal products company who claimed their products would get rid of pain. Although I was sceptical, my husband persuaded me to try the products. Two weeks later, I was completely pain-free after suffering for three years.

When my mother arrived later in the year for her visit, I ran to greet her at the airport.

She was astounded. 'You can walk again!'

It was a breakthrough for me. If these products could help change my life, then I could help others change their lives. I pursued a personal course of study, reading about health and well-being. It became a passion for me to know as much as I could about how to retain well-being and health and to help others do so as well. I felt I was in the right space.

In 2000, changes, challenges and new choices confronted me and although Mum had planned to come to Australia again, her doctor advised her not to travel. I wanted Mum here with me.

I sat at my bench at the beach and cried. 'Please, Mum, please come one more time. We need you here.'

I felt lost and lonely. Perhaps I was being selfish in my marriage, spending so much time now on my own. My husband and I now had separate interests; we were taking different paths in our lives. His was staying in the same direction – work and home, home and work. I was moving into new places.

Mum called the following day to say she would visit. That was the best news. Thank God!

During Mum's visit, my husband and I decided we needed to separate and live our own lives. I had Mum's moral support; this mother-daughter connection was utmost. She understood what I was going through. The marriage separation, although necessary, was experienced as a loss. Mum returning home to Germany was an added loss. I knew that, for our daughter, our separation would mean family loss; so it was for me. She, fourteen at this stage, was enthusiastic about the opportunity to travel to Austria for six months as an exchange student. What a terrific opportunity for her. We all agreed. Separation of parents is difficult for children and we all thought the exchange student opportunity had come at the right time.

My daughter was overseas. For me it felt like another loss. I missed her. Although I have had some very special close friends who are always there for me, I only share with people what I want to share. Personal life should stay personal, that's the way I am. Ultimately, I needed to sort myself out on my own. I decided to spend three months with my family and friends in Germany. A month after our daughter left, I arrived in time for Mum's eightieth birthday, which was special for us both.

Life wasn't easy. We all tried our best, but there were many challenges and difficulties. In October 2003, I had a serious car accident and my daughter was seriously injured. We survived, luckily. But life was never the same again. My goal was to be the best Mum to my daughter that I could be. Together we visited our clairvoyant, who was able to tell us that something serious had happened in October. How could he possibly know of the car accident? He predicted that Willi, our family dog, would not be with us much longer and that my 'little girl' would leave home at seventeen, and he was correct. I couldn't stop her from leaving, but my precious Schatzi is always close in my heart.

In recent years, I decided it was time to write my book. The time and environment needed to be perfect. I made an attempt to write on my last trip back to Germany. I received encouragement there from people involved in the publishing industry. Perhaps I had a fear of success. This project had been talked about so often since I defected. I'd lived more than half of my life in Australia now. That was the place I needed to be to write my book.

Finale

2020

Today I look over the sea from my favourite bench at the beach in Brighton, in beautiful bayside Melbourne, and it is a very different day from the one in 1980 when I faced that sea vista and decided that I would stay in Australia. To my right I can see St Kilda and the ever expanding city buildings. To my left, the masts of the vessels moored at the Brighton Yacht Club punctuate the skyline.

My bench has been updated in recent years, along with extensive foreshore works that have made this an even more beautiful stretch of beach than it was in 1980, when it was simply untouched nature, scrubby with native trees. I come here regularly.

I feel like I am the only person here today. The weather is very cold, windy and noisy from the stormy water, but there are few people passing by. Often I meet others, from all backgrounds, who walk every day, and we smile and say hello. Most days, I sit in silence on my bench in reflection, just feeling grateful for this special place and thinking about my life.

I still love Melbourne, this place I chose as my adopted home. I'm still learning to accept the way the weather can change here many times in one day. I love the people, I love my beach. I love the feeling of the raw wind blowing into my face. Every time I look at the sky, it is different. The appearance and colours of the water change constantly. I love all these changes. When the water is as still as a lake, the reflections fill me with delight. Swimming in the bay is wonderful and rejuvenating. My feeling of freedom and beauty is gigantic. Lying on the warm sand totally relaxes me.

Most days, I look out on the sea and see ships coming and going – that represents life today, tomorrow, ever evolving.

When I arrived in Australia in 1980, I thought there was not much culture and art life, and that was a disappointment. Over the years, I have watched especially Melbourne develop as the arts and culture centre of Australia and I am very excited about it.

At this stage in my life, I still feel enthusiastic and creative. I don't need too much sleep, never have – five to six hours is quite enough. I am very committed to maintaining my health, so I want to keep moving – physically, mentally and spiritually. My heart always sings and my soul dances when I listen to music. I love spending time with friends and family, travelling, being outside in nature, walking, dancing, reading, exercising and spending time in silence.

When you really want something deep in your heart, when you are certain about it, not having one per cent doubt, only one hundred per cent faith, I believe that anything is possible.

A newborn baby inspires me – what a miracle! A group of like-minded people involved in a hearty discussion inspires me. Stories of people who make a difference to other people's lives. Moments of joy. Beautiful music – classical or contemporary. The countless voluntary workers and organisations in Australia inspire me with the care they demonstrate, especially to children throughout the world.

Owning lots of clothes, jewellery and other possessions is not that important to me. Coffee, chocolate and ice cream are my favourite treats, especially dark chocolate which is bitter-sweet, just like life. All I really want is love, air, water – *Liebe, Luft und Wasser* – and lots of sunlight.

'Once a Berliner, always a Berliner...' I am a Berliner in my soul. Berlin, my *Muttererde*, mother earth, is where I was born, it is where I grew up. Now I've spent so many years of my adult life in Australia. Although I love travelling, for now Melbourne is still my much-loved adopted home.

Australia means to me freedom, space, beauty, love and harmony, possibilities and opportunities. It is still an amazing place on the earth to live in and make a difference. It is a country that has much history, deep roots and yet it is a very young country. Living here makes me feel young. In 2017, I was granted Australian citizenship. Even so, I have not let go of Germany – my mother earth. Australia has been absolutely wonderful to me. But I am global in my mind and respect the connections between all of us on the planet and our environment. I truly believe I am a citizen of the world.

In my view, everyone has a place in society. These days, there's much more categorising about people. Even in Germany, this has changed too, so I'm not just claiming this about Australia. For me, it's about appreciating that a dishwasher or a rubbish collector is as important as a wealthy person. They all teach me something. We are all interconnected like shiny facets of a diamond.

Mum asked me at different times during my life if I missed my father and wanted to see him, and I always answered I had no reason to. I didn't feel sadness. Mum had three children to raise, so she was driven to get on with life and taught us that we all should support each other. I just accepted it. I am a happy and compassionate person by nature.

I found my father in 2006 after forty-eight years and we spoke on the phone. By that stage, I'd reflected a great deal on my life and my defection. Today I understand that when he asked me who I wanted to live with, and I answered, 'Mum,' he gave me the freedom to follow my heart. He showed no anger about my choice. Most of my life I have followed what I have felt in my heart, not what I thought intellectually, but what I felt instinctively. I do not believe I would ever have decided to defect from East Germany to Australia unless I had followed my heart's desire. When I follow my heart, anything is possible.

Mama is now ninety-eight and has had many ups and downs. She has strength, resilience and courage and I admire, respect and love her. God bless her.

To my knowledge, none of my family, friends or colleagues have ever held my actions and decision to defect against me. Since the Berlin Wall has come down I have revisited Germany several times and reunited with old friends. I am nurturing old friendships and find it remarkable that nobody has ever said anything negative to me about my defection. Even though many colleagues were questioned by the Stasi about me after my defection, it is an incredible feeling to be loved for who I am.

So, do I feel guilty? No. The only thing I feel sad about is that I can't just pop in and visit my mother as my brothers do. I know she is happy when I am happy. She has always let me make my own choices. She taught me a lifetime lesson. I am reminded of this often now that my own daughter is making her own choices.

Today I'm certain it is my number one purpose to touch hearts, inspire and uplift people and make a difference in other people's lives. One of my dreams is to perform on stage again at some time in the future, even if it's only for a moment – every moment counts. Like my mother proudly said, 'With your art, your skills and honesty, you have made thousands of people feel something when you dance. You told stories with your body and gave them hope to take home.'

As my book goes to print, I recognise an unexpected experience of a very scary déjà vu. My dream of freedom was the reason I fled my home country of birth to this beautiful free country of Australia. What has happened to this country of freedom now that we are experiencing the corona virus pandemic? I feel trapped with the long lockdowns for an unpredicted time.

I have the utmost concern about the catastrophic consequences of this devastating situation we are facing in our entire country, especially in Victoria. My heart aches to witness the suffering of our entire nation, especially for all small businesses and the people who own them and those who they employ.

Coming from an artistic background, I have gained much knowledge about the painful and complicated survival of the whole arts sector in the best of times. Therefore, I am supporting the very well known

Stephanie Lake Dance Company with a contribution of ten per cent from my proceeds of the sale of this book. I will love to see the company back on its feet again when it can receive its well deserved applause on all stages in Australia and overseas. Toi Toi Toi – good luck and my best wishes.

I will travel soon, back to Berlin. Marlene Dietrich sang a famous song, *Ich Hab Noch Einen Koffer,* in Berlin, which means 'I Still Have a Suitcase in Berlin'. I too have kept a suitcase in Berlin.

How will the future unfold for me? I'm ready for the years ahead. The world is a huge stage. We are all players, let's play the game of life the best we can.

What became of that little three-year-old girl in the flat in East Germany who squeezed her eyes shut at the light of the camera flash? What became of the ballerina whose favourite role was Carmen, the proud, passionate gypsy woman?

Enough reflection for one day. It's time to leave my favourite beach bench, to stretch my legs, put my face to the wind and keep walking. Love, laugh and live an adventurous and committed life.

Interval

Acknowledgements

Thank you to all those people who I have known and those who are present in my life today. They all have become an important part in some way along my life's journey.

Thank you to all my schoolmates, friends and teachers with whom I shared an adventurous and interesting time in my childhood and as a teenager.

Thank you to Gerhard, my true best friend in good and bad times for over forty years. Our trust, integrity, loyalty and total honesty makes our friendship last over so many years. He believes that I am a legend and I believe that he's a genius.

Thank you to all the magnificent individuals of the ballet world. Special thanks to Teja Kremke, Lother Hanff and Eva Reinthaller; to Professor Tom Schilling, my director at the Komische Oper Berlin; to Graeme Murphy and Janet Vernon, who first welcomed me to join the Sydney Dance Company in 1980. I appreciate their professionalism and committed love towards ballet and the performing arts. They all had a profound impact during my passionate dance career, and encouraged me to be the very best I could be.

Thank you to Karl for the quality time we shared together as dance partners and friends. His respect and admiration made me feel so special.

Thank you to my countless friends and acquaintances here in Australia, which I call my adopted home. I am blessed with so many that if I named them all, the list would be endless. They all have a special place in my huge heart. Many of them welcomed me as a stranger into their families and have surrounded me with love, support and harmony.

Thank you to Paul and Helen – without them I would not be here today. Their ongoing guidance, encouragement and love is priceless.

Thank you N.B., for generosity, patience, honesty, support and for sharing pearls of wisdom in times when I needed it.

Thank you to Tom for his guidance and his book *The Joy of Perfect Health*, which taught me there is light at the end of a long, dark tunnel when I take the responsibility to heal my own mind and body and spirit in our precious environment.

Thank you to Mark and Alison and their gorgeous family, whose oceans of love and support infuse me with their courage and wisdom. Their ongoing great spirit and unconditional love is so nurturing.

Thank you to Dr John Demartini for his many books and life-changing program *The Breakthrough Experience*. His teachings of universal laws have had a miraculous impact on my life at the right time. I embrace his ongoing teachings, to believe in myself and 'to do what I love and to love what I do'. Here I am now with my first book!

Thank you to Carol for her intuitive nature, her gift to uplift me in a flash, for believing in me the moment we first met, her time, encouragement and advice to follow my dream. Thank you to Wolf for following Carol's intuition and agreeing to meet me. I appreciate that he believed in the possibility that my life experiences could make a powerful story, and for introducing me to my co-writer Janet Brown.

Thank you to Janet, writer and friend, for being inspired by my project when we first met, for her determination and patience to work with me to fulfil my dream. Thank you to Stephen and Ginninderra Press, my publisher. I am enormously grateful for your commitment and belief in my story, and for your professionalism.

Thank you to my sponsors – Jamie, Carol, Wolf, Barry, Graeme and Janet, Helen and Paul, Rosi, Renata, Pat and Don, Noala, Audrey, Joan, Hughan and Paula and Maurice. With their support, I was able to dedicate myself to working on this project. Especially a big thank you to Eva for her love, generosity, kindness and enthusiasm: an angel on my pathway to fulfilling my purpose.

Thank you to my family. I am certain that I am constantly blessed by them.

Thank you to Ernst for taking me onboard and for the dreams and years we shared together.

Thank you to my daughter. She is an inspiration to me and many people, no matter their background, age or who they are. I thank you for being you. You are my greatest teacher of all. You are the reason in the past, and now, why I never, ever give up. Thank you, Schatzi, you are my shining star.

Heidi Giersch

'Heidi, thank you for sharing your profound life story. I owe you a dept of gratitude as you have absolutely inspired and excited me as a result of sharing it.' – James, Australia

'Above all else, I drew strength, love and inspiration from your encouragement to keep dreaming and most importantly to never ever give up.' – Eva W, Australia

'Heidi, your artistry is remembered as absolutely brilliant. And your joyful personality is coined of loyalty, sincerity, bravery, determination, intelligence and love. Your fire within is infectious.' – Eva R, Hungary

'Heidi, thank you for renewing my faith that there are still more good than bad people in our world. God bless you.' – Warrick, Australia

'Heidi, we admire your attitude of gratitude and your kind words of honesty and truth. You are an inspiration to us all.' – Rosemary and Trent, Australia

'Heidi, you are the best friend and life coach under the southern hemisphere I've met.' – Anna, Germany

'Heidi, we love your professionalism, devotion, understanding, gentleness and happy nature.' Bryce, Australia

'Heidi, you are one of those people who learned to smile by instinct, you shared the beautiful kingdom of dance on earth with us and you see the magical beauty in everyone. Thank you.' – Marie, Sweden

www.ingramcontent.com/pod-product-compliance
Lightning Source LLC
Chambersburg PA
CBHW071812080526
44589CB00012B/768